Shortchanged

Howard Karger

Shortchanged

Life and Debt in the Fringe Economy

BERRETT-KOEHLER PUBLISHERS, INC.
San Francisco
a BK Currents book

Berrett-Koehler Publishers, Inc.
235 Montgomery Street, Suite 650, San Francisco, CA 94104-2916
Tel: (415) 288-0260   Fax: (415) 362-2512   www.bkconnection.com

ORDERING INFORMATION

Quantity sales. Special discounts are available on quantity purchases by corporations, associations, and others. For details, contact the "Special Sales Department" at the Berrett-Koehler address above.

Individual sales. Berrett-Koehler publications are available through most bookstores. They can also be ordered directly from Berrett-Koehler: Tel: (800) 929-2929; Fax: (802) 864-7626; www.bkconnection.com

Orders for college textbook/course adoption use. Please contact Berrett-Koehler: Tel: (800) 929-2929; Fax: (802) 864-7626.

Orders by U.S. trade bookstores and wholesalers. Please contact Publishers Group West, 1700 Fourth Street, Berkeley, CA 94710. Tel: (510) 528-1444; Fax (510) 528-3444.

Berrett-Koehler and the BK logo are registered trademarks of Berrett-Koehler Publishers, Inc.

PRINTED IN THE UNITED STATES OF AMERICA
Berrett-Koehler books are printed on long-lasting acid-free paper. When it is available, we choose paper that has been manufactured by environmentally responsible processes. These may include using trees grown in sustainable forests, incorporating recycled paper, minimizing chlorine in bleaching, or recycling the energy produced at the paper mill.

LIBRARY OF CONGRESS CATALOGING-IN-PUBLICATION DATA
Karger, Howard Jacob, 1948–
    Shortchanged : life and debt in the fringe economy / Howard Karger.
      p. cm.
    Includes bibliographical references and index.
    ISBN-10: 1-57675-336-0; ISBN-13: 978-1-57675-336-1
    1. Microfinance—United States. 2. Pawnbroking—United States. 3. Loans, Personal—United States. 4. Working poor—United States. 5. Marginality, Social—United States. I. Title.
HG178.33.U6K37 2005
332.3—dc22   2005040973

FIRST EDITION

10 09 08 07 06 05   10 9 8 7 6 5 4 3 2 1

Copyediting: Elissa Rabellino. Design: Richard Wilson. Index: Rachel Rice. Jacket design: Mark van Bronkhorst. Proofreading: Debra Gates.

For my father, Sam Karger, z"l.
May his memory be a blessing for us all.

Contents

Preface

Shortly after starting to work on *Shortchanged*, I visited a "buy here, pay here" used-car lot in Houston, Texas. Dressed in blue jeans, a T-shirt, and a baseball cap, I went to the lot to get a feel for how the system worked. The salesman showed me the typical overpriced $3,000–$5,000 used cars that were slightly sporty, with high mileage and interiors that had obviously hosted a few parties. Even the cleaner cars had hardened cola spills, cigarette holes in the seats, and a musty smell reminiscent of smoke and fast-food burgers. I popped hoods, kicked tires, and tried to be enthusiastic about my dire need for a vehicle.

The salesman was affable until I asked about financing. "It's only $60 a week," he said, "pretty good for a car like this."

I nodded and then mistakenly asked, "What's the interest rate?" The negotiations chilled as the salesman turned his back and walked away. I followed him, asking why I was suddenly getting the cold shoulder.

"I don't know who you are, but I know you're bullshitting me."

Sheepishly I asked, "How do you know?"

"None of my customers ever ask about interest rates. All they care about is how much they gotta pay each week." In a nutshell, that's how the fringe economy works.

For many years, I included a small amount of material on the fringe economy as part of my graduate course in social policy. Although I understood the general concept of the fringe economy, I wasn't fully aware of the details.

About five years ago, I arrived early for a dinner at a restaurant in a small, run-down Houston strip mall. With almost an hour to kill, I stopped in at a check-cashing outlet and browsed through the leaflets. Since it was tax season, many brochures advertised "instant tax refunds." Being the only customer, I asked the clerk how these refunds worked. Through a small hole in the bulletproof glass we chatted about tax refunds, check cashing, and payday loans. After hearing the details I was taken aback. While I understood the economics of higher risk and higher cost, the abuse of unregulated market power in regard to the economically fragile angered and dismayed me. I had always known that the poor got a raw deal in the fringe economy; I just hadn't realized how bad it really was.

Throughout the dinner my feelings alternated between outrage and relief. As a tenured college professor, I felt relieved that I'd never descend into that economic abyss. But, like much of the middle class, I had in the back of my mind that nagging "what if?" I knew that only a few shaky rungs separated me from the bottom of the economic ladder. Perhaps I'd knock the rungs out myself, or maybe they'd break because of events I couldn't control. This brief encounter led to my journey into the dark underbelly of America's fringe economy.

The first question I'm often asked is, "What's the fringe economy?" In the context of *Shortchanged*, I use "fringe economy" to refer to corporations and business practices that have a predatory relationship with the poor by charging excessive interest rates or fees, or exorbitant prices for goods or services. While some consumer groups use the term "alternative financial services sector," I prefer "fringe economy," because it better addresses the marginality of this economy and many of its customers.

After I list the visible parts of this economy—payday lenders, check cashers, rent-to-own stores, buy here, pay here used-car lots, tax refund lenders, and so forth—most people know what I'm talking about. But, as the book illustrates, these businesses are only the tip of a complex financial structure that engulfs virtually every area where people borrow, spend money, or purchase goods and services. At this point, a caveat is necessary. Some financial institutions that serve the poor—especially those in the nonprofit sector—are nonpredatory and are doing a remarkable job. Most for-profit businesses are not.

Despite its bland storefronts, the fringe economy is not composed primarily of family-run pawnshops, payday lenders, and check cashers. On the contrary, it's an industry increasingly dominated by a handful of large, well-financed national and multinational corporations with strong ties to mainstream financial institutions. It's also a comprehensive, mature, and fully formed parallel economy that addresses the financial needs of the poor and credit-challenged in much the same way as the mainstream economy meets the needs of the middle class. The main difference is the exorbitant interest rates and fees and the onerous loan terms that mark fringe economy transactions.

I had several goals in writing this book. My first was to shed light into this dark and shadowy sector of the American economy. Paradoxically, while the fringe economy is everywhere, it is hidden from public view. For instance, we've all passed the throngs of pawnshops, check cashers, payday lenders, rent-to-own stores, tax refund lenders, and buy here, pay here car lots that are increasingly populating America's cities and towns. While some of us have used these services, most of us don't really know what happens there. For others, fringe economy storefronts are like porn shops. We don't exactly know what goes on inside, but we're pretty sure it's unwholesome. As *Shortchanged* illustrates, this intuition is correct—there's indeed something seedy going on in most parts of the fringe economy. Behind this seediness are economic transactions marked by desperation and exploitation. It's a hidden world where a customer's economic fate is sealed with a handshake, a smile, and fine-print documents that would befuddle many attorneys.

My second goal was to show how poor and credit-impaired consumers are systematically exploited by a subeconomy with few restraints. Lawmakers and government officials have largely ignored much of the untoward activities of the fringe sector, instead focusing on protecting the financial interests of the rich. This has resulted in an economy with one set of rules for the rich and a different set of nonrules for the poor. For example, Wall Street brokers are prosecuted for complex financial crimes that most people can't grasp. At the same time, tax preparers and refund lenders are permitted to skim off $1.3 billion from the Earned Income Tax Credit, a program designed to help the nation's poorest families.[1] These nonrules have allowed a Wild West economy—one with an open season on the poor—to flourish.

My hope is that concerned citizens, advocates, and state and federal officials and lawmakers will be sufficiently alarmed by these activities to bring some measure of justice—or simple economic decency—into this sector. I am also hopeful that this book will further the ongoing dialogue about the need for alternative forms of credit and financial assistance, such as community banks, credit unions, and community development corporations. To further this goal, I've included suggestions for reform in most of the chapters.

My third goal was to make consumers aware of the inherent dangers of the fringe economy. Despite ads that promise to help people in need, fringe economy transactions are one-sided, and rarely do customers walk away better off financially. In most cases, the financial problems that drew people to the fringe economy are only exacerbated by overpriced goods and services, high interest rates and fees, impossible-to-meet loan terms, and short repayment schedules. This book may help friends, family members, and human-service professionals to steer financially troubled people away from the fringe economy. Some of this assistance might involve helping them find alternative and less predatory forms of financing.

In the avaricious world of the fringe economy, crafty merchants and economic institutions pander to the belief that everyone can have the American dream—only the poor have to pay more for it. In fact, the fringe economy leaves virtually no one without credit as long as they're willing to pay the price. Besides, if a transaction seems unaffordable, the down payment, interest rate, or terms can be adjusted to make it seem manageable, at least in the short run. While the fringe economy makes goods and services available to consumers who can't otherwise afford them, it also traps them in a cycle of debt.

The fringe economy is an unforgiving system that claims to give the poor and credit-challenged relief and a second chance. On the contrary, vulnerable customers are dragged deeper into a quagmire of debt. For most people, the greatest danger of the fringe economy doesn't lie in a single exploitive transaction, although it sometimes can. The real danger is becoming enmeshed in a subeconomy from which escape is difficult. For some at-risk consumers, fringe financial services are like an addiction—there's always money there when they need it. But, like most addictions, it comes at a high price.

A final goal was to show how the modern fringe economy reflects a break from the past. The availability of high-cost predatory credit is hardly a new phenomenon in the United States. On the contrary, the nation has a long history of indentured servants, debt servitude, company stores, loan sharks, pawnshops, and predatory finance companies. For example, company stores in mill towns, coalfields, and migrant camps have traditionally kept poor workers in a cycle of perpetual debt. Black sharecroppers were held in debt servitude to landowners by land and crop mortgages carrying exorbitant interest rates.[2]

What makes the modern fringe economy different is the level of organization, the corporate control, the presumed legitimacy of these enterprises, the growing appeal to large sectors of middle-income households, and the geographic reach of these companies. While older fringe businesses were local, the new fringe economy is national and even global in scope. And the fringe economy is not just an urban phenomenon. Many small towns and cities across the United States have multiple pawnshops, check cashers, payday lenders, and rent-to-own stores. Even a small town like Bay City, Texas (population 21,000), boasts two pawnshops, two check cashers, and four rent-to-own stores, including three of the biggest— Aaron's, ColorTyme, and RentWay.

Lending money has historically been profitable, and this didn't escape the notice of the underworld. For example, in 2003, six associates of the Colombo crime family were charged with illegal loan-sharking, among other crimes. According to the Justice Department, one underworld crew operated a large-scale loan-sharking and bookmaking operation that preyed upon young employees of stock-brokerage firms. Usurious loans were made at interest rates of 1%–5% a week, or the equivalent of a 52%–250% APR (annual percentage rate).[3] Ironically, a 52% APR loan would be a bargain for many fringe economy customers. Even the 250% APR charged by the Colombo loan sharks is less than the 470% APR charged by many legal payday lenders.[4]

Entrepreneurs soon realized that they could make vast sums of money by providing "legal" financial services to desperate borrowers. In turn, mainstream banks lent entrepreneurs the money to set up check-cashing outlets, rent-to-own stores, and payday lending operations. Illegal loan-sharking became redundant in many low-income communities as payday lenders took over. Consequently, some poor and middle-class consumers have simply shifted their borrowing habits from illegal to legal loan sharks.

A few notes on the book may be helpful. To begin with, I underestimated the difficulties I would encounter in the research. For example, when I started the book, I phoned an old friend whose daughter worked for a large payday lender in Arizona. Having known the family for 20 years, I was certain that Marcy would return my phone call. She never did. I phoned several more times, and still no return call. Finally, the family admitted that their daughter couldn't talk to me because she had signed an employee loyalty oath promising that she wouldn't discuss the business with anyone. Breaching that oath would result in dismissal, and she needed the income. I encountered the same refusal to discuss "the business" with employees in check-cashing outlets and pawnshops. In another instance, my wife, Anna, talked to a client whose daughter managed a pawnshop. The mother enthusiastically volunteered her daughter for an interview. When Anna followed up, she was told that her client's daughter couldn't discuss the pawnshop, and if I wanted more information, I'd have to contact the owner directly. The lack of transparency was striking, and I couldn't help but suspect that something was being hidden.

Some readers may be put off by the book's focus on the economic straits of the poor *and* the middle class, thinking that it minimizes the true impact on the poor. I had originally titled the book *Scamming the Poor*, but as I dug deeper, I soon realized that the fringe economy is also affecting a growing number of functionally poor households—those with above-average incomes but with little or no assets and high debt. Indeed, many financial transactions have become so tricky that the middle class, especially the functionally poor middle class, is also vulnerable to the predations of the fringe economy. As *Shortchanged* illustrates, the lines between the fringe and mainstream economies are blurred, and the interests of the poor and the functionally poor middle class are growing closer.

Several readers may find details about the fringe economy tedious. In the fringe economy, as in many things, the devil is in the details. Understanding the fringe economy requires a grasp of how financial schemes circumvent state and federal laws, and how consumers are becoming trapped in a cycle of indebtedness through loan rates and terms that are almost impossible to satisfy. In large measure, the fringe economy exerts its control by carefully manipulating the details of the financial transaction.

Some case examples are taken directly from interviews, while others are composites. Surrogate names are used throughout the book to protect the privacy of the interviewees. A few readers will notice variations in statistical data used in various parts of the book. These are due to the differences in data-gathering techniques used by different non- and for-profit organizations and federal agencies. Data discrepancies are often the most evident between fringe industry trade groups and consumer organizations. In those cases, I chose what I surmised to be the most reliable data.

Finally, the critical reader will certainly ask the challenging question, don't the credit problems of some fringe economy customers justify the high interest rates? The obvious answer is yes. Most of us wouldn't lend money to some fringe economy customers because it would be financially imprudent. But at what point does the profit so overshadow the risks that the transaction becomes predatory?

The answer is obvious in some cases. For instance, consumers who pawn their vehicle for one-third of its value, then pay 300% or more a year in interest to get it back, are exploited. Some consumers are forced to deposit hundreds or thousands of dollars into a low-interest-bearing savings account—which they aren't permitted to use to pay off their balances—to get a secured credit card. These cardholders then pay 30% or more in interest, plus monthly and sundry fees, for the "privilege" of using the card. They are exploited. Customers who take out a $200 payday loan costing almost $40 for 14 days at a 417% APR are exploited. Check-cashing customers who pay 3%—$30 on a $1,000 check—to cash a secure government check are exploited. Homeowners enticed into high-interest refinancing loans that systematically strip equity from their property are exploited. Still others who pay 28% in interest on a 10-year-old overpriced car are exploited.

The list goes on and on. Interest rates in the fringe economy are often in triple digits, and the grossly inflated prices of goods and services have no relationship to their real market value. The poor and credit-poor live in a world where borrowing means temporarily or permanently losing a valued possession or paying an exorbitant fee for a small cash advance.

■ ■ ■

The following is a brief roadmap to *Shortchanged*.

Chapter 1 looks at the scope and size of the fringe economy and the characteristics of its customers. It then examines the major players in the fringe economy, including mainstream financial institutions. Chapter 2 explores key factors that explain the phenomenal growth of the fringe sector, including stagnant wages, the rising numbers of working poor, the impact of welfare reform, immigration, and the rise of the Internet. Chapter 3 looks at the functionally poor middle class, an economic group increasingly targeted by the fringe sector. It also investigates the role of household debt in the growth of the fringe economy.

Having a credit card is almost a necessity in America's plastic-driven society. Without one you can't rent a car, book a room or flight, or order goods online. Chapter 4 examines credit and the credit card industry. Specifically, it explores how the credit industry makes the unaffordable seem affordable by artificially manipulating interest rates and terms, how creditworthiness is determined, and how the credit card industry works. It also investigates how aggressive marketing lures young adults into a credit card trap. Finally, the chapter examines the high costs of alternative credit and debit cards.

Rows of payday lenders, pawnshops, and tax refund lenders are increasingly lining the streets of American communities. Chapter 5 explores cash loans. One of the fastest-growing segments of the fringe economy is the payday loan industry. Despite the keen competition among payday lending corporations, the spectacular rise in consumer debt—around $9 trillion in 2004—portends a rosy future for this multibillion-dollar loan industry.

Pawnshops have historically assumed the role of the neighborhood banker, lending money to those frozen out of the economic mainstream. This chapter examines the high cost of pawn transactions and its economic effects on borrowers. In addition, it looks at the important role that mainstream and federally insured banks are playing in the fringe economy.

Tax time is feeding time for the fringe economy. From January to April, newspapers, television, and radio are buzzing with ads about "instant tax refunds." Brochures are placed in thousands of convenience stores and supermarkets. Abandoned stores are suddenly occupied, at least for a few months. Appliance stores, car dealers, and other merchants advertise "instant money" if you promise to buy their wares. Chapter 5 explores the real costs of this instant money.

Chapter 6 investigates check cashing and auxiliary financial services (money orders, electronic bill paying, and so forth) that are lucrative parts of the fringe economy. The chapter also looks at how the fringe economy provides consumers with necessities such as appliances and furniture by way of the rent-to-own industry. Like furniture and appliances, telephone service is a necessity for many people. Without phone service it is difficult to secure employment interviews, contact relatives, or be available for family emergencies. The chapter examines the alternative telecommunications sector, including prepaid home and cell phone service.

While payday lenders, pawnshops, and check cashers can boast high earnings, the biggest revenues come from housing. Simply put, it would take 500 payday loans of $200 each to equal one $100,000 home mortgage. Not surprisingly, the rapaciousness of the fringe economy is clearly evident in the housing area. Chapter 7 investigates the fringe housing sector, the difference between subprime and predatory mortgage lending, various kinds of risky home mortgages, and home equity and refinancing loans. Chapter 8 looks at housing speculation and foreclosures.

Those who live in urban or rural areas without adequate public transportation need a reliable vehicle for arriving at work on time, for picking up children from school or day care, for exercising family responsibilities, and for shopping in low-cost stores. Vehicle ownership is also an area where fringe economy abuses are evident in everything from car purchases to insurance. Chapter 9 investigates the fringe auto economy and explores the obstacles faced by the poor in finding and keeping basic transportation.

Americans are besieged by two contradictory messages: get more and cheaper credit, and get out of debt. Unfortunately, the first message appears to be the most compelling. If the getting-into-debt industry is growing, the getting-out-of-debt industry is following closely on its heels.

Chapter 10 examines the latter, including collection agencies, the organization and evolution of consumer credit counseling agencies, the structure and limitations of debt-management plans, the corruption of "nonprofit"-agency status, debt settlement, and debt dispute and file segregation.

Chapter 11 looks at what can be done to control the fringe economy. It examines various strategies for reforming the fringe economy, including government regulations, consumer education, the need for mainstream banks to better serve the poor, and the creation of alternative lending institutions. Finally, the chapter looks at the future of the fringe economy.

Acknowledgments

Many people helped bring this book to fruition. David Stoesz and Steven Rose provided steadfast support through the dark times. Maxine Epstein always asked how the book was coming along. It's the little things. Larry Litterst read and commented on the manuscript. A special thanks to the people who agreed to be interviewed.

Brett Needham worked tirelessly on many of the interviews. Mandi Sheridan did a wonderful job of researching fringe economy corporations. Their contributions helped make the book better.

Mark Dowie, Jeff Kulick, Gabriela Melano, and Steven Slattery went above and beyond what should be expected of reviewers. Their commitment to the book made it better, and their questions made me rethink things, often grudgingly.

Thanks to Steve Piersanti, Jeevan Sivasubramaniam, and the Berrett-Koehler staff for believing in the project. Steve's dogged pursuit of the "So what?" forced me to rethink the book. Their commitment to their books and their authors kept me going.

Writing can be selfish. Apologies to Aaron, Rafi, and Saul for a distracted dad. Thanks also to my father, Sam, who until his death always asked about the book. I miss him. Most of all, thanks to Anna, my wife, best friend, lover, critic, and loyal supporter. Whenever I got lost in the "Why the hell am I doing this?" she brought me back. Although undocumented, her astute insights infuse the better parts of this book. Without her I couldn't have completed it.

A debt is also owed to the excellent research done by the many think tanks, advocacy groups, and consumer protection organizations working on the problem of the fringe economy. A short list includes the Consumer Federation of America, the National Consumer Law Center, Consumer

Action, the Brookings Institution, the U.S. Public Interest Research Group, ACORN, the North Carolina Self-Help Credit Union, and Shore-Bank. Without their important work this book could not have been written.

SHORTCHANGED

Overview of the Fringe Economy

He That Goes a-Borrowing Goes a-Sorrowing.

–Benjamin Franklin

1

America's Changing Fringe Economy

Driving through low-income neighborhoods, you can't help but notice the large number of pawnshops, check cashers, rent-to-own stores, payday and tax refund lenders, auto title pawns and buy-here, pay-here used-car lots. We are awash in "alternative financial services" directed at the poor and those with credit problems. These fringe economy services are equivalent to an economic Wild West where just about any financial scheme that's not patently illegal is tolerated.

Elise and Bernardo Rodriguez are typical fringe economy customers. The Rodriguezes emigrated from Honduras to San Antonio, Texas, in the middle 1990s. Elise works for a company that cleans office buildings, and Bernardo owns a small landscaping company. They have two school-age children. Although the Rodriguezes are paid by check, they don't have a checking or savings account. Instead, they use ACE Cash Express to cash their checks and to electronically pay bills. When electronic bill paying is not available, the Rodriguezes use money orders. They also wire money back to their family in Honduras through ACE. In fact, ACE is an important part of the Rodriguezes' banking system. Occasional trips to pawnshops and check cashers round out their informal banking system.

There are several reasons why the Rodriguezes use check cashers. For one, they can't wait for checks to clear. Because they make so little money, they live hand-to-mouth, and waiting a week or more for a check to clear the banking system means not having food on the table. Second, their account balances are so small after the rent and car payments that there's almost nothing left after the second week of the month. Third, the Rodriguezes live in a cash economy, and many of the small shops where they buy food, clothing, and other necessities accept only cash. Checks are viewed skeptically and generally not accepted. The Rodriguezes don't trust banks, and they don't feel welcome there. They are also reluctant to write checks for fear of bounced-check fees from banks and merchants. All told, the Rodriguezes spend almost 10% of their net income on alternative financial services, which is average for unbanked households that rely on the fringe economy for their financial needs.[1]

OVERVIEW OF THE FRINGE ECONOMY

Defining the Fringe Economy

There is no generally agreed-upon definition of the fringe economy or of predatory lending. In fact, if a broad definition is applied that includes high-interest home refinancing and credit cards, then the fringe economy is used as frequently by the financially troubled middle class as by the poor. Nevertheless, in a public relations spin, the industry uses "subprime lending" to refer to "loans made to borrowers with credit problems by charging higher, but still fair, fees."[2] The Federal Reserve Board defines subprime lending as "extending credit to borrowers who exhibit characteristics indicating a significantly higher risk of default than traditional bank lending customers."[3]

Although a continuum supposedly exists between subprime and predatory lending, the delineation between the two is unclear. For example, what differentiates "expensive" or "very expensive" from "predatory" lending? When does an interest rate go from subprime to predatory? While not all subprime loans are predatory, all predatory loans are subprime. As Citigroup concedes, "There is no standard industry-wide approach to the definitions of either subprime loans or subprime lending programs, indicating that the meanings of these terms are institution specific."[4]

Under the Home Ownership and Equity Protection Act (HOEPA), a mortgage is considered high interest if the annual percentage rate (APR) is 8 points (8%) for first mortgages and 10 points for subsequent loans above the rate of return on Treasury securities for the same period, or if the fees and points at closing are 8% or more of the loan amount. This definition of a high-cost loan would be a bargain for the many fringe economy customers whose interest rates are measured in the hundreds of percent. A clear definition of predatory lending is important, since without it all manner of abuses can be overlooked.

The Scope and Profitability of the Fringe Economy

The spartan and often shoddy storefronts of the fringe economy mask the true scope of this economic sector. In 2003 government spending on social welfare programs included the following:

- $29 billion for Temporary Aid to Needy Families (TANF), the replacement for Aid to Families with Dependent Children (AFDC)

- $35 billion for Supplemental Security Income (SSI)

- $33 billion for food stamps, the Special Supplemental Food Program for Women, Infants, and Children (WIC), and school lunch programs

- $25 billion for the U.S. Department of Housing and Urban Development's (HUD) low-income housing programs

Altogether, the bulwark of America's public-assistance programs cost less than $125 billion. By comparison, check cashers, payday lenders, pawnshops, and rent-to-own stores engaged in at least 280 million transactions in 2001, generating about $78 billion in gross revenues.[5] If we add subprime home mortgages and refinancing, as well as used-car sales, revenues in the combined sectors of the fringe economy are several times higher than federal and state spending on the poor.[6]

About 22,000 payday lenders extended more than $25 billion in short-term loans to millions of households in 2004.[7] The 11,000 check-cashing stores alone processed 180 million checks in 2002, with a face value of $55 billion.[8] The sheer number of fringe economy storefronts illustrates the scope of this sector. For example, McDonald's has 13,500 U.S. restaurants, Burger King has 7,624, Target has 1,250 stores, Sears has 1,970, J.C. Penney has about 1,000 locations, and the entire Wal-Mart retail chain includes about 3,600 U.S. outlets. These combined 29,000 locations are fewer than the nation's 33,000 check-cashing and payday lenders, just two sectors of the fringe economy.[9]

ACE Cash Express, the nation's largest check casher, is an example of the scope, growth, and profitability of the fringe economy. In 1991 ACE had 181 company-owned stores; by 2003 that number had risen to 1,230 company-owned and franchised stores in 37 states and the District of Columbia. (ACE plans to add another 500 stores by 2008.) In 2000 ACE's net income was $8.3 million; by 2004 that had risen to $17.1 million. ACE claims about 1.2 million new customers a year, and in 2004 it served 38.2 million customers, or about 11,000 an hour. The company's revenue corresponded to its growth. In 2000 ACE's revenues were $141 million; by 2004 they had jumped to $247 million. In 2004, ACE

- engaged in 41 million total transactions worth over $8 billion,

- cashed approximately 13.2 million checks with a face value of $5.1 billion,

- made 1.9 million payday loans and earned $77 million in fees,

- completed 9.7 million bill-payment transactions,

- made 2 million wire transfers (worth $581 million) and sold 8.8 million money orders with a face value of $1.2 billion,

- added 53 new stores, compared with 14 in 2003.

ACE expects its total revenue for fiscal 2005 to range between $265 million and $270 million.[10]

Advance America, Cash Advance Centers, Inc., is the nation's leading payday lender, at least as measured by the number of its stores. By 2004 Advance America had 2,290 stores in 34 states. In 2003 it employed 5,300 people and had $489.5 million in sales with a net income of $96 million.[11] Advance America allied with out-of-state banks in 2002 to evade limits that some states imposed on the industry's excesses. After the federal Comptroller of the Currency cracked down on a bank that helped Advance America evade state regulation, the company affiliated with Federal Deposit Insurance Corporation (FDIC)–regulated state-chartered banks to further dodge regulation.

The company is a strange bird in the world of payday lending. William "Billy" Webster IV, Advance America's CEO and cofounder, was former president Clinton's director of scheduling and advance. Despite lending money to working people at exorbitant interest rates, Advance America partnered with seven nonprofit organizations in 2004 to "get out the vote." These nonprofits included the League of Women Voters, the National Urban League, the National Association of Latino Elected and Appointed Officials Educational Fund, People for the American Way Foundation, the League of United Latin American Citizens, the Southwest Voter Registration Education Project, and the Georgia Coalition for the People's Agenda. The drive signed on 110,000 new voters—double its original goal of 50,000—partly because of the availability of voter-registration forms in more than 2,000 Advance America locations in 29 states.[12]

Dollar Financial Corporation operates 1,106 stores—including 630 company stores—in 17 states, the District of Columbia, Canada, and the United Kingdom. Company stores operate under names like Money Mart, Loan Mart, and Money Shop. Dollar's 2004 revenues from its U.S. and international operations were $246.5 million. Unlike most fringe economy sectors, Dollar lost $28 million in 2004. Check into Cash has more than 700 stores, and CIC, its financial subsidiary, makes personal loans up to $1,000 in select markets.

In 1985 there were 4,500 pawnshops in the United States; by 2000 that number had risen to 14,000, including five publicly traded chains. The three big chains—Cash America International, EZ Pawn, and First Cash—had combined annual revenues of nearly $1 billion in 2003.[13] Cash America is the largest pawnshop chain, with 750 total locations in 17 states. It also offers payday loans through Cash America Payday Advance stores. In addition, Cash America provides payday loans and check cashing through Cashland and Mr. Payroll stores. In 2003 Cash America had revenues of almost $438 million, with a net income of $30 million. From 2001 to 2003 its revenues rose 23%, and net income was 60% higher from 2002 to 2003.

EZ Pawn owns 275 pawnshops in 11 states. Its 2003 revenues were $206 million, with a net income of almost $8.9 million. First Cash Financial Services, the nation's third-largest publicly traded pawnshop chain, has 280 pawnshops and check-cashing outlets in 11 states and Mexico. Its revenues totaled about $164 million in 2004.

The $6 billion–a–year furniture and appliance rent-to-own industry serves 3 million customers annually.[14] Rent-A-Center is the largest rent-to-own corporation in the world, employing 15,000 people. The company owns or operates more than 2,800 stores in the United States and Puerto Rico under the names of Rent-A-Center, Rent Rite, Rainbow Rentals, and Get It Now. It also controls 320 franchises through its subsidiary Color-Tyme. In 2003 Rent-A-Center's sales were about $2.3 billion, with $181.5 million in net income. Aaron Rents has almost 900 stores across the United States and Canada. In 2003 its gross revenues were $767 million, reflecting a net income of $36.4 million. In 2004 RentWay operated 753 stores in 33 states and had revenues of almost $504 million.[15]

Low-income consumers paid almost $1.75 billion in fees for tax refund loans in 2002, and the nation's largest tax preparers earned about $357 million from fringe economy "fast-cash" products in 2001, more than double their earnings in 1998.[16] All told, about 12 million consumers received tax refund anticipation loans in 2002, almost half through H&R Block, whose revenues jumped from $2.4 billion in 2000 to $3.8 billion in 2003.[17]

The fringe economy is also buoyant in the housing market, where subprime home mortgages rose from 35,000 in 1994 to 332,000 in 2003, a growth rate of 25% a year and an almost tenfold increase in just nine years. In 2003 these mortgages accounted for almost $300 billion[18]; by that year, almost 9% of all mortgages were subprime.[19]

One reason for the profitability of the fringe economy is the relatively low cost of starting and running these businesses. For example, few of the check-cashing and payday stores I visited had more than one employee working at a time. Usually I was the only customer, and I was hard-pressed to imagine a restaurant or retail operation surviving with so little traffic. I suspected that the profit margin was so high that it compensated for the slow traffic.

Unlike typical retail businesses that require a substantial inventory and a large number of employees, a new payday or check-cashing store can open with a relatively modest investment, although that varies based upon the size and type of store. For instance, starting a new check-cashing store requires about $65,000–$75,000, which is counterbalanced by incentives from corporations like MoneyGram. The basic startup costs include property improvements, computer equipment, and a security system. In addition, the typical check-cashing and payday storefront requires working capital of $80,000–$100,000 for operating expenses and to fund the store's loan portfolio. According to ACE, it takes about one year for a store to break even.[20]

There's considerable money to be made from the financial misery of the poor and credit-challenged. And if the fringe economy squeezes its customers, it's certainly generous to many of its CEOs. According to *Forbes*, salaries in many fringe economy corporations rival those at much larger companies. Sterling Brinkley, chairman of EZ Pawn's board of directors, earned $1.26 million in 2004. Cash America's CEO, Daniel Feehan, was paid almost $2.2 million in 2003 plus the $9 million he had in stock options. Feehan is also on the board of Radio Shack. James Kauffman, executive vice president of Cash America's international operations, received a paltry $932,000 but had $2 million in stock options. In 2003 First Cash Financial Services' board chairman, Phillip Powell, made $1.4 million along with the $19 million he had in stock options. Rick Wessel, vice chairman of First Cash's board, received $1 million in salary and owned $3.9 million in stock options.

According to ACE, "We also take great pride in being an active and empowering force in the communities in which we operate. That is why we give 1% of net income annually to support children's causes, education and financial literacy. We call it: Giving Back—The ACE Community Fund. . . . During fiscal 2004, ACE donated over $200,000 to various charities across the U.S."[21] In contrast to ACE's "generosity," its CEO, Jay Shipowitz, received $2.1 million in total cash compensation in 2004 on top of his $2.38 million in stocks.

Dollar's losses in 2004 didn't stop CEO Jeffrey Weiss from earning $1.83 million, of which $1 million was a bonus. Rent-A-Center's CEO, Mark Speese, made $820,000, with total stock options of $10 million. R. Charles Loudermilk, Aaron Rents' CEO, received a total cash compensation of $1.17 million in 2003 and had stock options of $5.8 million.[22] He also controls 60% of the company's voting power.

Billy Webster, Advance America's CEO, earned only $650,000 in 2003. However, the 4.6 million shares he owns in the company were worth almost $101 million in early 2005. (Webster's wife also owns considerable stock in Advance America.) Not to be outdone, George Johnson Jr., chairman of Advance's board and its other cofounder, indirectly owns about 10 million shares in the company worth $218 million in early 2005.[23] Inducted into the South Carolina Business Hall of Fame, Johnson served three terms in the South Carolina House of Representatives, having been elected as an independent, a Democrat, and a Republican. From 1984 to 1985 he was also a director of the Federal Reserve Bank of Richmond.[24]

America's fringe economy is clearly not a mom-and-pop industry composed of small storefronts that generate moderate family incomes. Instead, it is a fast-growing and highly developed parallel economy that provides low-income and credit-impaired consumers with a full spectrum of cash, commodities, and credit lines.

Fringe corporations argue that their high charges represent the heightened risks of doing business with an economically unstable population. While fringe economy businesses have never made their criteria for determining prices public, some risks are clearly overstated. For example, ACE Cash Express assesses the risk of each check-cashing transaction and reports losses of less than 1%.[25] Because tax refund loan companies prepare and file the borrower's taxes, they are reasonably assured that loans will not exceed refunds. To further guarantee repayment, tax refund lenders often establish an account into which the Internal Revenue Service (IRS) directly deposits the customer's refund check. Pawnshops lend about 50% of a pledged collateral's value, which leaves a large buffer if it goes unclaimed (according to industry trade groups about 70% of customers redeem their goods). Repayment of credit card debt by high-risk borrowers is guaranteed by a credit line secured through an escrowed savings account (see chapter 4). The rent-to-own furniture and appliance industry charges well above the "street price" for furniture and appliances, which is generally more than sufficient to offset losses. Payday lenders require a postdated check or electronic debit transfer to ensure repayment. In any case, losses are obviously not severe given the phenomenal growth of the payday lending industry.

While risks exist—as in all industries—they are mitigated by loan collateral, excessive markup in prices, and the socialization of losses among a class of borrowers. Put another way, enough people will make good on their payday loans to compensate for the bad ones—not difficult, given the extremely high industry-wide profit margins. In short, industry claims about the high risks associated with serving marginal populations are exaggerated.

The major profit in the fringe economy generally doesn't lie in the sale of a product, but rather in the financing. For example, if a used-car lot buys a vehicle for $3,000 and sells it for $5,000, its profit is $2,000. But if it finances that vehicle for two years at a 25% APR, the profit jumps to $3,242. This dynamic is true for virtually every sector in the fringe economy. A customer's paying off a loan or purchasing a good or service outright is far less profitable than an ongoing financial relationship. Consequently, the profitability of the fringe economy lies in keeping customers continually enmeshed in an expensive financial system.

Mainstream Financial Institutions and the Fringe Economy

By 2000 there were no banks left in Southwest Baltimore. They wanted no part of a neighborhood where the median income was $19,000 and 58% of the residents lived below the poverty line. When the last bank left in the late 1990s, the 21,000 residents were forced to make due with check-cashing outlets, payday lenders, and pawnshops. The same phenomenon exists in South Central Los Angeles, a low-income community of 400,000 that has 133 check-cashing outlets and 19 bank branches.[26] For Southwest Baltimore, South Central Los Angeles, and hundreds of other low-income communities across the nation, the fringe lending sector has become the modern equivalent of a local community bank.[27]

The consolidation in the banking industry over the past 20 years has reduced the number of banks in low-income neighborhoods, increased the focus of banks on corporate and high-income customers, and limited banks' interest in serving consumers with small accounts or less-than-perfect credit. To counter this trend, some scholars and community activists are encouraging mainstream banks to set up branches in low-income neighborhoods.

John Caskey argues that mainstream banks should develop innovative programs to help low-income households build savings, improve credit profiles, lower bill-payment costs, and gain access to lower-cost sources of credit.[28] He suggests that banks can open conveniently located branch offices, targeted at low-income households, that offer nontraditional services such as basic low-cost savings accounts that include access to money orders; deposit accounts designed to help low-income people accumulate savings; secured loans to individuals whose credit histories make them ineligible for mainstream credit; and budget-management and credit-repair seminars. Despite Caskey's optimism, when traditional banks serve low-income communities, they are frequently as predatory as fringe economy businesses.

OVERVIEW OF THE FRINGE ECONOMY

Rob Schneider, staff attorney for Consumers Union, maintains that banks have neglected low-income communities for years to concentrate on branches in more affluent areas. "Nowadays, banks are returning to the same neighborhoods to claim a piece of the pie once reserved for check-cashers, pawnshops, and payday lenders."[29] He says that the same banks now competing with check cashers had a hand in developing the industry. For example, many banks fulfilled their obligations under the 1977 Community Reinvestment Act (which required banks to serve low-income and minority communities) by investing in check cashers and other fringe economy businesses. To remain competitive in today's financial-services market, some banks are also tapping directly into the low-income market by providing check-cashing services and low-cost deposit accounts (see chapter 6).

Today's fringe economy is heavily dependent on mainstream financial institutions. For instance, ACE Cash Express has a relationship with a group of banks, including Wells Fargo and JP Morgan Chase Bank, to provide capital for its acquisitions and other activities.[30] Advance America has relationships with Morgan Stanley, Banc of America Securities, Wachovia Capital Markets, and Wells Fargo Securities, to name a few. Similar banking relationships exist throughout the alternative financial-services industry.

A growing number of mainstream financial institutions also serve high-risk consumers through their affiliates. Citigroup (the largest U.S.-based bank holding company) acquired Washington Mutual Finance in 2003, giving it 400 subprime lending offices in 25 states. Through its subprime flagship, CitiFinancial, Citigroup engages in subprime lending, and by 2000 it was America's largest subprime lender, with more than $16 billion in outstanding loans.

Subprime lending is clearly profitable. While Citigroup reported a 3% increase in income in 2001, CitiFinancial boasted 39%.[31] In 2002 CitiFinancial's income grew by 21% (more than $1.3 billion) and accounted for almost 10% of Citigroup's revenue.[32] Citigroup's 2004 net revenue was a staggering $21.89 billion.[33]

Some observers believe that the entry of mainstream financial institutions into subprime lending will help neutralize some of the worst features of the fringe economy, an optimism that may not be justified. In one of the largest consumer protection settlements in Federal Trade Commission history, CitiFinancial paid $240 million in 2002 to resolve charges that its units Associates First Capital and Associates Corporation systematically engaged in widespread deceptive and abusive lending practices.[34] In 2003 a $51 million verdict was awarded in a class action suit filed against Lehman Brothers, First Alliance Corporation, and MBIA on behalf of 7,500 homeowners. The plaintiffs claimed that First Alliance defrauded them on home equity loans and that Lehman Brothers assisted in fraudulent activities when it financed the lender.

Wells Fargo is involved in subprime lending through its subsidiaries Wells Fargo Financial and Wells Fargo Funding. The California Department of Corporations found Wells Fargo Financial, prominent on the Association of Community Organizations for Reform Now (ACORN) list of predatory lenders, guilty of charging predatory interest rates to 15,000 customers in 2001. After refunding more than $533,000, Wells Fargo Financial turned around and overcharged many of these same customers another $338,000 in 2002.[35] EquiCredit, a former subsidiary of Bank of America (BofA), was forced to pay back $2.5 million to 12,000 Philadelphia homeowners because of predatory lending practices. BoA's former subsidiary NationsCredit was stung with a $2.5 million verdict by an Alabama jury for fleecing a couple on a home repair loan.[36] In 2001 the cost and embarrassment of these lawsuits led BofA to supposedly divest itself of subprime lending and liquidate its $26.3 billion subprime real estate portfolio, losing about $1.25 billion. However, BofA reentered the subprime market in 2004 when it purchased Oakmont Mortgage Company, a subprime lender.

Although the current concern that federal and state officials have shown toward the fringe economy is partly triggered by a desire to protect the public interest, it is also motivated by the pressure exerted by mainstream financial institutions to appropriate important parts of this market. For example, the Financial Service Centers of America (FiSCA), an industry trade group representing check cashers and payday lenders, came out strongly against BofA's proposed acquisition of Fleet Boston. FiSCA demanded that "the Federal Reserve Bank should require, as a condition to approving the acquisition, that Bank of America make commercial banking facilities available to check cashers and prohibit the bank from enforcing its discriminatory blanket withholding of services from the entire industry."[37] Lest one believe that BofA's refusal to provide financial services to the check-cashing industry is grounded in corporate social responsibility, the bank charges $5 to cash checks in many states, which is the same as, if not more than, what many commercial check cashers charge. The fringe economy is clearly too profitable to be overlooked by mainstream financial institutions.

Our customer base is very large, diverse, and
rapidly growing—it's really mainstream America.

—ACE Cash Express, 2004 Annual Report

2

Why the Fringe Economy Is Growing

The almost exponential growth of the fringe economy during the mid-1990s was baffling, especially since real incomes were rising and the numbers of people in poverty were dropping. Nonetheless, many factors came together to foster the phenomenal growth of the fringe economy, including the rise in numbers of America's working poor, welfare reform, high levels of immigration, the growth of the Internet, the increased financial stress that slow wage growth and the rising cost of necessities placed on the middle class; and liberal federal banking laws. In simple terms, a major reason for the growth in the fringe economy is that 43% of Americans annually spend more than they earn. A full appreciation of the growth of the fringe economy begins with an understanding of its customer base.

Fringe Economy Customers

The fringe economy primarily targets those who make less than the median family income of $50,000 and live from paycheck to paycheck. A second target is immigrants who have little experience with banking institutions in their home countries, or who come from countries where banks cater primarily to the wealthy. Each month the amount of money they earn is equivalent to, or less than, their living expenses for rent, utilities, food, clothing, and other necessities.

According to the Consumer Federation of America, about 53% of us live from paycheck to paycheck, at least some of the time. Moreover, about 40% of all white children and 73% of all African American children in the United States live in a household with zero or negative net worth.[1] For these people, living on the economic edge means that there is no room for error. Any unforeseen expense, such as a car breakdown, a babysitter not showing up, or a bout of the flu, can become a cash crisis and lead to a trip to the pawnshop or payday lender. The traditional banking model doesn't work for many of these people. Having poor or no credit history makes them a high risk to banks, and minimum-balance requirements and high overdraft and check-bouncing fees often make a checking account unrealistic. The lack of a nearby branch or multilingual tellers, as well as limited hours of operation, further alienates some people from traditional banking

OVERVIEW OF THE FRINGE ECONOMY

services. Many banks also fail to adequately explain the banking system to immigrants from countries where banking is limited to the upper classes.

An important group of fringe economy customers is the "unbanked"— individuals or families without accounts at deposit institutions. Because the unbanked have no formal ties to mainstream financial institutions, they can't secure traditional credit, so they turn to the fringe sector for check cashing, bill paying, short-term payroll loans, furniture and appliance rentals, and a host of other financial services involving high fees and inter- est rates. When the unbanked are combined with the similarly large num- ber of people who are classified as "underbanked"—those who don't utilize or qualify for bank services beyond maintaining an account—the market for fringe services is even larger.

According to the U.S. General Accounting Office, as many as 56 million adult Americans—about 28% of all adults—don't have a bank account. Almost 12 million U.S. households (one-fourth of all low-income families) have no relationship with a bank, savings institution, credit union, or other mainstream financial-services provider.[2] Most of the unbanked say they lack a checking account because (1) they don't write enough checks to warrant one, (2) they don't have any month-to-month savings to deposit, (3) they can't afford high bank fees, (4) they can't meet minimum bank bal- ance requirements, (5) they want to keep their financial records private, and (6) they are uncomfortable dealing with banks. Almost 85% of the unbanked have yearly incomes below $25,000.[3] Many also have jobs for which they are paid weekly by check or cash rather than through direct deposit.

One industry-funded study found that the average payday customer was female with children living at home, was between 24 and 44, earned less than $40,000 a year, was a high school graduate, was a renter (most had lived in their homes for less than five years), and had little job tenure.[4] This group represents the lower- and moderate-income working class rather than the poorest of the poor. However, if the fringe economy is broadly defined to include consumers with higher incomes but no assets and high debt—the functionally poor—these customer characteristics dramatically change.

The Working Poor

The Danforths live in a small three-bedroom apartment in Chicago along with their three children. Robert works in the sporting goods department at Wal-Mart, America's largest private employer. (In 2004 Wal-Mart employed 1.2 million people and reported $250 billion in revenues, or about 2% of the nation's gross domestic product. By 2007 Wal-Mart is expected to control 35% of all U.S. food and drug sales.[5])

Despite having the title of "associate," Robert earns $9.75 an hour (11 cents more than the average Wal-Mart wage of $9.64), substantially less than when he owned his own small sporting goods store. Surrounded by big box stores like Wal-Mart and Target, Robert couldn't compete and was forced to close down. The prospects for him to get ahead at Wal-Mart are limited, since the average store has one manager, one to three assistant managers, 15 department heads, and 300–350 "associates." On the other hand, he is one of the lucky few who have a 40-hour workweek, as opposed to the average 32-hour workweek for most Wal-Mart employees.[6]

Robert is one of 47% of Wal-Mart employees who receive health care benefits. Therefore, his modest salary is eroded by large employee premiums and high deductibles—employee-paid premiums cover 42% of Wal-Mart's health plan, compared with the national average of 16%. In a worst-case scenario, Robert could spend about $6,400 before he sees a single benefit from the health plan. There are no free lunches, and one way or another, we all pay the real costs for Wal-Mart's "low prices." According to a study by the Institute for Labor and Employment at the University of California, Berkeley, California taxpayers subsidize $20.5 million worth of medical care for Wal-Mart employees. In fact, Wal-Mart personnel offices know that their employees can't afford the company health plan and encourage them to apply for charitable and public assistance.[7]

Unlike Robert, Betsy hasn't been able to find a full-time job and shuttles between part-time jobs at Target and Circuit City. Together, they scrape up a yearly income of $38,000, or $16,000 above the 2004 federal poverty line of $22,000 for a family of five. Despite their being above the poverty line, the Danforths' economic life is bleak. Rent is rising, along with the costs of utilities, gas, food, pharmaceuticals, and most other necessities. Their car is getting old, and they hope to send at least one of their children to college. The Danforths are America's working poor. They're also the propellant for America's fringe economy.

Almost one in four American workers lives in poverty or close to it. Thirty-five million people work full time but still don't make an adequate living. These workers are the nursing home aides, poultry processors, pharmacy assistants, child-care workers, data-entry keyers, janitors, and other employees of the secondary and tertiary labor markets. They are also the 53% of underemployed Wal-Mart employees with no benefits and a 32-hour workweek. As David Shipler writes, "The term by which they are usually described, 'working poor,' should be an oxymoron. Nobody who works hard should be poor in America."[8] Since the 1980s, the relative wages of these workers have declined.[9]

The growth of the fringe economy parallels the economic development of the 1990s and early 2000s. Specifically, during this time there were four distinct economic phases: a downward spiral from 1989 to 1993 (family income fell $1,572 from 1989 to 1992); a slow recovery up to 1995; rapid growth from 1995 to 2001 (family income grew $4,555 from 1995 to 1999); and another economic dip, starting in 2001.

One measure of the economic well-being of workers is the median hourly wage of male and female workers. The median male wage fell dramatically from the 1980s to the early 1990s, dropping 9.1%. While it rose 5.5% from 1995 to 1999, this was not enough to offset earlier declines. In contrast, the median female wage grew slowly over the 1980s, rising 5.7% from 1979 to 1989 and then dipping slightly in the early 1990s. Although there was a marked increase in wages during the mid-1990s, much of this increase was offset by the wage declines in the 1980s and early 1990s and by the higher prices of necessities such as housing, health care, education, and pharmaceuticals.[10] While corporate profits rose in 2003, median- and below-median-wage earners were losing ground as they had in the 1980s and early 1990s, and by 2003 the gains of the mid-1990s had all but evaporated.[11]

The problems of the working poor have been worsened by the inadequacy of the $5.15 minimum wage, which has been frozen since 1997. In 1999 about 3.3 million hourly workers (4.6% of the workforce) earned the minimum wage.[12] Among full-time workers age 16–24 that number was 10.2%, and among part-time workers it was almost 12%.[13] In 1997 the minimum wage brought a three-person family to only within 77% of the poverty line; by 2003 the figure had gone down to 67%.[14] Although the minimum wage only impacts a small portion of the workforce, it is used widely as a benchmark for setting wages in the secondary labor market.

The Economic Policy Institute estimates that households with one adult and two children require $14 an hour—far more than the current $5.15 minimum wage—to live barely above the poverty line. Sixty percent of American workers earn less than $14 an hour, and unskilled entry-level workers in many service occupations earn $7 an hour or less.[15] The working poor are also more vulnerable to the vicissitudes of life than the middle class. For example, more than 40 million Americans lack health insurance, and unanticipated events such as illnesses or family emergencies may require workers to take off time without pay, leading to a temporary short-fall in income and increased debt. Given the low incomes of the working poor, it's not surprising that a fringe economy that promises quick cash with few questions asked has become a high-growth sector. The growth of the fringe economy can also be partially attributed to the 1996 welfare-reform legislation signed by former president Bill Clinton.

Welfare Reform

Lavelle Brown, of Milwaukee, Wisconsin, is the mother of two children and a former Temporary Aid to Needy Families (TANF) recipient. In 1997 Wisconsin adopted the Wisconsin Works, or W-2, program, which is based on a "work-first" approach emphasizing the placement of recipients in unsubsidized employment or community-service jobs rather than educa-tion and training. Under W-2 there's no entitlement to income assistance; its goals are to promote self-sufficiency and to reduce welfare rolls. In 1997 Lavelle was forced to forgo public assistance for Wisconsin Works.

After cycling through three jobs since 1997, Lavelle finally ended up working as a certified nurse's aide. Although she started at $6 an hour, she is now making $7.75 an hour. In the past, Lavelle was able to supplement her income by working overtime, but in the last two years her employer virtually eliminated that possibility due to cutbacks. As a seasoned welfare recipient, Lavelle knew the ropes. Her low salary qualified her for food stamps, the Child Health Insurance Program (CHIPS), the Earned Income Tax Credit (EITC), and the Child Tax Credit (CTC). By combining benefits and occasional outside work, Lavelle raised her $15,000 salary to an income of $25,000 a year. Despite this, it was often too low to meet monthly expenses, especially when an unexpected crisis occurred. Without the public-assistance safety net to help her through the hard times, Lavelle was forced to turn to payday lenders and pawnshops.

In 1996 Congress passed the Personal Responsibility and Work Opportunity Reconciliation Act (PRWORA), which included the TANF program. Among other things, TANF mandated a five-year lifetime cap on public assistance, which states were permitted to reduce to two years. The soul of TANF lay in the compulsory work program that required states to place 50% of recipients in jobs by 2000. Since PRWORA's passage, welfare caseloads have dropped more than 47% nationally. From 1994 to 2002, caseloads dropped from 14 million to 5 million, with most of the 9 million former recipients ending up in the low-wage labor market. At the same time, requests for emergency food assistance surged 17% from 1996 to 2001—62% of those requests came from families with children and 32% from employed adults.[16]

According to the National Conference of State Legislatures, "Most of the jobs former recipients take pay between $5.50 and $7.00 per hour, higher than the minimum wage but not enough to raise a family out of poverty. Most jobs are in the services and retail trade. So far, few families who leave welfare have been able to escape poverty.[17] This finding is corroborated by other reports showing the following:

- Women leaving welfare earn an average of $6.75 an hour, barely enough to raise a family of three above the federal poverty line. Fifty-eight percent of employed former recipients have an income below the poverty line, and more than half are unable to pay rent, purchase food, afford medical care, or pay for utilities.

- Only former recipients with at least a two-year post-secondary or vocational degree are likely to escape poverty by earnings alone.[18]

Forced into low-wage employment, former welfare recipients are an important base for the fringe economy. Indeed, it's no coincidence that 60% of payday lending customers are women.[19]

Providing for the needs of the poor is like the game of hot potatoes. Government discharges the responsibility for the poor to the labor market through compulsory TANF work requirements, while the private sector employs them in low-wage jobs without benefits. The hot potato is then passed back to government, which institutes the benefit portions of labor-force participation—CHIPS for children; Medicaid; and EITC and CTC, for supplementing low wages. In the end, taxpayers continue to subsidize the poor, indirectly. In that sense, the major beneficiaries of welfare reform are not the poor or American taxpayers, but low-wage employers who can hire cheap hourly workers without the responsibility of providing anything beyond a weekly paycheck. In large measure, this represents the adoption of Third World labor standards into the American context.

Apart from the cash offered by tax programs like EITC and CTC, government is increasingly refusing to provide emergency assistance to the working poor. While TANF work requirements force former recipients into low-wage work, they also allow fringe economy businesses to assume some welfare-state functions, such as providing emergency cash assistance through payday loans, pawns, and other short-term credit. Hence, the fringe economy has taken on the functions of a privatized—and expensive—welfare state by offering former recipients emergency financial services no longer provided by the government. It's also one of the only economic sectors that primarily serve the poor.

Immigration

The Census Bureau projects that in less than 50 years the U.S. population will swell from 290 million to 400 million because of immigration. In 2002, 33.1 million people in the United States were foreign-born, or about 11.5% of the population. About 11.4 million of them had permanent resident status, and another 8 million were eligible to be naturalized.[20] Immigrants filled 4 of every 10 job openings in the mid-1990s when the

OVERVIEW OF THE FRINGE ECONOMY

unemployment rate hit record lows. In fact, when the labor force grew by 16.7 million workers in the 1990s, 6.4 million of them were foreign-born.[21]

The 1990s saw large-scale geographic dispersion among newly arriving immigrants. While in earlier years most new immigrants clustered in a few large cities, such as Los Angeles, New York, and Chicago, the 1990s witnessed a spread to the Midwest, New England, and the mid- and South Atlantic regions. In some parts of the country, almost the entire labor-force growth between 1996 and 2000 was due to immigration.[22]

New immigrants commonly fill low-skill, blue-collar jobs, since a large number have less than a high school education. About 33% of immigrants have not finished high school, compared with 13% of natives. Not only do immigrants possess fewer educational skills than native workers, but also many of their skills don't translate into the American workplace.[23]

Between 2000 and 2002, about 3.3 million illegal immigrants entered in the United States. Mexicans made up 57% of undocumented workers, with another 23% coming from other Latin American countries.[24] A significant portion of Hispanic poverty is attributable to these large numbers of illegal workers entering the United States and the low-paying jobs they occupy.

Although there is no reliable data about the number of immigrants who use the fringe economy, it is undoubtedly high. The 1996 welfare-reform bill had profound implications for both legal and illegal immigrants. Specifically, the bill disentitled most legal immigrants (including many who had lived in the United States for years but chose not to become citizens) from food stamps, TANF, and Supplemental Security Income (SSI).[25] The low wages paid to many immigrants, especially those from Latin America, the Caribbean, and Africa, put them squarely in the ranks of the working poor. Denied public-assistance benefits and other welfare subsidies, immigrants are the perfect customers for the fringe economy. This base is further expanded by immigrants who lack a basic knowledge of consumer financial services due to the lack of these services in their home countries.

Another reason why immigrants—especially undocumented workers—use fringe financial services is that they lack the requisite IDs (such as a Social Security card or driver's license) that many mainstream banks require for credit or other financial transactions. Instead, many Mexican immigrants have a *matricula consular* card, a photo ID issued by Mexican consulates. While in the past only fringe businesses recognized these cards as valid identification, today some banks and credit unions, including Bank of America, Wells Fargo, and Citigroup, accept *consular* cards. However, many illegal workers continue to steer clear of mainstream financial institutions for fear of being caught or exposed.

The Internet

The Internet is shaping our society in myriad ways, and its use is leaching down to America's poorest citizens. For example, computer and Internet use has risen dramatically among all racial and socioeconomic groups since 1994. Even in low-income central cities, 51% of residents now own a personal computer and 46% have online access.[26] The widespread use of the Internet has also promoted the growth of the fringe economy.

The Internet poses dangers for poor and credit-challenged consumers because of its reach and its cloak of invisibility. For instance, short of doing extensive research, users have little knowledge of whom they are corresponding with or where those businesses are based. This anonymity has proved useful for various fringe economy operators and scam artists, many of which operate offshore.

E-commerce accounted for nearly $6.8 trillion in international sales in 2004, with almost $3.2 trillion of that in the United States alone.[27] The use of the Internet for mortgages, home refinancing, payday loans, debt-management plans, credit-repair services, and tax refund loans has been exploding. For example in 2003, 9% of all mortgages—$150 billion—were initiated online, a number expected to reach 15% in 2005.[28] Despite this potential, the Internet is mainly useful for transactions that don't require the transfer of physical collateral, and it's less useful when a face-to-face exchange of physical goods is required, such as pawns, transferring auto titles, or renting furniture and appliances.

The Internet has fostered a proliferation of online payday lenders with names like Sonic Cash, MyPaydayLoan.com, WeGiveCash.com, PayDay OK, the Cash Station, CheckAdvance.com, and National Payday Loans. Some of these online lenders offer bigger loans than states allow—up to

$2,500—and charge interest rates exceeding state usury caps, sometimes in excess of 650%. Others make loans in states where payday lending is illegal, and in states that allow only brick-and-mortar storefront payday lending.

Some online lenders automatically renew loans if they're not repaid by debiting cash from the borrower's bank account. Using the cloak of invisibility, many online payday lenders don't provide phone numbers or physical addresses—only e-mail addresses—and borrowers may have trouble canceling transactions or resolving problems. Borrowers also face the security risk of sending bank account and Social Security numbers over the Internet to unknown lenders, which can result in identity theft or unauthorized debits.

The Internet has created a new playing field by enabling fringe corporations to skip over state commercial barriers, thereby providing fresh opportunities to circumvent usury laws. In fact, the Internet has allowed payday lenders, fringe mortgage lenders, and predatory credit card companies to operate not only outside of state laws, but sometimes even outside of U.S. borders. For example, payday lenders can use electronic transfers to send cash to borrowers through offshore banks.

State commercial barriers are being broken down in all areas, including credit cards. For example, consumers no longer have to apply for credit cards at local banks; instead, they can apply online to almost any bank in the United States. Some fringe lenders in states with strict usury laws have installed Internet kiosks that allow customers to apply for loans in states with liberal or no interest caps.

The technological revolution is increasingly making state usury laws almost anachronistic and is a factor in the explosive growth of the fringe economy. While the fringe economy is growing because of welfare reform, slow wage growth, the rising costs of necessities, and the Internet, it is also expanding because of increased use by the middle class, especially functionally poor middle-income families.

Debt – the frozen form of stored-up hierarchy.

–Rabbi Arthur Waskow, *Take Back Your Time*

3

Debt and the Functionally Poor Middle Class

Although the concept of "the middle class" is central to American life, there's no agreed-upon definition of the term. For example, the U.S. Census Bureau has no official income classification for the middle class.[1] Consequently, the middle class has come to represent a large portion of the population ranging from those with incomes at 200% of the federal poverty level to those in the nation's top 5% of income earners.

Some policy analysts classify households with a total annual income between $40,000 and $140,000 as middle class, while others categorize the middle class as having an annual income between $25,000 and $75,000. Still others use an annual income of $50,000 as a benchmark.[2] To complicate matters, middle-class incomes are not adjusted geographically or by an urban/rural designation. In short, the term "middle class" is virtually meaningless given the enormous income spread. For the purposes of this chapter, the middle class is defined as households with a yearly pretax income of between $25,000 and $75,000 — A group that occupies about the middle half of the Census income-distribution tables.[3]

Jon and Miriam Goldstein illustrate the growing group of functionally poor middle class households. Jon is a network systems administrator in the insurance industry. After the birth of their child, Ari, the Goldsteins agreed that Miriam would stay at home to care for the baby. Besides, Miriam worked in an office where she earned $21,000 a year, and after she paid $700 a month for child care and bought work clothes, lunches, and gas, her income would be so depleted that it made little sense for her to work.

After Ari's birth, the Goldsteins sold their small townhouse and purchased a larger but still modest home in a suburban Atlanta neighborhood. Jon had gotten a raise and was making $85,000 a year. Two years later he lost his job when the company outsourced its computer work abroad. Jon spent seven months looking for another job. In the meantime, the Goldsteins lived on help from their families and their small savings. When that proved insufficient, they used their credit cards, racking up almost $35,000 in debt.

The Goldsteins' monthly costs were high. In addition to a mortgage, they had loans on two newer cars that were "upside down" (the loan amount was greater than the value of the vehicles). After maxing out two credit lines, the Goldsteins were forced to refinance their home to draw out the little equity they had accrued.

Jon's new job paid $50,000 a year, 41% less than he had made in his former position. Miriam went back to work, but their joint income was still lower than what Jon had earned before. Faced with a large credit card debt, higher house payments due to refinancing, and less income, the Goldsteins were inaugurated into the growing class of functionally poor middle-class households.

There's a misconception that only the poor use the fringe economy. This overlooks the convergence of the traditional poor with growing segments of the middle class that have a moderate income but are asset-poor and debt-rich. Specifically, the functionally poor include homeowners who use their houses as ATMs, regularly drawing out equity to finance credit card debts or other purchases. It also includes middle-class people with tarnished credit who use high-interest-rate credit cards or finance their purchases through tricky time-deferred payments. In that sense, a burgeoning sector of the middle class is economically closer to the poor than to the traditional middle class. Arriving by different roads, they both risk ending up in the fringe economy.

Debt and the Fringe Economy

The ostensible cause of financial hardship among the functionally poor middle class is debt, which is endemic to all sectors of our society. In 2004 the federal debt was $7.5 trillion, a $2.1 trillion increase over 1997.[4] Each citizen's share of this debt totaled more than $23,000, or about 50% of the average American family wage.[5]

Consumer spending—much of it fueled by advertising and marketing—accounts for two-thirds of the nation's $11 trillion economy. In part, the success of these two industries has led us to become more indebted than ever. Consumer debt—excluding mortgages—almost doubled from 1994 to 2004 and totals about $19,000 per family. By 2004 we owed more than $9 trillion in home mortgages, car loans, credit card debt, home equity loans, and other forms of credit. We accumulated nearly 40% of that total in just four years. One-fifth of the $9 trillion was borrowed at variable interest rates, such as those on credit or store cards.

Because of this, middle-income consumers—the biggest users of variable-rate debt—are ten times more likely than upper-income families to devote 40% or more of their income to debt repayment.[6] (The average household now spends 13% of its after-tax income on debt repayment, the highest percentage since 1986.[7]) All told, family debt has increased a whopping 500% since 1957.

Consumer debt is aggravated by low rates of personal savings. Americans saved about 10% of their disposable income in the 1980s; by late 2004 that fell to a near-record low as we saved less than 1%.[8] Home equity was also the lowest in recent history due to feverish home refinancing. In 2002 homeowners initiated $97 billion in home equity loans, nearly five times the amount in 1993.[9] While home refinancing put about $300 billion back into the economy from 2001 to 2003, consumers spent almost all of it.[10] Not coincidentally, roughly half a million homeowners are currently in the foreclosure process.[11]

Credit card debt is another factor in the growth of the "new poor." Estimates of credit card balances per household range from slightly less than

Figure 3.1.
Average U.S. credit card debt per household (includes all credit cards and U.S. households with at least one credit card).[12]

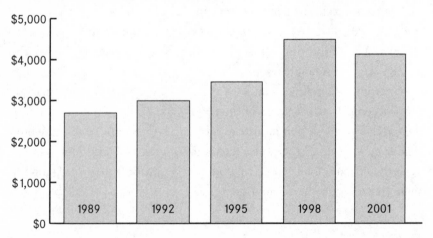

OVERVIEW OF THE FRINGE ECONOMY

$5,000 to almost $12,000, with the average American family spending about $1,100 a year in credit card interest alone.[13] Overall, credit card holders carried more than $1.7 trillion in debt in 2002, up from $1.1 trillion in 1995.[14] Debt is now cited as the number one problem facing newlyweds and is becoming a major cause of divorce.[15] Figure 3.1 illustrates a conservative estimate of the growth in credit card debt.

According to Elizabeth Warren and Amelia Tyagi, today's two-income family earns 75% more than its single-income counterpart did a generation ago but has less discretionary income after fixed monthly bills are paid.[16] Some of this is attributable to mortgage costs, which have risen 70 times faster than an average father's wages.[17] In addition, earnings of non-college-graduate males have dropped since the 1970s, forcing more mothers to work to make up the difference. This second income has not resulted in families' purchasing more; instead, it is used to pay for necessities. While a second income helps pay bills, the effect is diminished by day-care costs ranging from $340 to almost $1,100 a month, clothing expenses, and the need for a second reliable car.[18] For many families with young children, half or more of their second wage is consumed by the costs of holding a job, and after expenses they see only a small increase in family income. The impact of the second income is further diminished by the differential in male and female wages (women earn roughly 77% as much as men for the same job).[19]

Eileen Applebaum, Annette Bernhardt, and Richard Murnane argue that middle- and low-income families have maxed out their earnings capacity when the mothers have gone to work. Specifically, second incomes are no longer kept in reserve for family emergencies but instead are used to pay for day-to-day living expenses. The result is that families are left with no reserve income for emergencies. Home equity refinancing, high credit card debt, anemic savings rates, high housing costs, and little or no reserve income leave middle-class families in a precarious situation, and life events such as illness, death, desertion, or unemployment can easily push them into bankruptcy. Consequently, these families are forced to generate additional income by ersatz means such as mortgage refinancing.[20]

The Overconsumption Argument

Juliet Schor asserts that middle- and upper-middle-class consumers are participating in a national orgy of overspending and living beyond their means.[21] She maintains that the majority of American households have attained a level of affluence where added consumption no longer improves welfare. Despite the rising income of professionals, she notes, most don't feel better off and tell pollsters that they lack the money to buy everything they need. Surprisingly, they are almost as likely to report this whether they make $85,000 or $35,000 a year. Schor also points to studies showing that materialistic attitudes—wanting more and never being satisfied—increase the likelihood of suffering from depression, anxiety, and low self-esteem. (Alternatively, depression and anxiety may lead to over-consumption rather than the other way around.)

John de Graaf, David Wann, and Thomas Naylor also address the over-consumption argument. According to them, "affluenza" is a contagious, socially transmitted disease of overload, debt, anxiety, and waste that results from the frantic pursuit of *more*. Shockingly, we spend more for trash bags than 90 of the world's 210 countries spend for everything. "To live, we buy," they write, and we can't resist the "urge to splurge" on every-thing from food and good sex to religion and recreation. The price we pay is the suffocation of our intrinsic curiosity, self-motivation, and creativity.[22]

Although compelling, the overconsumption argument fails to address a major cause of indebtedness: the high costs of living in a privatized society. The critique fails to acknowledge that "fixed costs"—mortgage, child care, health insurance, vehicles, and taxes—take up 75% of the paycheck of today's two-income family. By contrast, those costs represented about half of a middle-class family's income in the early 1970s. For instance, Ameri-can families in 2002 spent 22% less for food (including restaurant meals), 21% less for clothing, and 44% less for appliances than in 1973. Adjusted for inflation, consumer expenditures are lower than a generation ago.[23] Blaming overconsumption for structural economic problems allows law-makers to admonish families for an economic reality they can't control.

An important cause of growing indebtedness is the rising cost of neces-sities. For the average middle-class family, indebtedness is due more to

OVERVIEW OF THE FRINGE ECONOMY

increases in fixed expenses than to spending money on designer clothes, luxury cars, exotic vacations, high-tech home entertainment centers, and expensive jewelry . Consider the following examples:

- Cuts in health insurance benefits nationwide resulted in a rise in worker contributions from $6,438 in 2000 to $9,068 in 2003. From 2000 to 2003, inflation-adjusted out-of-pocket expenditures rose by more than 7%. Costs for prescription drugs and medical supplies grew by 12.5%. In comparison, from 2000 to 2004, pay raises averaged less than 4%, and some workers received no increase at all.

- Between 1997 and 2001 the median household income rose about 14% to $42,228, while the median price of a new home rose 20% to roughly $175,200. The median rent in 2001 was about $535, up more than 17% from the same period in 1997. More than 13 million households pay over 50% of their income for housing.

- Public-college tuition costs rose 14.1% from 2003 to 2004.

- Property and car insurance costs rose 9% from 2003 to 2004. Average auto insurance costs grew from $668 in 1995 to $855 in 2003. Home-owners' insurance rose from $420 in 1994 to $603 in 2003. Property taxes in many urban areas rose more than 30% from 1999 to 2003.[24]

Indebtedness can lead to bankruptcy. In 2002 there were 1.4 personal bankruptcies for every 100 U.S. households. Every 15 seconds, someone in the United States goes bankrupt, a fourfold increase over 1980. About 1.5 million American households filed for bankruptcy in 2003, 400% more than in 1975.[25] In fact, more people filed for bankruptcy in 2004 than graduated from college or filed for divorce.[26] In examining bankruptcy filers, Teresa Sullivan, Elizabeth Warren, and Jay Westbrook found that they crossed all income and occupational levels and were not irresponsible spendthrifts. Instead, they had had insurmountable financial problems stemming from a life crisis such as divorce, job loss, or medical problems.[27]

Warren and Tyagi argue that two-parent middle-class working families are teetering on the brink of financial disaster. From economic data and 2,000 interviews, they found that families are not in financial trouble because they squander their second income on luxuries; instead, both incomes are used almost exclusively for necessities. When a crisis occurs, these financially overstretched families have no discretionary income to fall back on.[28]

The middle class is becoming an important customer base for the fringe economy. Although middle-class people are not yet flocking to pay-day lenders, check cashers, or pawnshops in large numbers, when their credit lines are exhausted, greater numbers will undoubtedly slide into more fringe economy services. This potential market is illustrated by television, newspaper, and radio advertisements run by large fringe corporations that are increasingly highlighting middle-class customers. The attempt is to normalize the fringe economy by changing its sleazy image and showing that it's respectable for the middle class to use these services. Even if this strategy doesn't yield immediate results, large fringe economy corporations have deep pockets and can wait for the new wave of consumers.

Cultural Change and the Fringe Economy

One way to understand the fringe economy is through economic stratification theory. Within that framework, the fringe economy represents the stratification of the mainstream economy into three separate economies: one for the affluent; one for the middle class with good credit; and a third for the poor, near-poor, or credit-challenged. But what was once a neatly stratified economy—with fringe services quarantined to low-income individuals—has now become more complicated as fringe services are leaching into the middle class. For example, a sign in one Wells Fargo bank advertised that home equity loans could be used to buy a new car, pay off bills, or go on a vacation. Just a few decades ago, drawing out home equity for these kinds of purchases would have been anathema to homeowners and the conservative banking industry. This represents a dramatic change in the culture of borrowing.

No single economic theory alone can explain the modern fringe economy, since its growth is as much a cultural phenomenon as an economic one. For example, while economic data explains why stagnant wages and rising costs have expanded the numbers of the working poor and driven them deeper into poverty, the data does not explain why a low-income family would pay $200 a month to rent an Italian leather couch from Aaron Rents. Nor does it explain why a poor family would rent a 45-inch high-definition television for the same monthly cost as buying a new, smaller set. Economic data also doesn't explain why a middle-class family would deplete its equity by refinancing its home to purchase a new automobile or to pay for an exotic vacation.

Traditional economic explanations don't address why families thirty or forty years ago were concerned about leaving their children with assets such as homes, stocks, or bonds, while today's families promise to leave heavily mortgaged houses and high credit card debt. Indeed, many of us have heard stories about how our grandmothers and grandfathers paid for everything in cash, including their cars. America has clearly undergone a major change regarding the acceptability of high debt and high levels of consumption. In that sense, the theory of overconsumption is correct.

The shift from the conservative financial culture of the 1950s and 1960s to the more freewheeling spending that characterizes the early 21st century can be attributed to several factors. First, advertising has been hugely successful in expanding the range of goods and services that people perceive as "necessary." These include cell phones, pagers, home entertainment centers, fast computers, cable television, blazing Internet access, video games, and so forth. Second, credit card companies and other financial institutions have helped redefine the concept of acceptable debt. As such, zero balances on credit cards are becoming increasingly rare as consumers rack up credit card purchases and play a shell game of shifting balances from one card to another.

Although stagnant wages coupled with increases in the cost of necessities drives the fringe economy, it is also driven by overconsumption, conspicuous consumption, status consumption, the inability to defer gratification, and impulse buying. Hence, it's not surprising that in surveys of children age 10 to 13, Juliet Schor found that their overriding goal was to get rich. In response to the statement, "I want to make a lot of money when I grow up," 63% agreed, and only 7% disagreed.[29] But even if most don't get rich, the fringe economy still allows them to live as if they were, albeit temporarily.

The driving vision of fringe economy entrepreneurs is to develop a fully formed subeconomy capable of meeting the financial needs of the poor, people with lower and moderate incomes, and the functionally poor middle class. While this is superficially a laudable goal, it is driven by maximizing profits from the economic desperation of these groups. The following chapters examine how this vision is being carried out within the various economic sectors, such as the credit, cash-loan, housing, and transportation industries.

II

The Fringe Sectors

Money can't buy you love, but a credit card can get you started.

−Robert D. Manning, *Credit Card Nation*

4

The Credit Card Industry

A profound revolution is taking place in the way we are meeting our financial needs. Although it is occurring largely off the radar screen, this change represents a fundamental shift in how a growing number of us access financial services and manage our day-to-day money matters. The basis of this revolution is the widespread expansion of credit.

Credit is the cornerstone of the modern U.S. economy. We can use it as a cushion for unexpected medical expenses, car repairs, the replacement of an appliance, an emergency family loan, or a trip to visit ailing or dying relatives. It is also a bridge between real household earnings and consumption decisions.[1] Credit allows us to purchase products or services immediately, some of which we would otherwise be unable to afford. Payment options are flexible for those of us with good credit, and collateral isn't required. Middle-class people can purchase goods or borrow cash while they retain their possessions, since loans are secured by the borrower's creditworthiness. Neither trust nor the presumption of goodwill exists in the fringe economy, however. A low-income or credit-challenged consumer who applies for a loan typically must provide collateral such as a secured bank account, a postdated check, household goods, or a car title.

There are two basic types of consumer credit: non-revolving and revolving. Non-revolving credit generally takes the form of loans—such as home mortgages, car loans, and student loans—with fixed balances and regular monthly payment schedules. The interest rate and the terms of the loan are typically fixed at the outset, and balances generally cannot be increased without initiating a new loan. Most non-revolving loans are for home mortgages, autos, and student loans. Revolving credit, the basis of credit cards and store cards, is used for open-ended loans with irregular balances that can change monthly. Balances on revolving loans grow with new purchases, and interest rates can change according to the market or the borrower's behavior.

Most of us have access today to consumer credit that was unimaginable only a generation ago. At the same time, debt has become increasingly common among those who can least afford it.[2] There is good and bad debt. Good debt builds physical or social assets, such as mortgages that lead to home equity or student loans that enhance human capital. Bad debt is generated by purchases that consumers can't afford, or by loans for month-to-month living expenses that regularly exceed income. Most revolving consumer debt fits in the latter category, and, as this chapter shows, it's accruing at a frightening pace.

The credit industry is based on a simple premise: in consumer loans, the economic interest of lenders lies primarily in the interest and fees they receive, not in having the original loan paid back. Lenders want the original loan paid back for only two reasons: if they think they can lend that money to someone else at a higher interest rate, or if they are concerned that they won't get their money back at all. Hence, the goal of a lender is to collect the most money possible through the highest interest rates and fees that the market will bear.

In that sense, the optimal lender scenario is for people to take on the maximum amount of debt they can handle at the highest interest rates and fees possible, and to keep that revenue stream flowing. The trick is to keep people paying this amount without pushing them to the point where they can no longer make timely payments or, in the worst-case scenario, they stop making payments altogether by declaring bankruptcy. Conversely, it's in our best interest to repay our debts in the most manageable way possible—that is, with the lowest interest rate and the fewest fees. Because of this dynamic, the relationship between creditors and borrowers is inherently adversarial.

Credit can be easily manipulated. Merchants and credit card issuers (CCIs) are continually developing innovative ways to lure us into buying more goods while going deeper into debt. For example, most large retailers offer financing programs that enable customers to buy merchandise they can't afford, such as furniture, electronics, and computers, that would otherwise wipe out their entire paycheck. This doesn't refer to charge cards or layaway plans where the customer pays for the merchandise before it is picked up, but rather to special promotions—usually advertised as "Buy now, pay later," "No interest for a year," or "90 days same as cash"—that let customers take possession of a product immediately but pay for it, interest-free, over a period of time. Some retailers require monthly payments, while others simply require payment in full before the grace period ends.

These promotions can be a good deal for those of us who can make timely payments, and a great deal for retailers, because a lot of us *can't* make the payments. Retailers like these plans because "no interest for 90 days" usually means "deferred interest after 90 days." For example, if you buy a $2,250 home entertainment center and the retailer doesn't receive your payment by the 91st day, you'll owe $2,250 plus three months of accrued interest. At a 23% APR—which is common—you'll pay an extra $129. There are myriad ways to make the unaffordable appear affordable.

An Overview of the Credit Card Industry

Jeanette Moseley and Wynne Chang bought a house together in Houston, Texas, in 2001. Because it was their first home, they went overboard in furnishing it, charging up $40,000 in credit card debt between them. Although they both earned an average income—about $40,000 a year each—they underestimated the expenses of home ownership and were unable to pay down their credit card balances. In fact, all Jeanette and Wynne could manage was to pay the minimum credit card balances owed. Barraged by credit card solicitations, they became "balance jumpers," going from one teaser rate to another just as the low rates were expiring. Jeanette and Wynne went through five promotional card offers but still couldn't substantially pay down their balances. Their mistake was in believing that they could borrow their way out of debt, something implicitly promised by the solicitations.

Credit cards are a way of life in the United States. Renting a car, reserving a hotel room, or booking a flight is almost impossible without a credit card.[3] The average American credit card holder has almost seven cards. Given this, it's not surprising that bank write-offs (that is, declaring a debt uncollectible) for credit card debt reached an 11-year high of 6.6% in early 2002.[4] While a large portion of the uncollectible debt can be traced to economically volatile card holders—many of whom were targeted by aggressive marketing campaigns to get new customers despite their shaky income or credit history—financially stretched middle-class households are responsible for a substantial amount of that debt. The statistics on credit card use are striking:

- Roughly 1.2 billion credit cards are in use in the United States. Eighty percent of households have at least one credit, debit, or retail card.

Plastic is used in 24% of all purchases, and by 2006 about 30% of all spending is expected to occur through credit cards. In 2004 the typical consumer had access to $12,190 on his or her combined credit cards.

- About 90% of Americans claim that credit card debt is not a source of worry. Curiously, 47% would refuse to tell a friend how much they owe. Eleven percent of Americans admit that their credit card debts went to collections, and 13% were 30 days late in paying credit card bills in 2003. Forty-eight percent of credit card holders carry a total balance of less than $1,000. However, 10% have total balances in excess of $10,000. About 12% of credit card holders use 80% or more of their credit card limit, and roughly 20% of all U.S. credit cards are maxed out. All told, in 2002 U.S. households owed an average of $8,940 on their credit cards compared with $7,842 in 2000. Credit card debt in 2002 was 173% higher than in 1992, and Americans paid $50 billion in finance charges, or about $1,100 per cardholder.

- Unpaid credit card debt, finance charges, and late fees are rising for those 35 years old and under. In 2003 the average balance-carrying consumer in that group owed $3,527, or almost 10% of his or her yearly income. Finance charges for the under-35 group were $456 in 2002, 18% higher than for older consumers.[5]

- Although much of the chronic credit card debt is attributable to the 45-and-under age group, credit card debt among senior citizens increased by 89% from 1993 to 2003, to an average of more than $4,000. The number of older Americans filing for bankruptcy has tripled, making them the fastest-growing age group in the bankruptcy courts.[6]

CCIs classify consumers by creditworthiness to determine the best way to profit from each level. Grouped by income and credit score, the top tier of consumers can get a platinum card with an APR of 12% or less. A gold card (which makes up half of all credit cards and requires only $10,000 in annual income) carries an average 15% APR, and a standard credit card has an APR of around 17%. Affluent or frugal consumers who use credit cards for convenience are offered preferred cards, often with no annual fees and including benefits such as frequent flyer miles and extended product warranties. Middle-class customers with good credit and college students with parental support are offered credit cards with little or no annual fees and an APR of 12%–26%. High-risk consumers—including those with a history of default or bankruptcy, low-wage earners, and new immigrants with sketchy credit histories—are offered high-interest-rate cards with a 25%–34% APR combined with annual or monthly fees.

Before discussing how the credit card industry works, we'll first take a look at how creditors assess creditworthiness.

How "Creditworthiness" Is Determined

The interest rate on credit cards, homes, automobiles, and so forth is based on your FICO (Fair Isaac Company) score, which is the numeric representation of your financial responsibility based on several factors. Your FICO score grades you on the likelihood that you'll repay a loan and is based on a standardized ranking system generated by the three major credit reporting agencies: Equifax, Experian, and TransUnion. Figure 4.1 shows the variables that go into calculating a FICO score. Table 4.1 examines the five FICO categories.

Figure 4.1.
How FICO scores are determined.[7] These percentages are based on the importance of the five categories for the *general* population, but they can carry different weight for particular groups, such as those who have been using credit for only a short time.

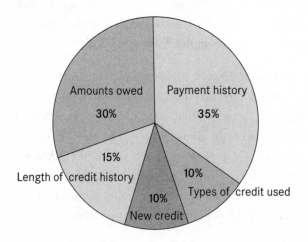

THE FRINGE SECTORS

Table 4.1.
Breakdown of the FICO categories.[8]

Payment history

Payment information on accounts, such as credit cards, retail accounts, and
    mortgages

Adverse public records (bankruptcy, judgments, suits, liens, wage attachments,
    etc.)

Collection and/or delinquency problems

Severity of delinquency

Amount past due on delinquent accounts or collection items

Time since past-due items, adverse public records, or collection items

Number of times that items were past due

Number of accounts paid as agreed

Amounts owed

Amount owing on accounts

Amount owing on specific types of accounts

Number of accounts with balances

Proportion of credit lines used to total credit limits on revolving accounts

Proportion of installment loan amounts still owed

Length of credit history

Time since accounts were opened

Time since account activity

New credit

Number of recently opened accounts and types of accounts

Number of recent credit inquiries

Time since new credit inquiry(s)

Time since the re-establishment of a positive credit history following past payment
    problems

Types of credit used

Number of various types of accounts

FICO scores can range from a high of 850 to a low of 350. About 1% of the population has a FICO score above 800. The bottom 20% of the population scores below 620. Based on FICO scores, the credit industry uses an A, B, or C ranking to classify borrowers. The higher the ranking, the cheaper the loan. For example, a FICO score of 720 or above typically translates into relatively low loan rates. Conversely, a score below 620 results in a more expensive subprime loan. Because lenders have some leeway, the relationship between FICO scores and interest rates can vary. Each time a credit report is accessed, the FICO score can drop by as much as 5 points. Merchants, landlords, and others who regularly run credit checks hurt our credit ratings.[9]

The Major Players in the Credit Card Industry

Bank of America began the first mass mailing of credit cards in 1958, sending some 60,000 into the mailboxes of unsuspecting families in Fresno, California. The plastic cards caught on, and a little more than a year later, over 2 million were circulating in California. Banks initially saw credit cards as a favor to their clients and a way to build customer loyalty by making small loans. Despite some scattered resistance, the convenience of charging and the lure of easy money prevailed.

The credit card idea was a brilliant innovation, because banks can make money on two fronts: from participating merchants, who are charged a fee for every credit card transaction; and from cardholders, who pay annual fees and interest on credit card balances. On the merchant side, MasterCard and Visa charge 1.5%–2.6% of the total sale, though fees are often adjusted based on the merchant's volume. Some merchants also pay a small (25–30 cents) transaction-processing and bank statement fee. In some cases, merchants must purchase an electronic terminal and software to process transactions.[10] Visa claims to have 1 billion cards in circulation, and its vast worldwide network processes more than 3,700 transactions a second.

The credit card industry is an oligopoly: Visa controls 50% of the market; MasterCard controls another 25%; and American Express, Discover, and other smaller companies share the remaining 25%. Contrary to popular misconceptions, neither Visa nor MasterCard issues credit cards; instead, they provide advertising, credit authorization, and payment services for their financial members. Visa credit cards are issued by individual banks that are part of the Visa network.

Visa is a for-profit corporation jointly owned by 21,000 banks, each of which issues and markets its own Visa products. Each financial institution also sets its own credit card terms, interest rates, fees, and penalties. MasterCard International, on the other hand, transfers profits directly to member banks. The loose structure of Visa and MasterCard explains the vast range of credit card terms, fees, and interest rates that are available.

Visa and MasterCard are owned and operated by the same group of major banks. They are also one of the most effective cartels in the United States. Responding to this, the U.S. Justice Department filed an antitrust suit in 1998 alleging that Visa and MasterCard cooperate rather than compete with each other. The government lawsuit also alleged that Visa and MasterCard's bylaws include illegal exclusionary rules that allow member banks to issue both major cards but no rival cards, such as Discover or American Express. In 2003 the federal courts struck down the exclusionary rule, and banks were permitted to offer competing credit cards.[11]

Wal-Mart and thousands of other retailers won a class-action lawsuit against Visa and MasterCard in 2003 claiming that the companies—individually and in conspiracy with their member banks—violated federal antitrust laws by forcing merchants who accept Visa- and/or MasterCard-branded credit cards to also accept their branded debit cards. The retailers claimed that Visa and MasterCard had conspired to monopolize the market for general-purpose debit cards, resulting in excessive fees for these transactions. The credit card companies agreed to settle the case for $3 billion and to cut debit card merchant fees by at least 33%. Retailers also won the right to refuse to accept debit cards.

The credit card industry is the nation's most profitable banking sector. At least 720 million credit cards are used each year in $860 billion worth of transactions from 15 million merchants worldwide. In 2003 the industry took in $31 billion in fee income alone, 2.5 times more than in 1993. Some of this profit is attributable to late fees, which now represent the third-largest source of revenue for credit card issuers, following interest and merchant fees.[12]

How the Credit Card Industry Works

Negotiating the credit card terrain is tricky. For instance, many lenders offer three different plans for credit card interest rates: a fixed rate, a variable rate, and a tiered rate. A fixed APR refers to an interest rate that is fixed until the bank decides to change it. A variable interest rate is tied to an index (such as the prime rate, treasury bills, or LIBOR[13]) and changes based on the index's direction. Although some banks claim to charge variable interest rates, many have a floor that keeps rates from dropping below a certain level. In a tiered interest rate, different rates apply to different levels of the outstanding balance. For example, you may be charged a 16% APR on balances of $1–$500; 17% on balances above $500, and so forth. Once you determine the best interest rate, you need to know the criteria that a lender applies to the balance. What you don't read in the fine print can cost hundreds a year in unnecessary expenses.

The heart of the credit card transaction is in the fine print. For example, some of us who want to pay off a high-interest credit card look for cards with a teaser or promotional rate into which we can transfer our outstanding balances. Most teasers have time limits and a *real* APR that's charged once the introductory period ends. While teaser rates may be appealing, the non-promotional APR is usually higher than for non-teaser-rate cards. Teaser rates often don't apply to new purchases, and just one late payment can cancel your teaser rate so that the card goes to the higher APR. A low introductory rate to transfer credit card balances can also include a balance-transfer fee of 3%–5%—for example, $30–$50 to transfer a $1,000 balance to a new credit card. Sometimes teaser-rate cards use bait-and-switch tactics. For example, you get a solicitation advertising a credit card at an incredibly low interest rate. But the fine print states that the company can issue you a more costly card if you fail to qualify for the premium card. Many, if not most, of us will get the card with the higher interest rate.

What's in the fine print also results in thousands of us paying millions each month in fees we didn't expect or don't consider reasonable. By invoking clauses tucked into the fine print of contract agreements, lenders can—and are—doubling or tripling interest rates with little warning or explanation.[14] For instance, a typical Visa contract issued by Bank One states, "We reserve the right to change the terms at any time for any reason."

Every bank performs periodic credit reviews on cardholders. Some pull credit reports monthly, while others do it quarterly or annually. Lenders have raised customers' rates because of a late payment on a phone or utility bill, or simply because they felt a customer had taken on too much debt. Called "universal default," this practice started after a rash of bankruptcy filings in the mid-to-late 1990s and has since become the industry standard.

A Consumer Action study found that 43% of CCIs raise cardholders' rates if they have credit problems with other lenders, even if they have no late payments on the CCI's card.[15] Other banks, such as Bank of America and Fidelity National, may use a credit request as a reason to lower a cardholder's credit limit.[16] The Consumer Action study also found that 85% of the banks surveyed had penalty rates that are triggered by one or two late payments made within six months to a year (the industry calls this "re-pricing"). Penalty rates—which permanently replace lower interest rates—range from APRs of 12%–30%.

Sixty-two percent of banks said they charge cardholders a late fee if payments are not received on or before the due date. Twenty-nine percent of CCIs had tiered late fees based on a cardholder's balance. For example, Wells Fargo charges a $20 late fee on balances up to $100; $29 for balances up to $1,000; and $35 for $1,000 or more.[17] Consequently, cardholders with smaller balances pay proportionally higher fees. In 2003 the most common late fee among major CCIs was $35. Some CCIs, like Bank of America and MBNA, have upped their late fee to $39 or more on balances over $1,000. From 1999 to 2003 late-payment fees rose 23%.[18] Combined credit card fees cost cardholders about $15 billion in 2004. In fact, fees are so profitable that in 2002 CCIs collected $7.1 billion in penalty fees alone.[19]

Credit cards can also contain hidden costs. For instance, a grace period lets a cardholder avoid finance and interest charges by paying the balance in full before the due date. Grace periods have been shrinking from a historic high of 30 days to the current 23-day average. Some CCIs have even whittled down the grace period to 20 days. Other cards have no grace period at all, and interest begins at the time of purchase. (Grace periods don't apply to cash advances or certain balance transfers that accrue interest from the date of the transaction.) Some CCIs charge an annual fee—averaging about $36 nationally—even if a credit card is never used. Credit card companies don't make money if cardholders don't use their cards, and infrequent use can incur a fee of as much as $15 if the card has been inactive for six months. Still others impose a minimum finance charge when a balance is carried over, a transaction fee for cash advances, and an over-the-credit-limit fee. If a credit limit is exceeded by even a penny, the cardholder is hit with an over-the-limit fee of $25–$39. To compound the injustice, a $39 late fee can trigger a $39 over-the-limit fee.[20]

A typical credit card purchase ends up costing 112% more than if cash were used. Another way CCIs make money is by requiring cardholders to pay only a small monthly minimum (about 2%) toward their balance. The consequences of minimum payments become obvious as the balance increases. For instance, if we owe $5,000 at a 16% APR and pay only 2.2% of the balance, it will take 47 years to pay off the debt. We'll also have paid $12,003, with $7,003 of that going for interest payments. Making low minimum payments keep us in debt longer and substantially increases our interest costs.

Added together, these fees have a profound impact on credit card debt and can lead to "negative amortization," which occurs when you make payments but your balance continues to grow because of penalties and other fees. For example, penalty interest rates can range from 30% to 40%, over-the-limit fees are about $35, and late-payment fees can cost another $35. In only a year, this $75 in fees (minus the higher interest rates) can add $900 to your balance. With a 30% penalty interest rate, even more money could be tacked on to the balance.

In a *Washington Post* article, Katherine Day and Caroline Mayer examine the case of special-education teacher Fatemeh Hosseini, whose $25,000 credit card debt nearly doubled to $49,574 (even though she stopped using her credit cards) because of late fees ranging from $25 to $50, and interest rates that doubled to nearly 30%. In fall 2004 Cleveland Municipal Judge Robert Triozzi ruled against Discover in the case of Ruth M. Owens, who had tried for six years to pay off her Discover card balance of $1,900. Owens had sent Discover a total of $3,492 in monthly payments from 1997 to 2003, yet her balance grew to $5,564 even though she had stopped using her card. Of that amount, $1,158 was for over-the-limit penalty fees alone.[21] Ironically, a debtor might be better off paying nothing at all, since the CCI would write off the debt and sell it to a collection agency, which might settle on the original balance.

The average credit card APR reported by the Consumer Action study was 12.19%, or almost three times the 4.75% prime rate in 2003. This is in contrast to the 6%–7% APR that consumers pay for mortgages and auto loans. Given this high interest rate, a case can be made that CCIs are actually predatory lenders who operate without the stigma associated with the fringe economy. Payday lenders charge about $37 for every $200 borrowed for two weeks. Credit card issuers charge 2%–3% for a cash advance plus a 30% or higher APR. Disturbingly, they hook in borrowers for longer periods than payday lenders do. Consumer Action's Linda Sherry maintains, "Every year we uncover more anti-consumer practices in the industry. So many of these policies seem greedy and shortsighted. If you look at them as a whole—tiny minimum monthly payments, outrageous late fees and significantly higher penalty rates—they seem designed to drive cardholders into bankruptcy."[22]

There are other tricks of the trade. For instance, the credit card industry doesn't appreciate responsible cardholders. Frugal credit card users who pay off their balances monthly (thereby accruing no interest charges) are viewed as freeloaders. Conversely, profitable customers carry over monthly balances and pay interest charges. A freeloading cardholder with a no-annual-fee card may suddenly find an annual fee tacked on. Or the CCI may eliminate the grace period so that interest begins from the date of purchase. Some CCIs entice customers to use a cash-advance check or to skip a payment and then increase their interest rate or lower their credit limit because they have a higher debt-to-income ratio. Still other CCIs add penalty fees for account inactivity or charge for canceling a credit card.

Balance-jumping—or transferring credit card balances from one promotional offer to another—is becoming common for those with high credit card debt. About 10% of customers who open promotional accounts transfer balances to another card when the low rate expires. Roughly 50% of consumers who transfer high balances to a new card still have those balances when the card jumps to the higher interest rate.[23] Some banks and

CCIs are protecting themselves by instituting a time limit on balance transfers. For example, a consumer transfers a large balance from a high-interest card to a promotional card, and after six months the APR on the new card jumps to a post-promotional interest rate of 14%–22%. Although the cardholder has another low-interest promotion lined up, he or she is retroactively assessed the post-promotional rate because the fine print states that formerly transferred balances cannot be shifted for a year.

Another trick is to send customers blank credit card checks, called "convenience" or "access" checks. These printed checks are tied to a credit card account and can be used like a personal check to make purchases, pay bills, or make a credit card payment. CCIs claim that convenience checks provide extra access to the customer's credit card line and allow the customer to pay for goods or services at locations that won't accept credit cards. The checks are typically sent out when consumers are the most vulnerable—Christmas, tax time, and vacation periods. Convenience checks are actually cash advances that carry a higher APR and accrue interest immediately.[24]

Credit card companies are always searching for the ideal customer: someone who keeps high credit card balances, pays only the minimum, and frequently pays late. In other words, charging high late fees and high interest rates allows credit card companies to keep people at the point where they get behind in their bills but can still make the payments. Except the payments aren't enough to substantially reduce their debt.

Setting the Hook Early: College Students and Credit Cards

Josh Wisnowsky is a recently married 28-year-old middle manager in a large retail corporation. Although Josh earns $70,000 a year, he's unable to buy his wife a diamond wedding ring because he maxed out his credit, owing $45,000 among five credit cards. Despite Josh's high income, his huge credit card debt precludes him from purchasing little beyond the essentials. He's in the growing legions of the credit-poor.

Josh's entry into the world of credit card debt began when he got his first card in college. Seduced by claims such as Chase's "It [Platinum for Students] comes with a 5.99% introductory APR on purchases and balance transfers, no annual fee, and tons of other cool benefits, like . . . ," Josh overlooked the fact that cash advances carry a 20% APR, late fees can add up quickly, and it's easy to reach the credit limit.

After hitting his $2,000 credit card limit, Josh applied for another card. He maxed out the second credit card in six months. Facing $4,000 of credit card debt, Josh took a leave from college to work full time. He never returned.

Although Josh was working full time, his credit card debt continued to soar. For a while, he played the credit card game and began shifting balances from one introductory card to another, never paying off any of them. Meanwhile, he bought a house and a new car, which only aggravated his debt. The credit card merry-go-round finally caught up with Josh as he sent in his payments later and later and began using cash advances for credit card payments.

Josh's late fees were mounting while his interest rate was rising sky-high, finally reaching nearly 30%. Collectors started calling him at work and at home. Desperate, Josh went to a credit counselor, who put him on a strict no-credit diet. Even so, it will take Josh years to pay off his credit card debt, reclaim his income, and achieve some sense of financial stability.

The credit card market is virtually saturated, and almost every adult eligible for a credit card already has one. To compensate, CCIs mailed out more than 4.3 billion solicitations in 2003 to approximately 200 million Americans. They also compete by stealing away customers through temporarily low promotional rates (0%–2.5%) on balance transfers or new purchases. To drum up business, CCIs relentlessly mine potentially lucrative populations such as college students.

College students are among the most prized of the new customers. The average graduate student has six credit cards, and one in seven of them owes more than $15,000. Despite their lack of credit and income (an important criterion for other customers), the industry wants college students because of their high future earnings and lifetime credit potential. To access their prey, CCIs hunt directly on campuses. Young recruiters staff tables outside of university bookstores and student centers, feverishly pitching the importance of credit cards while handing out free Frisbees, candy, and soda. The aggressiveness of these recruiters has led a few colleges to ban credit card solicitors from campus. "This is a terrible thing," said Indiana University administrator John Simpson. "We lose more students to credit card debt than academic failure."[25]

According to a U.S. Public Interest Research Group (U.S. PIRG) study, student credit card debt is increasing, and many college students are falling into the credit card trap well before they graduate. The U.S. PIRG study found that only 15% of students who obtained credit cards in their own names held a full-time job when they applied. Thirty-eight percent of those responsible for their own cards reported paying off their balance each month, while 36% paid as much as they could. More than 25% reported that they either paid the minimum or paid late.[26] The CCI strategy of hooking in college students has paid off. By 2004 nearly three-quarters of college students had credit cards, with an average balance of $3,100. This may partly explain why in 2000 the number of bankruptcy filings for those under 25 was 150% higher than in 1990.[27]

Secured and Unsecured Credit Cards

There are two basic categories of credit cards: traditional, or unsecured, cards and secured cards. Unsecured credit cards are offered on trust, and the cornerstone is the cardholder's presumed creditworthiness. Secured credit cards require borrowers to guarantee the credit line—thereby making default difficult—by providing cash collateral through an escrowed savings account.

The subprime credit card market is attractive for those banks experiencing shrinking or razor-thin profit margins. However, this enthusiasm has been tempered over the last few years by a growing default rate in the subprime market, reaching 19% in 2003.[28] Banks have compensated for their losses by hiking up interest rates and fees for the remaining 80% of high-risk borrowers. Hence, creditworthy but low-income consumers face discrimination by being forced to pay exorbitant interest rates and fees to counterbalance the banks' freewheeling lending policies. In effect, this constitutes class-based economic discrimination against the poor.

Unsecured Credit Cards

As the credit card market became more competitive, banks began to examine ways to make money from riskier consumers. Since Chapter 7 bankruptcy laws prevent refiling for seven years, they began to promote "special offers" to newly bankrupted consumers with an income source.[29] Although the default rate is high, these cards carry such low credit lines— coupled with extremely high interest rates and fees—that banks can still make money.

Some subprime credit cards require no security deposit, but credit limits are low (in the $100–$500 range), and cardholders must earn at least $12,000 a year. Fees on these unsecured cards are high, and interest rates are close to 30%. Centennial MasterCard/Visa advertises a low 9.9% APR. However, two late payments in six months results in a rate jump to almost 24%. Initial fees for this credit card are $178, plus $120 a year in annual

Table 4.2.
Costs for First Premier Bank's unsecured credit card.

Type of fee	Fee amount
Account setup fee	$29 (onetime fee)
Program fee	$95 (onetime fee)
Annual fee	$48
Participation fee	$72 annually (billed at $6 a month)
Additional-card fee	$20 annually
Minimum finance charge	$0.50
Credit limit increase	$25 each time an account is approved for a credit increase
Internet access fee	$3.95
Copying fee	$3 per item
Returned-item charge	$25
Autodraft fee	$11 per payment requested through an autodraft service
Autodraft payments requested through automated systems (voice response or Internet):	$7 per transaction
Express delivery fee	$25 for the delivery of card(s) sent by Priority Mail

fees. An additional $25 is charged for each late payment or if the balance exceeds the credit limit. The minimum credit limit is a paltry $250. Visa fees for the Plains Commerce Bank are $281 on a card with a credit limit of $300, leaving only $19 of available credit when the card first arrives. Credit card charges by South Dakota's First Premier Bank reflect a veritable swamp of fees (see Table 4.2).[30]

The remainder of First Premier's terms are equally harsh. The $178 of combined fees appears on the first billing statement, reducing the $250 credit line to only $72. Cardholders will therefore have accrued interest even before the card arrives. This is clearly predatory lending by any definition.

SECURED CREDIT CARDS

Responding to consumers with even more problematic credit, the industry created a class of credit cards secured by customer collateral. Like their unsecured cousins, secured cards are emblazoned with a Visa or MasterCard logo. Although these cards require a credit check, they are actually quasi–debit cards, since no line of credit is actually extended. For banks, the major advantage of secured cards is that they can easily liquidate a cardholder's collateral and apply it toward the outstanding balance.

Consumers wanting a secured credit card are required to open an interest-bearing savings account for the amount of the credit line, usually a minimum of $200–$5,000. (Some banks allow customers a credit line equal to only 50% of their collateral.) Funds in the savings account are escrowed by the bank and cannot be accessed by the cardholder. In turn, cardholders are given a Visa or MasterCard with a credit line equal to or less than the collateral. Credit card balances are not withdrawn from the savings account; instead, cardholders pay those charges as they would for any other credit card. Despite holding the customer's collateral, the bank charges high fees and interest rates. For example, Cross Country Bank charges a $50 origination fee, a 24% APR, and a hefty late fee. There is also a 50-cent minimum finance charge and a $10 monthly fee. Cross Country has no grace period, so interest charges begin with each purchase. Orchard Bank's secured card has a 19% APR, a $79 annual fee, and a $3.50 monthly fee. Wells Fargo's secured card has an $18 annual fee, a $300 security deposit, a late and over-the-limit fee of $30, and a 17% APR for purchases and 21.8% APR for cash advances.[31] Added together, these fees make for an expensive card.

Since the credit line is guaranteed by collateral, banks cannot argue that high costs reflect exceptional risk, and the most viable explanation for the difference in cost between the prime rate and the rate on secured credit cards is simply avarice. In addition, secured credit cards are often marketed as a way to build or rebuild credit histories. But if the CCI doesn't report to a credit bureau (many don't, since the transaction isn't really a loan), responsible cardholders cannot build or rebuild their credit history.

Secured credit cards reflect the injustice of the fringe economy. For instance, if banks demanded that the middle class secure their $10,000 Visa or MasterCard credit lines, most would return instantly to cash or checks. In the virtually unregulated fringe economy, however, banks are allowed to charge cardholders exorbitant fees to borrow against their own money.

Preloaded or Stored-Value Debit Cards

Another innovation is the preloaded debit card, sometimes called a "stored-value card" (SVC). Refillable, SVCs function like regular debit cards, allowing cardholders to do almost anything they could with a credit card, such as make purchases over the Internet, buy groceries, or pay for car repairs. In some cases, cardholders can arrange for direct payroll deposits, withdraw funds from ATM machines, pay bills online, and buy money orders from the post office.

Money can be loaded directly into SVCs through payroll transfers and government checks, and customers can add cash at various locations. The available balance and transaction history can be viewed through a Web site or an ATM machine. When the funds are exhausted, the card must be reloaded—for a fee—or it becomes inactive.[32] Unlike secured credit cards, prepaid cards are not dependent on credit or banking history, since they do not involve credit transactions and are not linked to a bank account. The SVC market is growing dramatically in both the number of providers and the number of customers.[33] Visa estimates that by 2008 this market will generate $77 billion, resulting from 2.5 billion transactions a year.[34]

SVCs have certain advantages for consumers. Low- and moderate-income consumers have different financial needs than higher-income ones. In particular, they often can't wait a week or two for a check to clear. SVCs can potentially give consumers the services they're getting from storefront financial-services operations, but at less cost. In addition, customers can use the entire amount loaded onto the card without paying any interest charges and without having a debt to repay. Eventually, immigrants may be able to send a second card back to their home countries so that family members can make direct withdrawals from their accounts.[35] SVCs can potentially provide credit-challenged consumers with an efficient way to store funds, make purchases, pay bills, and, in some cases, build credit. But while some SVC issuers claim to report transactions to a credit bureau, it is unclear how these transactions are recorded, since they're not really loans.[36]

While there are several variations of SVCs, the two most common are nonbranded and branded cards. Nonbranded cards use PIN technology (signature-based transactions are unavailable), and transactions are allowed only through point-of-sale (POS) or ATM networks. Branded cards are backed by Visa or MasterCard for universal acceptance.

SVC products are being aggressively pitched to immigrants, the under- and unbanked, and those with problematic credit. One example is the La Raza Personal Advantage Media MasterCard, marketed by the Spanish Broadcasting System. The MagicCash and Rush cards, being marketed primarily to African American consumers, are two more examples. Issued by Bank of America, the MagicCash card employs the image of Magic Johnson. The Rush Card uses hip-hop personality Russell Simmons. In fact, tax preparer Jackson Hewitt partnered with Russell Simmons to make the Rush Card available at all of its locations. These cards allow customers who opt for tax refund anticipation loans (RALs) to receive their refunds through an SVC. Not to be outdone, H&R Block partnered with Bank of America to provide a Visa-branded SVC on a pilot basis in Washington, DC, El Paso, and Fresno. In addition, H&R Block is considering making

Table 4.3.

Costs for Four Oaks Bank's stored-value card.

Action	Fee
Card-to-card reload	$1.00
Bank account–to–card reload	$1.00
Direct-deposit reload	$1.00
Purchase at merchant	$0.50
Purchase online	$0.50
Telephone purchase	$0.50
ATM withdrawal	$1.50
Live-teller withdrawal	$1.50
ATM balance inquiry	$1.00
Online balance inquiry	$0.10
Automated telephone inquiry	$0.50
Customer service live call	$3.00
Automated telephone service	$0.50
Online customer service	$0.10
Paper statement (special request)	$5.00 each
Cancel card	$5.00
Reactivate card	$5.00
Inactive account per month	$5.00
Monthly maintenance fee	$3.95

the cards reloadable for nonrefund transactions.[37] ACE Cash Express is planning to vigorously pursue its own SVCs.

As with all fringe economy transactions, there is a downside to SVCs. For example, Wired Plastic charges an initial $50 fee, a one-time activation fee, a monthly maintenance fee, and a $2 cash-withdrawal fee (plus any other fees assessed by ATM owners/operators). Four Oaks Bank & Trust Company, another SVC issuer, offers an even more expensive debit card. Four Oaks' initial setup charge is $159—$59 for the application, $90 for processing, and $10 toward the opening balance.[38] Table 4.3 lists Four Oaks' other charges.

Banks and retailers make money from SVCs in several ways. First, SVC cards accrue no interest, and banks get the float on the customer's unspent money. Given millions of customers, this float can be substantial. Second, there's a difference between how much retailers and distributors pay for an SVC card and how much they sell it for. Third, retailers and merchants can receive a commission on sales made using an SVC card with their imprint. Taken together, this represents a profitable industry.

SVCs are designed only to facilitate spending. Hence, most cards fail to provide an opportunity for savings, asset building, or credit restoration, since they are essentially in the same category as gift cards. As in much of the fringe economy, resources go only one way.

Reforming the Credit Card Industry

Like all economic sectors, the credit card industry must maintain growth to ensure its profitability. As American society becomes saturated with credit cards, the industry is forced to aggressively seek out new customers or find ways to "rehabilitate" existing ones who are less than creditworthy. In the process, CCIs have extended credit to those formerly denied it. For instance, consumers with an income below the poverty level more than doubled their credit card debt during the early and mid-1990s—the sharpest increase of any income group. By the late 1990s, the wealthiest Americans were using credit cards less, while the poorest were using them more.[39]

The credit card industry is in dire need of reform on several levels. Aggressive credit card marketing targeted to young people and economically volatile consumers should be abolished. Credit cards are open-ended loans that should be given only to those with the financial means to repay them. Marketing credit cards to students and others who lack the financial capacity to repay the debt is predatory. To avoid creating a credit trap, the CCI industry should be prohibited from issuing credit cards with limits that exceed a percentage of a household's income or assets. In the end, extending credit without considering the borrower's ability to repay only leads to crushing debt for many lower- and moderate-income households.

CCIs should be held accountable for their aggressive marketing. If they choose to entice unemployed college students and economically unstable consumers into high-interest credit cards, they should take responsibility

THE FRINGE SECTORS

for their actions. Namely, if these borrowers are delinquent, federal banking laws should limit the actions allowed to CCIs.

Consumer protections have been eroding for decades, and instead of vigorously regulating fringe economy transactions, the government has demanded that lenders provide mountains of interest disclosure and consumer information that virtually no one reads, least of all those in the heat of a sizable purchase. Providing information is no substitute for regulatory action.

Interest rates are regulated by state usury laws. However, fewer than half of all states cap credit card interest rates, and few CCIs are based in those states. Most large CCIs are located in states with liberal or no interest-rate caps. The 1978 Supreme Court decision in *Marquette v. First Omaha Service Corp.* stated that national banks can charge the highest interest rate allowed in their home state to customers living anywhere in the United States. After the Marquette ruling, major CCIs began moving to states with liberal usury laws. For example, Citibank moved its credit card business to South Dakota in 1981, while the four largest Maryland banks relocated their credit card operations to Delaware.[40] This has resulted in a banking loophole that can be corrected only by standardizing and regulating interest rates nationally.

The fact that the credit card industry consists mainly of two large players—Visa and MasterCard—partly explains why credit card interest rates are double (sometimes four to five times) the rates on mortgages and car loans. These high-interest rates are even more troubling because CCIs generate revenues from both merchants and cardholders. Consequently, there's little reason to believe that high interest rates reflect real costs. For example, Arkansas has some of the lowest credit card rates in the nation because it caps interest at 5% above the federal discount rate. Despite this cap, CCIs have not apparently lost money there.[41] This credit card oligopoly needs to be broken, and the industry should be opened up to more competition.

The interests of low-income and credit-challenged consumers require protection. Charging an APR of 25%–35% on credit cards secured by a borrower's collateral is clearly predatory. Because secured credit cards represent minimal risk, their fees should be commensurate with, or lower than, those on normally issued cards. Few middle-class consumers would tolerate secured credit cards, no less ones that carry a 30% APR.

The minimum payment required by a growing number of CCIs is about 2% of the outstanding balance, which is inadequate to pay off a credit card debt in a reasonable time. Instead, minimum payments should be increased to 4% per month. Also, CCIs should disclose how long it would take cardholders to pay off their balances (and the interest costs) using minimum payments.

CCIs should be prohibited from raising the interest rates of cardholders who have credit problems with other lenders.[42] At a minimum, they should be required to notify cardholders of an impending rate hike based on their credit records. They should also be required to provide cardholders with an opportunity to explain changes in their credit scores.

Finally, CCIs should be required to provide a five-day grace period before charging late fees. Because CCIs are often located in remote parts of the country, slow mail plus delays in recording payments can result in expensive penalties and late fees.

Despite aggressive credit card marketing, large numbers of people fall through the cracks. Lacking even minimal credit, they are forced to resort to the pawnshops and payday lenders of the storefront loan industry. It is to this group that we will now turn.

Anyone who has ever struggled with poverty knows
how extremely expensive it is to be poor.

—James A. Baldwin

5

Storefront Loans: Pawnshops, Payday Loans, and Tax Refund Lenders

All of us need cash at one time or another, and the cost of raising it depends on who's asking for it. For creditworthy consumers, cash is secured through bank lines of credit, overdraft protection, signature or home equity loans, or credit card cash withdrawals. For those with compromised credit, the essential condition for raising cash is a "no-credit-check" transaction, which translates into a high-interest predatory loan.

Collateral-based cash loans serve the same purpose for the poor as bank overdrafts or credit card cash advances do for the middle class. Namely, they provide cash for an emergency or when income is temporarily insufficient to make ends meet. Cash loans fall into two categories: (1) unsecured or promissory loans and (2) secured collateral-based loans. With an unsecured loan (such as a credit card, a signature loan, or a bank overdraft), the borrower promises to repay the lender, and no collateral is required. With secured loans, the borrower provides the lender with collateral (either property or a check) worth at least as much as the loan. The poor and severely credit-challenged are generally eligible only for collateral-based or secured loans requiring the temporary loss of property or guarantees such as postdated checks. Interest rates (sometimes called "fees") on these loans are extremely high.

Pawnshops: The Historical Neighborhood Banker

Pawnshops date back at least 3,000 years to ancient China. The word "pawn" is derived from the Latin *patinum*, meaning "cloth" or "clothing," since in earlier times people pawned their clothes to borrow money.[1] Historically, pawnshops were both exploitative and egalitarian. For instance, when African Americans were refused loans by mainstream financial institutions, pawnbrokers crossed the color line and lent money to any customer willing to pay the interest rate. They were one of the few institutions that minority groups could turn to for loans.

Pawnbroking declined from the 1930s to the mid-1970s as other credit alternatives became available, such as consumer finance companies and credit unions, and as personal incomes rose. However, by the middle 1970s the pawnshop industry began to grow dramatically. By 2004 there were 14,000 pawnshops nationwide (double the number in 1985) and five publicly traded chains (EZ Pawn, Cash America International, Express Cash, Famous Pawn, and First Cash Pawn).[2] Traditionally located in low-income minority neighborhoods, pawnshops now outnumber both credit unions and banks across the United States.[3]

Pawnshop loans are fairly simple economic transactions. A pawnbroker, sometimes called a "collateral loan broker," makes a fixed-term loan to a consumer who uses his or her collateral to guarantee the loan. (There is no credit check, since the loan is secured by the collateral.) Customers receive a pawn ticket with their name and address, a description of the item, the loan amount, and the maturity date. (With the exception of firearms, anyone who possesses a pawn ticket can redeem a pledged good (that is, a pawned item). The local police get a copy of the receipt. A customer's property is returned when the pawn ticket is presented and the loan and interest are repaid. If a loan is not repaid, the broker appropriates the property and cancels the debt.

Pawnshops allow customers to borrow on the appraised value of an item for a period of time (often 30 days), which is renewable. Some pawnshops allow customers to extend the loan indefinitely by paying only the interest. As one pawnshop manager put it, "It's not unusual for customers to renew their loans for a year or more."

The pawnshop loan is typically about 33%–50% of what a broker expects to receive if he or she sells the item.[4] Appraisals are low—jewelry appraises at wholesale value, guns at 60% of blue book value, and appliances at 10%–30% or less of their original cost.

Mary Bradley's sister, Lucy, is a recovering drug addict who, like many addicts, frequently stole money and "pawnable" goods from her family. Since Mary's family was wealthy, the pickings were good. Mary got to know pawnshops well, because after things disappeared, she and her mother regularly visited them to recover their missing goods. Mary was amazed at the low prices the pawns had brought. On one occasion, Lucy received $285 for her mother's ruby and diamond ring, which had appraised for $6,000.

Interest rates on pawn loans vary from 1.5% to 25% a month, depending on the state's usury laws.[5] Besides interest, some states allow pawnshops to add charges such as storage, insurance, or service fees. Other states allow pawnshops to require a new service fee each time a loan is renewed, and still others have a one-to-three-month grace period, during which a pawnbroker must keep a pledged good after the loan expires. While the average pawnshop loan is about $75, it can go as low as $15 or as high as $1,000.[6]

Pawnshops are regulated or licensed by state or local governments and are required to cooperate with local police departments to prevent the fencing of stolen goods. However, most police pawnshop details are small and cover only a fraction of the hundreds of pawnshops in major cities. For example, there are roughly 150 pawnshops in Houston, 200 in Chicago, and 300 in Los Angeles. Some larger pawnshops take in as many as 200 pawns a day. Retired Houston police officer Kamil Obedja has an insider's take on the issue.

> When someone goes in and pawns something, the clerks are supposed to get a valid ID from the customer. The information on their ID—by the way, it's really easy to get a fake ID—and any serial numbers or identifying information are written on the pawn ticket. These thousands of tickets are taken downtown, where people making minimum wage enter the information into a database. The information can then be checked against a list of items reported stolen. . . . But the thing is that there are so many stolen items and so much that winds up in pawnshops, there's no way the police can deal with the problem. If you've had something stolen and you want to get it back, you'd better go out and look for it yourself.

Jewelry accounts for more than 50% of pawns, and pieces of jewelry are some of the most difficult items to recover. Stones can be removed and reset, and without an inscription there's usually no way to identify jewelry unless the owner has photographed it. Even then, police have a hard time identifying one item amid the hundreds of jewelry pieces lying around a pawnshop.

Most pawnshops will buy goods outright, especially jewelry. In some instances, stolen jewelry will turn up at a pawnshop down the street, but, according to Obedja,

> there's a better chance that the shop is going to box up jewelry like that and store it in some warehouse until they can move it to another

location in the state. This is especially true of pawnshop chains where the business is highly organized with many locations. . . . A lot of merchandise has turned up far away from where it was stolen. It's a pretty good bet that a criminal who steals your jewelry in Houston isn't going to make the effort to pawn it in another part of the state. It's a concerted effort [on the part of pawnshops] to protect their investment. There's no law against it, but there is a law against receiving stolen property. If they can get it out of the neighborhood where it was stolen, there's less chance the victim is going to be able to find and claim it. Pawnshops hide behind the idea that they're providing a service to people, but you'll never convince me of it.

Large pawnshop chains can also ship jewelry out of state, where the stones are removed and the gold—at several hundreds of dollars an ounce—is melted down. At that point, all traces of the jewelry have vanished. In some cases, a pawnshop can't display an item until it has been deemed unclaimed, usually in 30 days. By that time, the trail is cold. Indeed, the *legal* fencing done by some pawnshops, including large chains, may help explain their growth and profitability.

Maria Olivera lives with her parents and two brothers in Brownsville, Texas. Her family recently emigrated from Mexico and is struggling economically because her brothers and father rarely have steady work as day laborers. Her mother occasionally works as a seamstress.

Maria has two part-time retail sales jobs, neither of which includes benefits. Although relatively young, Maria's parents have chronic health problems requiring frequent physician visits. Medical expenses are paid for out of pocket. The Olivera family doesn't have a bank account, and everything is paid in cash. Because of this, the Oliveras have no credit and therefore are ineligible for a bank loan.

Maria received a diamond necklace from her grandmother, a family heirloom. Her mother recently needed outpatient surgery costing $2,000, and the family had saved $1,000, but the only way to raise the additional money was to pawn Maria's necklace and any other collateral they owned. Although the necklace was worth $2,000, Fast Cash Pawn Shop would lend only its maximum of $500. To secure the remaining $500, the family pawned their television set and VCR, an older computer, and sundry tools.

The Oliveras' $1,000 loan was for 30 days and carried $150 a month in interest, or a 180% APR. As with most pawnshop loans, the family could extend the due date. At the end of 30 days they would pay $1,150 to redeem the collateral, after 60 days it would be $1,300, and at the end of 90 days it would be $1,450. If the family renewed the loan for a year, they would pay $2,800 to retrieve pawned items worth $1,000. Had the Oliveras lived in a state with different pawnshop rules, they might have paid 25% a month ($250 on a $1,000 loan) and, at the end of a year, shelled out $4,000 to reclaim $1,000 worth of collateral.

Although the Oliveras retrieved Maria's necklace, they were unable to get back the remaining items. Perhaps more disturbingly, the family began a pattern of using Maria's necklace for short-term loans, pawning it three times in two years. Maria's family heirloom quickly became little more than a piece of constantly traded collateral.

Cash America International's 2003 annual report states, "We help people get where they're going by providing a financial bridge. Providing our customers a solution to get from one point to another." The "financial bridge" that the Olivera family crossed only impoverished them more, as interest charges on each pawn made a poor family even poorer. On the other hand, without Fast Cash, Maria's mother would not have gotten the operation.

Perhaps the most dangerous part of the fringe economy is the psychological trap it sets for borrowers. According to Nancy Morrow, a professional musician from Kerrville, Texas,

> Once you get sucked into a pawnshop, it's like a loan shark without the strong arm. . . . It gets to the point where you have no other place to turn to get money. No bank account, no credit. You've used up all your sources as far as people to borrow money from. You can't borrow any more. You still owe. So what do you have that's valuable?
>
> I always established good rapport with my pawnshop people. They could go back and look at my file history and see that I always came back and got my stuff. . . . I got to the point with this one pawnshop where it was almost like Norm on *Cheers*—"Hey Nancy!" It's a bad habit to break. I was literally in debt thousands of dollars to one single pawnshop. . . . It finally took someone to bail me out.

THE FRINGE SECTORS

Despite Nancy's experiences, she still has a hard time letting go of the fringe lending culture.

I have until January 28 to come up with $80. Here's the thing . . . $80 to get it out, or I could just pay the $20 interest to keep them from selling it. I always push it to the last possible day—"OK, well, tomorrow the computer is spitting it out. It's going to be on the floor. It's ten days past the last grace day." Most pawnshops are the same. I've got ten days past this date. They don't say it, but they won't put my stuff out. As long as I come in—it's worse than a drug habit.

Convenience is an important factor in pawnshop transactions. For Jill Daugherty "it was ridiculous. I would borrow $200 and wind up spending $375—$175 interest on $200 over a six-month period. The pawnshop was right there. I could just drive there, drop it off, get the money, and go. It was the convenience factor."

Pawnshops are major players in the cash-lending economy. They're also one of the few stable industries in hard economic times. High unemployment means more borrowers, and since only about 30% of customers abandon their pawn, the high interest paid by the other 70% more than compensates for any dead merchandise.[7] Moreover, pawnshops lend money at an APR of 120%–300%, while the industry borrows at interest rates of 9% or less. The pawnshop industry is partly insulated by the huge difference between the cost of borrowing money and the price of lending it. Also, pawnbroking is a cash business with few worries about suppliers, late payments, or slow deliveries. There are no bad loans. If a customer defaults, the collateral is quickly sold for more than the loan amount. This helps explain the rapid growth of the industry.[8]

The pawnshop industry is evolving from a monoline (single consumer product) to a multiservice industry, one that also provides payday loans and other financial services. The major driving forces in this transformation are the crowded pawnshop market and the pricing pressure exerted by large discount stores. For example, browsing through pawnshops in Texas and New Mexico, I was struck by the high prices of used goods, many of which could be purchased new for the same price at Wal-Mart or Kmart. Moreover, mass-produced durable goods, such as appliances and tools (except in the case of expensive professional tools), are no longer being made as strong. Products with a short operational life are less valuable as used articles. Hence, purchasing used pawnshop merchandise has become an unattractive option for many shoppers.

Pawnshop transactions are some of the least complicated and dangerous of all fringe loans. Because these transactions are collateral-based, they don't foster a debt trap like unsecured loans. There's no follow-up, no credit agency report, no collection agencies, no harassing phone calls, and no future debt obligation. In comparison, payday advances create a debt trap that allows interest obligations and a borrower's future indebtedness to grow.

Payday Loans

Ralph Johnson lives in Bloomington, Indiana, and is employed as an assistant manager for a convenience store chain. He earns $12 an hour, plus occasional overtime. His wife is a file clerk and earns $8 an hour. The Johnsons and their two children live on a family income of about $40,000 a year, well above the 2003 federal poverty line of $18,400 for a family of four. Despite this, they periodically borrow from payday lenders to tide them over until payday. Ralph is a classic payday loan customer in an industry that targets low-income workers, single mothers, women on welfare, senior citizens (many on Social Security), and military personnel.

An established payday customer, Ralph borrowed $500 for 14 days, for which he owed $100 in interest. Because Ralph couldn't repay the $500, he paid the $100 interest fee and rolled over the loan for an additional two weeks. The original $500 loan now cost $200 in interest for 30 days. If Ralph rolled over the loan for yet another month—or two more 14-day cycles—he would've paid $400 in interest on a $500 loan for 60 days. (Some payday lenders permit only four rollovers or loan extensions.)

While pawnshops often lend to the poorest of the poor, payday lenders typically serve those one rung up on the economic ladder. For example, pawnshop customers aren't required to have a bank account or employment since the transaction is solely based on collateral. Since payday lenders generally deal with the working poor or those with compromised credit, they require an active checking account and a source of income. A Georgetown University study found that more than half of payday loan customers came from households with yearly incomes of between $25,000 and $50,000.[9]

The Growth and Profitability of Payday Lending

Payday lending is one of the fastest-growing businesses, not only in the United States, but also in Canada, Australia, England, New Zealand, South Korea, and other countries. In the United States, the number of payday lenders grew from a few hundred in 1990 to more than 25,000 in 2002, with the industry expecting to double in size over the next few years.[10] In fact, there are now more payday loan shops in America than McDonald's restaurants.[11] The largest payday lenders are Advance America (1,375 stores in 30 states); ACE Cash Express (1,000 stores in 30 states); Check 'n Go (800 stores in 26 states); Dollar (700 stores in 24 states); Check into Cash (650 stores in 24 states); and Cash America International (470 stores in 18 states).[12]

The growth of the payday industry has been explosive, with loan volume rising from $10 billion in 2000 to $25 billion by 2003. This $25 billion included 83 million payday loans costing 7.6 million customers about $3.4 billion.[13] Surprisingly, this growth occurred despite 19 states' prohibiting payday loans at triple-digit interest rates.[14]

Payday loans (also known as "payday advances" or "deferred deposit loans") are about twice as profitable as standard pawn-based loans.[15] In 2002 the percentage of payday loans charged off as uncollectible in Virginia was 3.4%. In North Carolina, only 6% of payday checks were returned for insufficient funds (NSF). Lenders recovered 69% of the value of those checks.[16] According to the Center for Responsible Lending, payday lenders report losses of 10–12 cents for every dollar lent and a 34% pretax return on investment. The Tennessee Department of Financial Institutions reported that payday lenders earned a return on investment of more than 30% in the first nine months of legal operation.[17] One company selling payday lending manuals lays out the profitability:

> Losses? It's part of the business. But they can be kept to a very minimum. Less than 2% is easy if you do not break your rules and your

underwriting criteria is conservative. Four percent to 8% is quite normal. . . . The average payday advance (PDA) is $276 and rising. You would tie up approximately $200 for 8 days on average. You write a check for $175.95 for their check in the amount of $217. That is an annual percentage rate in excess of 800%. It's obvious tremendous returns are possible![18]

HOW PAYDAY LOANS WORK

Payday loans are relatively small, and the average is $300—although loans of $500 to $1,000 are becoming more common—with a loan period of 14 to 18 days. The national average for payday loan fees is $18.28 per $100 (a 470% APR) for two weeks, although they can range from $10 to $40 per $100.[19] Payday lenders don't require credit reports, and borrowers don't need a good credit rating or even a credit history. However, most payday lenders subscribe to Teletrack, or a similar service, which evaluates the borrower's check-writing history and likelihood of writing a bad check.

Payday loan customers must provide valid identification, recent pay stubs, a bank statement, proof of address and phone service, and the names of six or more references. To qualify, they must have a bank account from which a check is issued (or an electronic debit is authorized) to cover the interest (sometimes called a "fee" or "finance charge") and the loan principal.

Borrowers typically give the payday lender a postdated personal check and then receive cash, minus the fees. For instance, the customer will write a $200 check but receive only $160 in cash for a payday loan that charges $40 in interest. When the loan comes due, the borrower can (1) repay the $200 in cash and take back the original check, (2) allow the lender to deposit the check, (3) renew or roll over the loan if unable to repay it, or (4) default and pay NSF fees to the payday lender and the bank.

In states where payday loan extensions are prohibited, some lenders will use back-to-back transactions, whereby the borrower writes a check for a new loan and then uses the money to repay the old loan. In these transactions, the borrower receives no new money but pays an additional interest fee. In addition, some payday lenders charge a $10 to $15 "startup fee" for new customers. Many payday lenders consider benefits as income and lend to those on public assistance and disability, recipients of child support or alimony payments, and Social Security beneficiaries.[20]

Holding a "live" check or an electronic debit gives lenders significant leverage, because most borrowers will repay their loan when faced with the threat of criminal prosecution and penalties. Nevertheless, collection tactics for payday loans can be aggressive. If a borrower can't repay a loan, it may be turned over to a collection agency, which leads to a poor credit score or even the loss of a house or a car or to garnisheed wages. The collection agency sometimes adds its own interest charges or fees to the loan.[21] Particularly vindictive lenders may continually redeposit the check, thereby causing borrowers to accrue multiple NSF fees from the bank and the lender. Some states allow payday lenders to prosecute a borrower for writing a "hot check" even if they knew beforehand that the customer had insufficient funds to cover it. Even in states where this is illegal, payday lenders may still threaten to file criminal charges.

Many payday lenders require borrowers to agree beforehand to pay all fees related to the collection of their account. These payday lenders will simply deposit the check and then proceed under "hot check" laws to collect the principal and interest, the bounced-check fees, and attorney and court costs.[22] Since defaulting on a payday loan involves writing a bad check, some states allow for triple damages if it's used in a retail transaction. Lenders may also require customers to sign a statement authorizing employers to directly deduct a payday loan from the borrower's paycheck. According to the Center for Responsible Lending, one industry plan advised payday lenders to "Help them [non-paying customers] visualize a uniformed, gun toting U.S. Marshal arriving at their place of employment. Emphasize to them that this U.S. Marshal will first ask for their immediate supervisor!"[23]

THE SPIRALING CYCLE OF PAYDAY LOAN DEBT

The real danger in payday loans doesn't lie in a single transaction where the borrower is exploited; instead, it lies in creating a spiraling cycle of debt. An extreme example is the situation of Lisa Engelkins, who entered into 35 back-to-back payday loan transactions over 17 months, paying $1,254 in fees to extend a $300 payday loan.[24]

Table 5.1 is an example of a hypothetical payday loan history.

Ralph Johnson takes out 10 payday loans a year, which is close to the national average. Despite admonitions by payday lenders that "a cash advance is a short-term solution to an immediate need, it is not intended for repeated use in carrying an individual from payday to payday,"[25] these loans are generally not used this way. Payday lenders maintain that the industry provides needed credit for emergencies. However, a 2003 study by the Southwest Center for Economic Integrity found that 67% of payday borrowers used their loans to pay general nonemergency bills.[26] For many people, payday loans lead to a pattern of chronic borrowing and chronic debt.

Table 5.1.
Connie's $300 payday loan.

		Interest paid
November 1 (date of original loan)	Connie takes out a $300 payday loan and writes a 14-day postdated check for $300 to cover the loan plus the $60 in interest charges ($20 per $100 borrowed). She receives $240 in cash.	$60
November 15 (due date for original loan, and first extension)	Connie cannot repay the loan and pays another $60 in interest fees to extend it. She receives no additional money but has now paid $120 in interest charges on the original $300 loan.	$120
November 30 (second extension)	Connie extends the loan again and pays another $60. She has now paid $180 in interest charges on the $300 loan.	$180
December 15 (third extension)	Connie still can't repay the original $300 loan, so she pays yet another $60 to extend it. In only eight weeks Connie has paid $240 in interest charges on the $240 she received.	$240
December 30 (loan due in full)	The payday lender deposits Connie's last check. If there are insufficient funds in her account, she will be charged an NSF fee by the bank and the lender. The lender will pursue Connie for the original $300, which she still owes.	$240

THE FRINGE SECTORS

According to the Center for Responsible Lending, only 1% of all pay-day loans go to one-time emergency borrowers who pay their loan within two weeks and don't borrow again within a year. Conversely, 66% of borrowers initiate 5 or more loans a year, and 33% take out 12 or more loans a year. Ninety-one percent of all payday loans are made to borrowers with five or more loans a year. On average, payday customers receive 8–13 loans a year. These chronic borrowers form the backbone of payday-industry profits. For example, borrowers who receive 5 or more payday loans a year account for 91% of payday lenders' revenues, and 56% of this revenue is generated by customers who take out 13 or more loans a year.[27]

Payday loans exacerbate credit problems by postponing the inevitable for two weeks at an exorbitant cost. The Southwest Center for Economic Integrity found that 60% of payday customers didn't pay off their loans within the allotted two-week loan period, and 30% took more than seven weeks to repay it.[28] Other studies found that 75% of customers renew their payday loans.[29] Some borrowers trapped in the debt cycle get loans from one payday lender to repay another and end up with multiple renewal fees. About 47% of payday borrowers use more than one payday lending company, many taking out a whopping 14–22 loans a year.[30]

The payday loan industry argues that the interest and fees it charges are cheaper than the cost of bouncing checks. It may be right. A bounced check can cost up to $60 in bank and merchant fees (banks earn $7 billion a year in bounced-check fees). According to the Community Financial Services Association of America (CFSAA), a $100 payday loan with a $15 fee carries a 391% APR. In comparison, a $100 bounced check with $48 in bank and merchant fees translates into a 1,251% APR. A $100 utility bill with a $50 late/reconnect fee is equivalent to a 1,304% APR.[31] While this may be a compelling argument for those who wrote the 600 million bounced checks in 2003,[32] it's cold comfort for borrowers faced with paying $900 for a $500 payday loan rolled over for two months.

CASH LEASING

The most expensive loans are those obtained through cash leasing. Lenders use radio and print advertising to target low-income groups, with a particular emphasis on working-class minorities and, more recently, on college students. The advertising promises to "help you out during those cash crunch periods."[33]

This relatively new financial product offers a small, short-term cash advance that is a cross between a payday loan and a pawnshop loan. So that lenders can evade state usury laws, money is technically "leased" rather than lent, and costs 30% in interest for 15 days (a 730% APR). To qualify, borrowers must have held the same job for at least six months, verify a monthly income of at least $1,000, have a phone in their name, and have an active checking account.[34] Additionally, borrowers must own at least three major electronic items, each less than five years old and worth $200 or more. These items are then sold to the lender for a cash settlement and leased back to the borrower for a daily rental fee. After the lease ends, the borrower incurs a "rental" charge and is liable for the initial loan. Since ownership of the items is transferred to the cash leaser, lenders avoid state usury laws, interest caps, and other regulations.[35]

RENT-A-BANK

Responding to high profits in short-term consumer loans, several smaller Federal Deposit Insurance Corporation (FDIC) banks are partnering with fringe lenders to offer "agent-assisted loan programs." Under the National Bank Act, nationally chartered banks are permitted to export the interest rates charged in their home states to customers in other states. In these partnerships, the bank sets the credit criteria and funds the loans. Fringe lenders then market and distribute them. Lenders with rent-a-bank partnerships often charge higher interest rates, make larger loans, or make repeat loans that violate state laws. Despite warnings from federal bank regulators, FDIC-insured bank involvement in fringe lending may be continuing. In turn, consumer groups have criticized the FDIC for being too lax in ending rent-a-bank arrangements.[36]

A RACE TO THE BOTTOM

A key reason why consumers use payday lenders is to avoid bounced-check fees. In 2003 banks charged $30 billion in ATM, bounced-check, and overdraft fees, accounting for 30% of their operating profit.[37] Federal law allows banks to process checks in any order they choose, and some maxi-

THE FRINGE SECTORS

mize their NSF profits by using a big-to-small processing system.[38] For example, if a bank customer writes four checks in one day, many banks will clear the largest check first, even if it was written last. Hence, if a checking account has sufficient funds to cover the three smaller checks but not the larger check, the smaller checks will bounce and the customer will pay three NSF fees. At $30 for each bounced check, the consumer pays $90 instead of the $30 if only the larger check bounced. This accounting system can generate huge profits when applied to millions of customers.

Not to be outdone by payday lenders, some 1,000 banks nationwide are offering expensive overdraft or bounce-protection plans. These plans allow customers to overdraw their accounts using automated teller machines and debit cards. However, instead of charging a 20% APR as with traditional lines of credit, the new programs charge a flat fee (roughly similar to an NSF charge) for each overdraft, which translates into an APR similar to those offered by payday lenders. Unlike traditional lines of credit with limits of $1,000 or more, new programs cap overdrafts at $100–$300, after which the checks bounce. Also unlike traditional lines of credit that allow a flexible repayment schedule, these overdraft programs often require customers to balance their accounts within a few days. Because this plan is promoted as bounced-check protection rather than credit, mainstream banks can earn millions in new fees while skirting state and federal regulations. Consumer groups charge that these programs, which include fees as high as $35 for each overdraft, are essentially high-interest payday loans aimed at working-class customers.[39]

Tax Preparation and Refund Loans

Tax time is feeding time for the fringe economy. From December to April, the media are buzzing with ads about "instant tax refunds." Brochures are conspicuously placed in thousands of convenience stores and supermarkets. Leaflets are tacked onto telephone poles. Abandoned stores are suddenly occupied, at least for a few months. Appliance stores, car dealers, and other merchants will help you get instant money, if you use it to buy their stuff. There's a wild frenzy about instant money. But like all things in the fringe economy, "instant money" isn't free, even if it's your money.

Judy Williams is a single mother of three who lives in rural Arkansas. She works as an office clerk in a small machine shop and earns $7.50 an hour, or roughly $14,400 a year, which is near the median income for this region. Judy makes up the difference between her income and her day-to-day living expenses with federal Earned Income Tax Credit (EITC) and Child Tax Credit (CTC) refunds.

Until recently, Judy had her taxes prepared by a local accountant. However, he closed shop because he couldn't compete with the H&R Block and Jackson Hewitt offices that opened nearby. Judy shifted her business to Jackson Hewitt.

The transaction that had been relatively simple between Judy and her former tax preparer became more complicated with Jackson Hewitt. She was now faced with a staggering array of options. Should Judy choose the Money Now program and get an instant advance against her EITC and CTC refunds? Should she get a MasterCard Cash Card? Should she get an Accelerated Check Refund? Judy was confused. The only certainty was that she would be paying much more than the $75 fee she had paid her former tax preparer.

Jackson Hewitt's tax preparer asked Judy if she wanted a refund anticipation loan (RAL). In the past, Judy had filed her taxes and waited for the refund check. However, the prospect of an instant refund was appealing. Plus, she couldn't afford the tax preparation fee. (Her former tax preparer had let her pay the fee after the refund arrived.)

Judy received an $800 CTC refund and a $2,700 EITC refund, for a total of $3,500. She paid Jackson Hewitt almost $300, which covered the tax preparation fee, the RAL fee, the electronic filing fee, the document preparation fee, and a Gold Guarantee, which promised to protect her in the event of an audit. The $3,500 refund suddenly became $3,200. Since Judy had no bank account, she went to a check-cashing outlet (CCO), which charged 3.9%, or $125. The $3,200 refund was now reduced to $3,075. All told, Judy lost more than 12% of her tax refund. David Shipler summarizes tax time for the poor:

> Tax time in poor neighborhoods is not April. It is January. And
> "income tax" isn't what you pay; it's what you receive. As soon as the

W-2s arrive, working folks eager for their checks from the Internal
Revenue Service hurry to the tax preparers, who have flourished and
gouged impoverished laborers since the welfare time limits enacted by
Congress in 1996. . . .

With cunning creativity, the preparers have devised schemes to
separate low-wage workers from as much of their refunds . . . as
feasible. The marvel of electronic filing, the speedy direct deposit into
a bank account, the high-interest loan masquerading as a "rapid
refund" all promise a sudden flush of dollars to cash-starved families.
The trouble is, getting money costs money.[40]

The EITC is the nation's largest and probably most effective
antipoverty program. In 2002 EITC benefits provided more than $30 bil-
lion in refundable tax credits to almost 20 million low-income taxpayers.
Under EITC, the working poor receive refunds that exceed what they paid
in taxes. Income and family size determine the amount of the EITC
refund. In 2003 the maximum income was $29,666 ($30,666 if filing a joint
return) for a family with one child, and $33,692 ($34,692 if filing a joint
return) for those with two or more qualifying children.[41] In addition to the
EITC, low- and moderate-income families with children are also eligible
for the CTC, a federal tax credit worth up to $1,000 per child. The amount
a family receives under CTC is based on the number of dependent children under age 17 and the amount of federal income tax paid. Most CTC-
eligible families also file for the EITC.

The EITC program has important economic consequences for rural
and metropolitan areas. For instance, Los Angeles County received nearly
$1.3 billion in EITC refunds in 1998, and nearly 25% of families got an
average tax credit of $1,700.[42] Not surprisingly, the more than $30 billion in
EITC and CTC refunds has created a keen interest among fringe lenders
with established footholds in low-income communities. It has also created
a powerful temptation for mainstream tax preparers like H&R Block and
Jackson Hewitt.

Sixty-eight percent of EITC- and CTC-eligible families use tax preparers, and most choose electronic return originators (EROs)—tax preparers
or tax preparation services authorized by the IRS to electronically transmit

federal income tax returns. Low-income consumers use tax preparers for several reasons. For one, the EITC and CTC filing process is complicated. Second, many tax preparation storefronts offer fast cash, and because many low-income working families receive a large EITC refund, they're eager to claim it quickly. Third, tax preparation storefronts are ubiquitous in lower-income neighborhoods. According to one study, zip codes with high numbers of EITC recipients house 50% more tax preparers than zip codes with fewer recipients.[43] Finally, many of the working poor use tax preparers that offer RALs because they can't afford the $100-plus in tax preparation fees upfront.

The tax and RAL sectors of the fringe economy operate in the following way: A low-income tax filer visits an ERO and is charged a tax preparation fee of $100 and upward, which he or she is expected to pay out of pocket.[44] To offset the costs, tax preparers offer a "refund anticipation check." They may also offer a refund transfer, which is not a loan per se, since the filer pays a fee to establish a bank account into which the IRS deposits the tax refund check. After the IRS deposit, the tax preparer withdraws the fee, issues a check, and closes the account. This fee, often around $28, is high for a 10-day bank account designed for a single lump sum. However, the advantage to low-income consumers is that tax preparation fees can be deducted directly from the account. Another variation is an "assisted refund transfer," or, as Jackson Hewitt calls it, IRS Direct. Simply, the tax filer pays the tax preparer to be an intermediary in processing a tax refund into the filer's *own* bank account.[45]

According to a Brookings Institution study, more than 50% of EITC recipients in some large cities receive RALs.[46] The advantage of RALs is that filers can get tax refund loans on the spot or within a few days. Like most fringe economy loans, they include multiple costs. For example, a tax filer eligible for an EITC refund of $1,900 who took out an RAL would pay a total of $248, including the tax preparation fee (see Table 5.2).[47] This cost would be incurred simply to get an EITC refund a few days earlier than if filing in the normal manner. If low-income tax filers seeking an RAL are fleeced in a tax preparation office, they're exploited again on their way out. Namely, about 45% of RAL customers use CCOs to cash their refund checks, paying fees of 3%–10% of the checks' face value. ACE check-cashing machines in H&R Block lobbies charge about 3% to cash a secure refund check. All told, EITC-eligible families using EROs and check-cashers can lose more than 16% of the total value of their tax refunds.

RALs can be risky for low-income tax-filers. Since an RAL is a loan from a bank in partnership with a tax preparer, it must be repaid even if the IRS denies the refund or if it is smaller than expected. If a borrower can't repay the RAL, the lender may forward the debt to a collection agency. Plus, when filers apply for an RAL, they give the lender the right to use the tax refund to pay the filer's old tax preparation debts that the lender may claim are owed.

Many consumers are unaware that RALs are actually loans. Some of this deception is engineered by tax preparers who advertise RALs as "Quick Cash," "Super Fast Refunds," and "Instant Money." In April 2001 H&R Block received 2,230 citations from the New York City Department of Consumer Affairs for misrepresenting RALs and luring customers into accepting loans they didn't fully understand. The company settled for $4 million and paid $2.4 million in restitution to 61,700 New York City customers. Block also settled an RAL-related 700,000-member class-action suit in Texas for $41.7 million. As of 2004, similar class-action suits were pending in Maryland, Illinois, and Alabama.[48]

High tax preparation and RAL fees hurt poor working families and substantially diminish the economic impact of the EITC and CTC. In 2001 tax filers paid $907 million in RAL fees plus $484 million in electronic filing fees. Other sundry tax-related fees added another $400 million, for a total of $1.8 billion, which represents 6% of the $31 billion EITC program targeted for the poor.[49] Table 5.2 examines the impact of tax preparation fees and RALs on tax filers and the EITC program.

The nation's largest RAL lenders earned $357 million from "fast-cash" products in 2001, more than double the $138 million earned in 1998.[50] H&R Block is the dominant player in the tax preparation industry. About 11 million taxpayers received RALs in 2000, almost half through H&R Block. At the same time, Block's revenue rose from $2.4 billion in 2000 to $3.8 billion in 2003. Block's profits came largely from preparing 16.3 million individual tax returns, or 15% of all personal IRS returns in the United States. By 2003, Block had 9,300 tax offices in the United States, along with

Table 5.2.
Draining EITC: 2002 tax preparation, RAL, and check-cashing fees.[51]

Type of Fee	Cost to tax filer	Drain on EITC program (in millions)
RAL loan fee	$75	$363
Electronic filing fee	$40	$194
Document preparation/ application/handling fee	$33	$160
Tax preparation fee	$100	$484
Check-cashing fee	$57	$110[52]
Total	**$305**	**$1.31 billion**

1,000 offices in Canada, Australia, and the United Kingdom, and more than 21 million customers worldwide.[53] Jackson Hewitt (the second-largest tax preparation company) did more than 2.2 million tax returns in 2002, or about 1.7% of all returns filed. It is also the fastest-growing tax preparation company, with more than 4,000 franchised offices in 48 states.[54]

Apart from the two big companies, the remaining taxes are prepared by individual tax filers or by a variety of professionals, such as certified public accountants, attorneys, and fly-by-night amateurs. RALs are also offered by some mainstream banks, payday lenders, pawnshops, CCOs, and even used-car lots. Lending people their own money at high interest rates is quickly becoming a big business in America.

Reforming the Storefront Loan Industry

Pawnshops exist on the periphery of respectability, and their image conjures up Dickensian scenes of desperate families pawning their last goods to buy groceries. The challenge for the industry is to dispel these stereotypes by making this business appear respectable. Corporate owners hope that brightly lit stores, cheerful sales help, new locations in upscale neighborhoods, and a carefully manicured corporate image will change the public's perception. Only time will tell whether this strategy will be successful.

Nevertheless, excessive interest rates in low-to-moderate-risk pawnshop loans should be controlled more tightly. Lending risks are principally determined by the incidence of borrower default and whether the loan is backed by collateral. In view of those criteria, interest rates charged for pawned goods far exceed the risks of loss for pawnshop owners. Therefore, these interest rates should reflect the relative security of pawnshop loans.

Serious reform of the payday lending industry should incorporate at least some of the following: First, the minimum loan term should be no less than 90 days to enable a borrower to recover from an emergency. Few borrowers facing an acute financial dilemma or cash crisis can achieve financial equilibrium in only 14–18 days. Second, repayment should be permitted in installments so that borrowers can systematically pay down their loan principal. Payday rollovers or back-to-back loans are not installments, since borrowers are only paying the interest on the initial loan, not reducing the principal. Third, loans should be made only to borrowers who have the income or liquid assets to repay the debt. Loans that disregard a borrower's income and existing financial obligations will only cause a borrower to go deeper into debt. Fourth, loan churning and back-to-back credit transactions should be prohibited. Florida prohibits the initiation of a new payday loan while another loan is outstanding with a different lender. This prohibition is enforced by a statewide database that tracks individual borrowers. Florida's system represents a model that other states should consider. Finally, borrowers should not be prosecuted for using "bad checks" for payday loans. Payday lenders are not duped in accepting bad checks, since they know beforehand that postdated checks have insufficient funds to cover them.[55] In that sense, payday lenders can't claim duplicity on the part of borrowers.

The Office of the Comptroller of the Currency, the Office of Thrift Supervision, and the Federal Reserve Board have taken significant steps to prevent the institutions they regulate from continuing rent-a-charter relationships with payday lenders. In March 2005 the FDIC adopted restrictive guidelines, requiring banks to ensure that payday loans aren't given to customers with outstanding loans for more than three of the previous 12 months. It is too early to assess the impact of this policy on the industry.

Several things would help lessen the financial burden of tax preparation for low-income families. First, Congress should remove rules that prohibit the IRS from directly competing with the tax preparation industry. This would allow the IRS to provide free software and online filing. Second, Congress should simplify the EITC and CTC refundable tax credits, thereby eliminating needlessly complicated rules and paperwork. Third, low-income taxpayers should be provided with more free tax help, and the IRS Volunteer Income Tax Assistance (VITA) program should be expanded.[56]

In 2001 the federal Office of Budget Management (OMB) established several policy initiatives to improve efficiency. One such initiative instructed the IRS to provide free online tax return preparation and filing services. Complying with this directive, the IRS partnered with the tax-software industry to form the Free File Alliance. The public-private partnership called for the alliance to provide free tax preparation and electronic filing to at least 60% of taxpayers, with each participating software company setting its own eligibility requirements. Unfortunately, this partnership was similar to having the fox guard the chicken coop. Almost immediately, several consumer groups sent a letter to the Treasury Department charging that commercial tax preparers participating in the program were using confidential information to cross-market financial products. One of the key "perps" was H&R Block.[57]

Although there's no easy way to curb the excesses of fringe banking, federal and state regulators must be more vigilant in enforcing usury and federal banking laws. Consumer groups, legislators, and policy makers should strive for stricter usury caps, comprehensive disclosure laws, and enforceable anti-predatory-lending legislation. However, the primary thrust for change must occur at the federal level. As this chapter demonstrates, the fringe economy is increasingly being dominated by large, well-funded national and multinational corporations with the ability to circumvent state laws through loopholes and partnerships with state-chartered banks. Individual states cannot compete effectively against the juggernaut of this well-funded industry.

The millions who are poor in the United States tend to become increasingly invisible. Here is a great mass of people, yet it takes an effort of the intellect and will even to see them.

–Michael Harrington, *The Other America*

Alternative Services: Check Cashers, the Rent-to-Own Industry, and Telecommunications

A robust and growing industry has emerged in America for those with bad or no credit. Most services, such as telecommunications, apartment rentals, and store credit cards, require a credit check. Those who score low on this check are forced into the alternative services sector. This chapter examines how America's down-and-out are shortchanged through expensive alternative services, such as furniture and appliance rentals and telecommunications.

Check Cashers and Auxiliary Financial Services[1]

ACE Cash Express, Check 'n Go, Mr. Payroll (Cash America International), Dollar, and Money Mart are familiar sights in inner-city neighborhoods and strip malls. Behind these 14,000-plus storefronts lies an industry that cashed upwards of 180 million checks in 2001 with a face value of $55 billion. These check-cashing outlets (CCOs) generate nearly $1.5 billion a year in revenues, coming largely from the 20%–40% of the unbanked who regularly use these services to cash their paychecks.[2]

Chuck Waldron is a recovering alcoholic and former inmate at an Arkansas state prison. Although he's now gotten his life back on track, he still remembers the past:

> I used check cashers when I first got out of jail. I got a job and had a normal paycheck every week that I used to support my alcohol habit. I didn't have a checking account. I didn't use anything like that, so I used the check-cashing place and paid their fees. It wasn't extreme, but there was a bit of a charge—I think 50 bucks on a thousand-dollar check. I just paid it and got my 950 bucks. I did that for like six to eight months. Then I started adding things up. After four or five months I realized that I just lost 500 dollars. It's the equivalent of throwing half my paycheck into the trash. At that point I started taking it to the bank the check was drawn on. I don't know why I went to the check-cashing place in the first place. I guess it was out of convenience, since the bank was across town. So I started to go to the bank, and I realized they had branches all over. They asked me if I wanted an account, and sure enough, on the next street over from my house,

there was a bank branch. And then direct deposit came along. I did that, but it really screwed me up. I was writing checks the day before the deposit hit the bank.

Consumers use CCOs for a variety of reasons. A Financial Service Centers of America study asserts that CCO customers use the service because of convenient locations, longer hours (some are open 24 hours), good customer service, reasonable fees, and a safe environment.[3] Despite the industry spin, many customers use CCOs because they lack savings and require immediate cash to cover their living expenses. Many can't wait a day or two until their paycheck clears, so instant check cashing is attractive. For some, cashing a paycheck and getting the money instantly is the difference between eating and not eating that day. Others have been denied a checking account by a mainstream bank—sometimes due to an overdrawn account or too many bounced checks—and have no alternative.

Many of those denied a checking account are identified by Chex-Systems, a national database containing a history of consumer checking accounts. The company provides deposit-account verification services to its financial institutions to aid them in identifying applicants who have a history of account mishandling, such as having overdrawn accounts closed by a bank. In addition, ChexSystems is a licensed collection agency that provides debt-collection services to participating members. Each report submitted to ChexSystems remains in its files for five years unless the bank or credit union that filed the report requests its removal. ChexSystems also helps banks discriminate against the poor. In particular, some banks use ChexSystems not only as a tool for reducing risk, but also as a way to eliminate the bottom tier of account holders who maintain low balances.

CCOs provide an expensive form of check cashing. Eighteen states don't regulate CCOs, and most check-cashing fees range from 1% to 10% (plus a service fee in some states) of a check's value.[4] Fees for cashing personal checks can run as high as 10%–12% of a check's value. Check-cashing charges are often based on a sliding scale. Dollar, the second-largest CCO, charges 3.5%, or $35 to cash a $1,000 check. If a customer cashes 12 $1,400 paychecks a year through Dollar, he or she will pay $580, far more than the costs of even a deluxe checking account. The price list posted at

Table 6.1.

2004 price list for ACE Cash Express.

Type of charge	Fee
Cashier's check	5.0%
Government check	2.7%
Handwritten payroll check	2.7%
Insurance draft/checks	5.0%
Money order	5.0%
Tax refund check	3.9%
No I.D. check	5.0%
Special risk	5.0%
Bank processing fee	$0.49
Minimum charge per item	$1.99
Returned-check charge	$25

one ACE Cash Express in Houston, Texas, is typical of the industry (see Table 6.1).

Roughly 70%–90% of all checks cashed at CCOs are relatively secure payroll checks with an average face value of $500–$600.[5] Losses are low. For example, ACE uses a system for assessing the risk of each check-cashing transaction and reports losses of less than one-quarter of 1%.[6]

Check cashing is a large and profitable business. In 2002, 797 ACE company-owned stores posted average revenues of $237,000, or a store profit of almost 43%.[7] In 2003 ACE—the largest franchiser of check cashing and related financial services—had 90 franchise owners operating in 206 locations. This was in addition to 968 company-owned stores in 36 states and the District of Columbia. ACE shares a strategic partnership with Travelers Express, and in 2003 it sold $1.6 billion in money orders and $400 million worth of MoneyGram money transfers.[8] Dollar, ACE's chief competitor, is the industry's only international CCO. In 2004 it operated or franchised almost 1,100 stores in 17 states, Canada, and the United Kingdom.

Like most of the fringe economy, the CCO industry has undergone spectacular growth. In 1993 ACE owned 276 stores in 10 cities; by 2000 it had 850 stores in 272 cities. Dollar owned six times as many stores in 2000

THE FRINGE SECTORS

as in 1995.[9] Cash America International located its Mr. Payroll check-cashing kiosks in 150 convenience stores, such as Toot'n Totum, Allsups, Cracker Barrel, EZ Mart, and Jet 24, and in major gas stations such as those owned by Texaco, Conoco, BP, and Total. According to the company, "The Mr. Payroll kiosk is a boon to the convenience store because it adds customers inside the store with cash in hand." Cash America's strategy creates a double whammy for low-income consumers by combining high check-cashing fees with the "convenience" of buying overpriced goods at minimarts and gas stations.[10]

The profits in check cashing are attracting even non-finance-related corporations, which is blurring the boundary between mainstream retailers and fringe-market CCOs. For example, the Eastern Division of the Safeway supermarket chain is the largest CCO in Maryland. Other supermarket chains, such as HEB and Randalls, have also established check-cashing operations, although they often charge 1%, rather than the 2%–5% charged by commercial CCOs. As a testament to the profitability of the fringe sector, even retailer giant Wal-Mart has initiated a payroll and government check-cashing service, an express bill-paying service, money orders, and international money transfers in some of its stores. Wal-Mart also provides fee-for-service credit reports. For example, the Wal-Mart in Giddings, Texas, charges $3 to cash a check up to $1,000, the maximum amount that can be cashed every seven days. (I wouldn't be surprised if Wal-Mart were soon to offer payday loans.) 7-Eleven stores provide check cashing through ATM terminals (generally charging about 2% of a check's value), plus money orders and transfers.

Mainstream banks are also directly competing in the check-cashing market. For example, Bank One charges a $3 check-cashing fee; JPMorgan Chase charges 1.5%, with a minimum $5 fee; and Bank of America levies a $5 check-cashing fee. These fees go beyond covering expenses. A 1999 Federal Reserve Bank report noted that big banks pay only 36 cents to cash a check drawn on a customer's account, an amount already figured into the checking-account-maintenance fee.[11] While check cashing is lucrative, auxiliary services, such as the sale of money transfers and electronic bill paying, are potentially even more profitable because they incur less risk.

The High Cost of Auxiliary Financial Services

There is a growing population of immigrants from Latin America and other nations who are unable or unwilling to use traditional financial services. These individuals frequently send part of their paycheck to family members in their homelands. According to the Pew Hispanic Center and Multilateral Investment Fund, money transfers to Latin America by individuals living in the United States are expected to grow to $25 billion by 2010. While international remittances have usually been handled through Western Union outlets and other money-transfer services, deposit institutions such as banks and credit unions are increasingly offering them. When they're provided through the fringe economy, the fees for these transactions can be extremely high—in some cases, as much as 28% of the remittance.[12]

In international money transfers the customer pays a transfer fee plus a fee for the currency exchange. If a customer used Western Union to wire $500 from Ohio to El Salvador, he or she would pay $51 in fees, or more than 10% of the transfer amount. In addition, U.S. currency is converted to foreign currency at an exchange rate set by Western Union. Any difference between the rate charged a customer and that received by Western Union or MoneyGram is additional profit. For example, if a Western Union customer wired $500 to Mexico on December 12, 2003, the company's exchange rate was 10.85 pesos to the dollar, while the actual rate was closer to 11.21 pesos. Spread over millions of customers, this rate differential represents significant profit for Western Union. Profit can be made at the other end, too, since some wire services also require the recipient to pay a fee.

Another source of income for CCOs is electronic bill paying. For example, ACE partnered with Travelers Express's MoneyGram to create the first universal bill-payment service for walk-in consumers. In 2004, 9.7 million bills were paid electronically at ACE stores. Like all fringe economy services, bill paying comes at a high cost. In 2004 ACE charged 75 cents a transaction, and Western Union charged up to $2 per bill. MoneyGram charges were $8.95 for an electronic bill payment. Even Wal-Mart's Express Bill-Payment service cost $8.50 a bill in 2005.

While CCOs charge for electronic bill paying, the major banks, including Bank of America, Citibank, Chase, and Wells Fargo, provide this service free for their checking account customers. Electronic bill paying is provided free because it saves money for banks. The Federal Reserve estimates that it costs $1–$5 to process a paper check, but electronic payments cost as little as 7 cents each.[13] Banks derive another important benefit from electronic bill paying: free use of the customer's money. For example, with electronic bill paying, money disappears from a customer's account several days before a bill is actually paid. During this time, the bank is using the customer's money without paying interest. The lag time between the request for funds and their release is called "float." While a bank obviously doesn't make a huge profit from the float on a single utility bill, multiplied by 12–15 bills a month and millions of customers, the money that the bank can earn is considerable. In contrast with middle-class bank consumers who lose only the float, fringe economy customers pay twice: once for the bill-paying service and then again for the hidden cost of the float.

Rent to Own: The Furniture and Appliance Rental Industry

Without cash and mainstream credit, many consumers are forced to turn to the furniture and appliance rental industry. This industry encompasses two types of companies: high-end businesses designed for short-term corporate or other temporary relocations, and the rent-to-own (RTO) industry, which targets low- and moderate-income consumers. RTOs advertise that no credit checks are required; they take weekly or monthly payments; and they can offer a wide variety of appliances, furniture, and jewelry that many low-income consumers couldn't afford to buy outright.

Janis Gardner lives with her two young grandchildren on her salary as a nurse's aide. She has no car, relies on Dallas public transportation, and shops at convenient but expensive local shops, which substantially increases her cost of living. Janis needed furniture for her grandchildren, including beds, dressers, and lamps. Without cash or credit, she turned to a Rental Centers store that was only a few blocks from her home. The salesperson treated Janis courteously and seemed sympathetic to her plight. After Janis filled out the paperwork and provided the names of six references, she was promised that the furniture would be delivered by the end of the day. Rental Centers kept its word.

Not much was explained about the terms of the transaction, except the amount of the weekly payments. Besides, Janis didn't read the fine print, and, like most low-income customers, she was mainly concerned about how much she'd have to pay each week. Janis owed $30 a week, and the salesperson encouraged her to pay in person. Every time she stopped in to pay, she was treated well, although the salesperson was always trying to push more rentals. When Janis's refrigerator went out, she turned to Rental Centers. Although she wanted a basic unit, the salesperson used upselling tactics to persuade her to rent a better model. Janis also ended up renting a television set. In less than two years, her payments jumped from $30 to $120 a week.

When Janis's youngest grandchild became ill, she was forced to cut back on her work hours. Not long afterward, she was unable to pay Rental Centers. Janis's salesperson called with friendly reminders, but after a while the tone became harsh and nasty. After returning from church one day, Janis found her apartment almost empty—the bedroom set, the television, and the refrigerator were gone, and the food was sitting on the kitchen table getting warm. All the money that Janis had faithfully paid for these goods over a year and a half was lost. Sadly, Janis had already spent enough to buy the furniture and appliances outright at a discount store.

Janis eventually returned to work full time. Not long afterward, she received a Rental Centers mailing saying that they wanted her back. Janis marched down to Rental Centers and rented a similar bedroom set, television, and refrigerator. But this time, because of Janis's spotty payment history, she had to pay for three months in advance. Why did Janis do it again? Because she still had no cash, no credit, and no other choice. For Rental Centers, it was just business. Joe Marolian, a former Rent-A-Center manager and now the owner of an RTO company, sums up the nature of the industry:

> When you go into homes that you're delivering furniture or merchandise to, you have to step over something, like a hole in the floor. Those old wood houses they live in, definitely living week to week, paycheck to paycheck. But they were sure to have their $10 rental payment to the store for that 19-inch TV that was for 78 or 91 weeks, and cost them $900 instead of $200, which in itself is criminal. But it's the way

THE FRINGE SECTORS

it was and still is. . . . These customers come in, and I can tell you I've seen customers come in for 91 weeks on a 19-inch TV and spend $1,100. Could they do it any other way? Could they save that money up? Yes. Probably with some help, someone to help them with their finances. . . . But they've been paying things weekly for years; their family's been doing it that way for years. Every single week they have to pay a good portion of their income to the rental store. Some of them will be paying the store $1,000 a month. That's a lot of money. And they do it religiously.

On the positive side, Janis didn't take on intractable debt—as she would with payday loans or credit card purchases—and she could voluntarily return the rentals when the payments became unaffordable. Nor did she face a potential lawsuit and hounding by collection agencies. The repossession also didn't affect her future credit.

GROWTH AND PROFITABILITY IN THE RTO INDUSTRY

The RTO industry is a major player in the fringe economy. In 2004 the $6.2 billion-a-year industry served 2.7 million customers through 8,300 stores. The rapid growth of the RTO industry parallels the overall growth of the fringe economy. Rent-A-Center began with eight stores in 1986; by 2003 it had more than 2,500 stores in 50 states. The company was bought in 1987 for $594 million by Thorn EMI plc, the record company of Frank Sinatra, Tina Turner, and the Beatles. With the backing of Thorn, Rent-A-Center became the largest RTO corporation in the world, with revenues of more than $2 billion in 2004.

Aaron Rents started in 1955 by renting folding chairs to auction houses for 10 cents a day; by 2004, it had 644 stores with almost $1 billion in annual revenues. RentWay grew from a single store in 1983 to more than 1,000 stores with revenues of $626 million in 2003.

Business is brisk in the industry. In 2003 Rent-A-Center shares rose 70%, the company's stock price having climbed 153% since 2001. Shares in Aaron Rents rose 60% in 2003 and were 114% higher than in 2001.[14]

The fringe economy is highly competitive, and to survive, corporations must always be on the lookout for new opportunities. So in addition to rentals, many RTOs also offer alternative local phone service, check cashing, prepaid phone cards, and income tax refund anticipation loans.[15] The larger RTOs offer these services to help meet their goal of becoming full-service financial centers for the poor and credit-challenged.

The High Cost of Rentals

The RTO industry employs two approaches to transactions. In the first, customers simply rent goods and pay weekly or monthly fees. In the second, they rent to own, and payments are extended from 12 to 24 months. In either case, customers can usually cancel the agreement without further cost or obligation, or can renew the contract by making another payment. Customers take ownership of the property once they complete the lease agreement, although many never get that far. No credit bureau reports are filed, since RTO customers make advance payments.

While the rental option is expensive, the RTO industry claims that its high prices reflect the cost of repairs and the risks of doing business with customers who have poor credit histories and unstable incomes. According to the Consumer Federation of America, customers with RTO contracts pay between $1,000 and $2,400 for a television, stereo, or other major appliance worth as little as $200 used and seldom more than $600 new.

Rainbow Rentals, the nation's fourth-largest RTO chain, advertises a Frigidaire washer and dryer for $19 a week, or $69 a month for 21 months. The total cost is between $1,450 and $1,600 for a washer and dryer that could be purchased new for about $800 at a local discount store like Best Buy or Circuit City. A Compaq Presario notebook with an inexpensive Celeron processor rents for $38 a week or $144 a month for 24 months, raising the total cost to about $3,500. The same computer can be bought for less than $900 at major retailers. A 32-inch Toshiba flat-screen television costs $1,800 to rent for 24 months. Best Buy sells the same set for $650. A Philips DVD player costs $228 to rent for 12 months. It can be bought outright for $100 at most discount stores. At a minimum, RTO customers pay at least two to three times more than the retail price.[16] Advertised RTO payments also don't include sales tax, service fees (about 10%), late fees, or "customer protection plans."

RTOs gouge consumers in other ways. For example, they offer merchandise at a "cash and carry" price. According to a 1997 U.S. PIRG study, the typical RTO cash price on an item was $389, compared with the average department store price of $217.[17] One Aaron Rents store in Houston was selling a used GE refrigerator for $1,134—about the same price as a new one at a large discount store like Circuit City.

RTOs also make money with repossessions and re-rents. For instance, a 32-inch Toshiba television may cost the RTO $500. If the set is rented for $69 a month, the RTO will make back the $500 in seven months and realize a gross profit of $1,173 at the end of a two-year lease term. (Gross profits don't take into account the cost of repossessions, servicing merchandise, salaries, and the overall expenses in running the store.) If the set is repossessed after seven months, the retailer can re-rent it for another two years at a slightly lower price. Merchandise can therefore be recycled several times. Alix Freedman reported that one Rent-A-Center store had a $119 VCR that brought in more than $5,000 over a five-year period.[18] Typical RTO stores record yearly revenues of almost $500,000.[19]

CUSTOMER SERVICE

Janis Gardner's experience mirrors that of thousands of other Americans. RTO stores are used not only by the chronically poor, but also by temporarily poor college students. Kyle and Marti Johnson were students at the University of Oklahoma when they rented furniture from a large RTO. For them, the experience "was horrible, absolutely horrible. They give you the weekly payment. . . . They charge you interest; the payments are ridiculous. And they harass you. They come to your door. We were two or three days behind. Phone calls every five minutes. Once they start coming to your door, they leave nasty notes on it, like 'We're going to come pick up your stuff if you're late again.' We were definitely treated with disrespect." John Walker had a similar experience:

> I needed a couch really bad. And I thought, rent to own, why not? I wanted a new couch, since I didn't want some piece of crap somebody gave me. I was tired of that. The only way for somebody in my income bracket to buy things is to make payments. I went in and they had this nice big sectional with a couple of recliners. They wanted $600 if you paid right then. I had the $66 every two weeks. By the time I finished

paying it off in a year and a half, I had forked over $1200 for that couch. I ended up throwing it away, since it was such a piece of shit. It wasn't even worth the $600 they were asking for it. Maybe a couple hundred bucks. Yeah, there were times where I would forget to go in and pay it, and they'd be knocking on the door with their little truck outside ready to take my couch away even though I'd already paid for this couch twice over. I'd have to come up with the money right there. It sucked. I'll never do it again.

RTO transactions are a mixed blessing for low-income consumers. A Federal Trade Commission (FTC) study found that 75% of rental customers were satisfied with their transactions. These customers gave a variety of reasons for this satisfaction, including the positive aspects of the sale, the merchandise and services, and the good treatment they received from employees. On the other hand, 27% of RTO customers—including nearly 70% of dissatisfied customers—complained about high prices. The high satisfaction rate is not surprising, since many fringe businesses long ago realized the importance of treating low-income customers respectfully. They also realized that customers like the folksy "we understand what you're going through" approach. Rent Rite's store brochure is an example of this approach:

What's the EZ-est kind of payment for most people? Weekly payments, of course. TeenZ-weenZ, low, low weekly payments—not those high priced, jaw-dropping monthly payments those other companies push on you. Weekly payments are what Rent Rite specializes in. Because c'mon, who has lots of money left after rent, groceries, car payments and stuff like that? And you know that when you get your rental payment taken care of each week, it's just plain EZ-ier to manage.

Rent-A-Center also understands "folksy" and uses John Madden as its TV spokesman. A multimillionaire sports commentator, Madden uses his blue-collar, just-plain-folks image to convince poor people that paying $2,500 for an $800 product is a good deal. "Hey," Madden quips, "Rent-A-Center has a holiday gift for you. But you gotta be quick."

Despite vying for a more upscale image and a large middle-class customer base, the fringe economy still has the poor and credit-challenged as its bread and butter. RTO marketing predominantly targets low-income consumers by advertising in media located in buses and around public housing projects that target people of color. The industry also promotes features attractive to low-income consumers: quick delivery, weekly payments, no or small down payments, quick repair service, no credit checks, and no harm to one's credit if one cancels the transaction.

While all consumers appreciate good customer service, it's especially important for low-income consumers who have been humiliated by mainstream merchants after bad credit checks. Some low-income consumers are so sensitive to poor treatment that they'll pay more, sometimes much more, just to feel they are being respected. As one former Rent-A-Center manager stated, "If you treat the customer like royalty, you can bleed them through the nose."[20]

Prepaid Telecommunications

Telecommunications are a necessity in modern American life. Without a home telephone, you can't schedule job interviews, make doctor's appointments, contact family members, or even call for emergency assistance. Nor can you get credit—including payday or fringe economy auto loans—without a home phone.

Consumer telecommunications are divided into two types of services: postpaid and prepaid. For postpaid (that is, paying *after* a charge is accrued) services, customers are required to undergo credit checks, and those with poor scores are typically denied phone service. In fact, the first thing a salesperson does with a potential customer in a mainstream cell phone store is run a credit check. Low-income or credit-impaired consumers classified as unworthy of credit are forced into the more expensive prepaid sector.

ALTERNATIVE LOCAL TELEPHONE SERVICE
Telephone service providers fall into two categories. The first is ILECs (incumbent local exchange carriers), telephone companies that already

provided local service when the Telecommunications Act of 1996 was enacted. The second category is CLECs (competitive local exchange carriers), or companies that began after passage of the telecommunications act and compete with traditional regional local telephone companies, such as the Bell companies and GTE. Consumers who fail a credit check or whose service has been disconnected for nonpayment can opt for alternative prepaid local phone service from CLECs.

Mary Bradshaw needed telephone service after hers was disconnected by Southwestern Bell for nonpayment. Although she had responsibly paid her bills in the past, her neighbors had used her phone to make several hundred dollars' worth of long distance calls. Since Mary works for a temporary-employment agency, she needs a telephone to know when and where to show up for work. Plus, she's a single mother with two kids in day care.

A friend referred Mary to Get-A-Fone, and she signed up for prepaid telephone service costing $30 a month plus taxes and other fees. In addition, she paid a $40 startup fee. Installation was supposedly free but operated in the following way: Get-A-Fone charged Mary $160 in cash for the line installation. Her account was credited $10 a month toward the $160 until it was paid off. The remaining line-installation fee was due in full if she decided to transfer her existing service to another provider but was not due if Mary's line was fully disconnected. Get-A-Fone also charged her $25 in additional line fees.

Like many fringe economy customers, Mary didn't read the fine print. For one, she had to purchase a long distance service package separately from her local phone service. Local service also didn't include directory assistance, operator-assisted calls, or the ability to make or accept collect calls. As part of the long distance package, Mary's home phone was basically treated like a calling card. In other words, she had to pay a "bong" charge ("bong" being the sound of coins entering a pay phone) of 25 cents per long distance call plus 19 cents a minute. To make matters worse, all long distance calls were subject to a one-minute charge, even if the number she called was busy or no one answered. Long distance calls were also rounded off to the next minute, and Mary's unused minutes expired in 30 days. Mary didn't realize that she had to make three monthly payments of $30 (plus taxes and other fees) before disconnecting the service or transferring to another company. This was in addition to a $40 disconnect fee.

Mary didn't understand that her telephone service could be suspended or disconnected if her line was used for the transmission of data, such as faxes or Internet services, or if she exceeded the number of local calls or minutes included in her basic monthly service package. Get-A-Fone also reserved the right to change her local service to a different calling plan, which could result in higher monthly charges. All told, Mary's phone charges doubled.

THE ALTERNATIVE PHONE MARKET

The industry estimates that about 5 million households don't have dial tone service because of nonpayment, translating into a market of roughly $2 billion. About 2 million of those households fit into the prepaid market, estimated to be worth $800 million annually. DPI Teleconnect estimates that prepaid CLECs have fewer than 300,000 customers. In other words, over 80% of the potential market is still untapped.[21]

In 2004 DPI served 58,000 customers and was marketed at more than 3,000 locations. DPI has an ongoing relationship with large pawnshop chains, check cashers, and payday lenders, demonstrating how intertwined are the different parts of the fringe economy. DPI charges $39 a month (excluding taxes and access fees) for basic local phone service. Others, such as Direct Telephone Company, charge $50 a month for local service (bundled with some options); 1-800 Reconex charges $46.50. In addition to these charges, low-income customers pay sundry connection, processing, and service fees ranging from $39 to $60 a month.[22] Qtel charges $35 a month for basic service (excluding surcharges and fees), plus an initial $25 startup fee and another $5-a-month fee for the first five months. In comparison, Southwestern Bell charges about $19 a month for a full-service unlimited local telephone plan.[23]

There's no magic to setting up an alternative phone system. According to DPI, "The equipment needed to maintain operations consists of a personal computer network and a telephone system to support the Customer

Service Representatives, 800# in and out and overall communication needs. These unique features make the business profitable in its early stages of growth."[24]

High monthly service and startup fees represent only one way that prepaid telephone companies profit from low-income or credit-challenged consumers. In large measure, the real profit lies in the fine print. For example, Dallas-based Qtel charges a $15 nonrecurring fee for each option added to a telephone, such as call-waiting and caller ID. Late fees for Qtel cost $10 for the first to the seventh day late, and $25 from the eighth day forward, or the maximum allowed by law. There's generally no grace period with prepaid services.

CELL PHONE SERVICE

Postpaid cell phone service depends on good credit. Creditworthy customers can get Sprint's $35 postpaid cell phone service, which includes 300 daytime minutes and unlimited nighttime and evening minutes. Cingular's $30 plan includes 200 anytime minutes and 1,000 night and weekend minutes.[25] The deal for the poor isn't nearly as good.

Poor and credit-challenged customers are a lucrative market for the wireless industry. In fact, prepaid cell phone service is one of the fastest-growing segments of the wireless market and has almost 17 million customers nationwide. Prepaid cell phone service is expensive. One study found that 300 minutes cost 25 cents a minute more for prepaid customers. Minutes in a prepaid plan cost twice as much as minutes in a postpaid plan from the same carrier.[26] In addition, most prepaid cell phone minutes expire every 15–60 days. Although some companies offer "rollover" minutes, the prices on these plans are typically very high. Getting set up is also expensive. The typical startup package, including the phone, charger, and a handful of minutes, can cost $100 or more.

Unlike postpaid cell phone service with set minutes, prepaid cell phone airtime can cost anywhere from 12 to 60 cents a minute. In 2004 Verizon charged prepaid customers 10 cents a minute and 25 cents for each call. Cingular charged 35 cents a minute on weekdays, 10 cents a minute on weekends. In 2004 the prepaid pricing at AT&T (now owned by Cingular) was based on the amount of refills that a customer bought. For example, those who could afford only a $10 refill paid 50–85 cents a minute, while the minute charges for those who could afford a $100 refill dropped to 12–22 cents a minute.[27]

The Evolving Fringe Economy

While the last two chapters have examined pawnshops, payday lenders, CCOs, and tax refund lenders separately, the lines between them are blurring. For example, pawnshops are increasingly offering payday loans and check-cashing services along with traditional pawn loans. Many CCOs also offer payday loans, auxiliary financial services, and RALs.

The fringe economy is undergoing a dramatic change marked by the widespread consolidation of financial services. For example, corporations like Cash America International, ACE Cash Express, and EZ Pawn are aggressively purchasing mom-and-pop pawnshops, CCOs, and small payday lenders. Their driving vision is to become full-service financial centers. In time, these centers could well offer a complete line of financial products, including pawns, auto title and payday loans, auxiliary financial services, auto and home insurance, tax preparation and RALs, secured credit cards, telecommunication services, and even large-scale subprime lending for vehicles and homes. In that sense, well-financed fringe lending operations would become a complete—and expensive—"poor person's bank."

To expand its market even further, the fringe economy must overcome the stigma associated with being viewed as predatory. Always concerned about its image, the industry tries to distance itself from the view that it targets mainly poor and desperate consumers. Hence, RTOs try to demonstrate their respectability by portraying their customers as just "plain folks." Industry statistics are often slanted to reflect that point. For example, the Association of Progressive Rental Organizations (APRO)—the industry trade group—claims that 50% of RTO customers are between the ages of 25 and 44; 70% are white; 25% are African American; and almost 40% have completed at least some college.[28] While the APRO also claims that 70% of customers earn more than $25,000 a year, an FTC study found that 59% had yearly household incomes of less than $25,000.[29] This hardly constitutes a group of middle-class consumers on the lookout for buying alternatives.

As part of the strategy to redefine itself, the industry has located a few pawnshops, payday lenders, and RTO stores in more upscale locations. It is also targeting its advertising to the younger middle class. One attempt to reach a larger market is Jackson Hewitt's strategy of putting tax preparation centers inside high-volume retail outlets like Wal-Mart, Kmart, Staples, Kroger, Value City, and General Growth malls. Housed in highly traveled and respectable middle-class venues, these tax centers are the perfect place for Jackson Hewitt to hawk its profitable fringe lending services to both the poor and the financially overstretched middle class.

Struggling for respectability, the fringe sector hopes that by shedding its sleazy image it can evade the continued scrutiny of consumer groups and federal and state regulators. Laudably, Financial Service Centers of America, a professional trade organization representing CCOs and payday lenders, offers a national scholarship program for college-bound high school seniors. Funding for FiSCA's scholarship program comes from member contributions and vendors like Western Union and Travelers Express.[30] Even Household International—a notorious subprime lender—spends $15 million a year making "cash and in-kind contributions to local nonprofit organizations that serve our communities and best respond to the issues and needs of our customers and employees."[31] The H&R Block Foundation funds $18 million in grants in the Kansas City area. ACE Cash Express gives 1% of its net profits—$200,000 in 2004—to charitable causes. Despite these modest attempts at charity, fringe lending is a legal and virtually unregulated form of loan-sharking. Fringe economy lenders neither provide nor offer any savings-based financial products that can build assets, increase household wealth, or build strong communities. Money flows in only one direction—from the pockets of low-income consumers to the coffers of fringe economy corporations.

Although the fringe economy saps the income and assets of poor families and communities, no simple or effective alternative to fringe lending has arisen that doesn't harm low-income people. Fringe economic institutions are important to low-income neighborhoods because they function like community banks. They also address a real need for cash, credit, goods, and other financial products not currently being provided by the government or mainstream banks. In the end, low-income consumers need the fringe economy as much as the industry needs them.

Reforming the Alternative Services Sector

Several changes are necessary to reform the fringe economy. For one, banks and credit unions should be prohibited from charging fees on checks drawn from their banks. This position is based on two principles: (1) a check is a promissory note from a bank customer to a payee, and by charging a fee to the payee the bank reduces the funds that the account holder promised to pay, and the promissory obligation is not met; and (2) check-cashing costs are already included in the fees (or float) paid for by the account holder. When a bank charges a fee on checks drawn from it, it is essentially being reimbursed twice for the same financial transaction.

Consumer advocates argue that rent-to-own transactions are credit sales rather than leases, and should be subject to federal and state consumer credit laws. A key issue in this debate is the extent to which customers purchase rather than rent merchandise. The APRO doggedly claims that 75% of renters return items within the first four months and the vast majority view the transactions as short-term leases.[32] Conversely, an FTC study found that renters bought 70% of RTO merchandise, and 67% of customers intended to purchase the merchandise when they began the transaction. The study also found that 90% of the merchandise on which customers had made substantial payments toward ownership (six months or more) was purchased.[33]

Rent-to-own arrangements should be treated as credit transactions, since that's essentially what they are. Even if a consumer enters an RTO agreement without the intent to eventually purchase the item, the structure of the transaction is usually predicated on the assumption of eventual ownership. Consequently, RTO contracts should be subject to the same federal and state laws that affect credit sales, including interest-rate disclosures, prohibitions against unfair credit practices, and state usury laws.

The argument over whether RTO transactions are credit versus lease transactions may be largely academic, since even in fringe economy areas where interest rates are spelled out, such as payday loans, consumers have not been deterred from using the services, nor have those disclosures hampered the growth of the industry. As noted throughout this book, what's important to low-income consumers is not the interest rate per se but the size of the weekly and monthly payments they have to make. Also, usury laws in some states are so liberal that most RTO transactions would be largely unaffected. For instance, many states permit triple-digit interest rates for payday and pawnshop loans. If RTO transactions were classified as credit sales, the same criteria would presumably be applied. Even if RTO transactions were covered under the federal Truth-in-Lending Act and various state laws, the deep pockets of the $6 billion RTO industry, its lobbying power, and its ability to hire high-priced legal talent to find loopholes would work against successful enforcement.

Consumers who are required to prepay for telecommunications services face several inequities. First, prepaid services help providers cut losses and ensure an uninterrupted revenue flow by holding customers' money even before they incur any charges. (It's difficult to imagine that these companies have a similar financial relationship with their lenders.) But even though these customers guarantee their bills by their prepayment, they're still charged more than postpaid customers. This is doubly unjust because the corporations presumably experience fewer losses from prepaid customers. Less risk should translate into lower, not higher, rates. At a minimum, prepaid customers should receive interest on their payments, which could then be deducted from the costs of the service.

Moreover, corporations keep the float on a customer's money without paying interest, which inadvertently increases the customer's cost for the service. Prepaid consumers are therefore penalized twice—once by paying higher prices, and then again by the company's using their money without paying them interest. Finally, consumers trying to build or rebuild their credit history will also derive little benefit from prepaying, since no credit is extended, and thus there's nothing to report to a credit agency.

Whether low-income consumers use check cashers, payday lenders, or banks, they pay more than the middle class for financial services both in absolute dollars and relative to their income.[34] These costs are symptomatic of the division of financial services that has led to even greater economic inequality: banks for the middle class and check cashers for the poor; access to savings tools for the middle class and barriers to savings for the poor; low-cost financial services for the middle class and high-fee-based services for the poor.

Although market specialization, competition, and innovation have vastly expanded credit to virtually all income classes, under certain circumstances this expanded access may not be entirely beneficial. . . . Of concern are abusive lending practices that target specific neighborhoods or vulnerable segments of the population and can result in unaffordable payments, equity stripping, and foreclosure.

−Alan Greenspan, "Economic Challenges in the New Century," Annual Conference of the National Community Reinvestment Coalition, Washington, DC, March 22, 2000

Congress knows predatory lending is a problem. The Clinton administration knows this is a problem. Now the chairman of the Federal Reserve himself is saying this is a problem. So, when are we going to see laws, regulation, and enforcement to put a stop to it?

−Frank Torres, legislative counsel, Consumers Union, March 22, 2000

7

Fringe Housing

Housing represents the biggest chunk of a family budget and is the single largest asset for the majority of American homeowners. Home mortgages and refinancing is a multibillion-dollar business in the United States, and in 2002 home equity hit a record high of $7.6 trillion.[1] Housing is also a sector highly susceptible to the predations of the fringe economy. For example, Eric Stein estimates that U.S. borrowers lose $9.1 billion annually to predatory mortgage practices.[2] The robust and dangerous fringe housing economy encompasses everything from subprime to predatory lending, and from legal, to quasi-legal, to outright illegal speculation and lender-initiated scams. This chapter examines the differences between subprime and predatory lending; various kinds of home, refinancing, and home equity loans; housing speculation; and the foreclosure process.

Purchasing or selling a house can be a scary experience, and buyers and sellers often leave a closing in a stupor, unsure of what they signed and why. My wife and I recently bought a house in Houston, Texas. Like many home buyers, we didn't retain an attorney to read the closing documents. The title insurance company set aside one hour for the closing. During that time, we were given more than 125 single-spaced pages of documents (much of it in small print) on legal-size paper. More than 60 pages required our signature or initials. It would've been almost impossible for us to digest those documents in 24 hours, let alone one hour. When we asked to slow down the process, we were met with perplexed stares, which later turned into impatience. On leaving the closing, Anna looked at me and asked, "What did we sign?" I shrugged. We were both in a fog as to what we had signed or why. We felt vulnerable, since unbeknownst to us they could've slipped in almost anything. In the end, we resigned ourselves to trusting the process. For most prime-rate mortgages the process is aboveboard, and there are few surprises.[3] It's another story for the poor and credit-challenged who rely on subprime or predatory mortgages.

The cost of housing in the United States is rising faster than the wages of middle-income families. In fact, housing prices since the early 1970s have risen 70 times faster than a father's wages.[4] Median family income was flat during the early 2000s. At the same time, housing prices rose faster in 2002 than at any time since 1978.[5]

The mortgage finance market has responded to the disparity between stagnant income, high debt, low savings rates, and rising housing prices by developing creative financing schemes designed to squeeze potential home buyers, albeit often temporarily, into unaffordable homes. It has been a sleight of hand requiring imaginative financing strategies that have been risky for both home buyers and financial institutions. While purchasing a home has been easier as lending strategies have become more creative, staying in it is quite another matter.

The Subprime and Predatory Housing Market

A first-time home buyer is struck by two things: the mountain of paperwork and the large number of people paid through the sale. For example, a typical mortgage involves paperwork an inch or more thick, with many pages containing fine print. New home buyers are often surprised to see the fees they paid to people they never met. Two real estate brokers often share the 6%–7% commission paid out of the seller's proceeds. Other costs can include attorney, appraiser, or surveyor fees; tax escrows; loan discount points; and mortgage and property insurance. There are 95 categories for payments or reimbursements on a Texas home closing statement.

The closing process is straightforward for most middle-income home buyers. However, the complexity of the mortgage process provides ample opportunities for subprime or predatory lenders to exploit unknowing borrowers. For this group, mortgages are fraught with dangers, such as prepayment-penalty clauses, loan packing (adding unnecessary charges to a mortgage such as life insurance and other "extras"), or loan terms that are impossible to meet. Before turning to the predatory housing sector, we'll first examine the difference between subprime and predatory housing loans.

THE LINE BETWEEN SUBPRIME AND PREDATORY LENDING

In studying the fringe economy, one of the most difficult things is distinguishing between legitimate subprime loans and predatory loans. Federal Reserve Bank governor Edward Gramlich points out a clear boundary: "As the Federal Reserve has begun studying these mortgage market developments intensively, we have been made all the more aware of the vast difference between the two. It is important that the distinction between the generally beneficial subprime market and destructive predatory lending be kept clear."[6] In the Federal Reserve Bank's definition, predatory lending involves at least one of the following: (1) loans to borrowers based on their assets rather than their ability to repay; (2) inducing borrowers to repeatedly refinance and then charging high points and fees for each refinancing (called "loan flipping"); or (3) engaging in fraud or deception to conceal the true nature of the loan.

Gramlich defends subprime lending by arguing that this market "gives people from all walks of life a shot at the American dream—owning a home and getting capital gains."[7] He applauds the expansion of the home mortgage market to all socioeconomic classes, citing studies showing that lower-income and minority consumers received loans at record levels. Indeed, home mortgages to low-income borrowers increased nearly 75% from 1993 to 1998, compared with 52% for upper-income borrowers. Gramlich attributes the increase in low-income borrowers to the subprime mortgage market, which grew from 80,000 loans in 1993 to 790,000 in 1998, a rise of 880%.[8]

Congress passed several laws that attempted to address the difference between subprime and predatory lending. One of the most important was the Home Ownership and Equity Protection Act (HOEPA) of 1994. HOEPA is not a usury law per se, since it permits high-cost loans. Instead, its purpose is to spotlight excessively high-interest loans and to ban egregious practices such as short-term balloon payments and various prepayment penalties. Under HOEPA, high-cost loans are defined as those with either (1) interest rates that are eight percentage points higher than comparable treasuries (for first-lien loans) or (2) total points and fees exceeding 8% of the total loan amount. HOEPA also limits the refinancing of a high-cost loan with another high-cost loan within the first year unless it's in "the interest of the borrower."

In effect, HOEPA implicitly accepted that low-income people could pay twice the monthly payments of those with good credit. This differential makes it prohibitive for low-income consumers, in Gramlich's words, to "get a shot at the American dream." It also makes it difficult to hold on to that dream. While the line between subprime and predatory lending is

THE FRINGE SECTORS

clear where fraud and deception is involved, it is blurrier in other areas. Specifically, when does an interest rate go from subprime to predatory? Until the criteria are firmed up, the difference between subprime and predatory lending will remain largely subjective.

THE GROWTH OF THE SUBPRIME MORTGAGE MARKET

Predatory lending is a subset of the subprime mortgage industry and can involve APRs of 18% or more, plus onerous loan terms. Subprime mortgages are marked by high interest rates and sundry fees for borrowers classified as credit risks. For example, borrowers with good credit could secure a prime-rate mortgage in 2005 with an interest rate of 6% or less. In contrast, those with problematic credit were forced into the subprime market and paid 9%–18% or more for a mortgage. On a $100,000 mortgage amortized over 30 years, prime-rate borrowers with a 6% mortgage would pay $599 a month in principal and interest. Subprime borrowers with a 10% mortgage would pay $878 a month, and those with an 18% predatory mortgage would pay $1,507, or two and a half times more than a prime-rate borrower.

Subprime lenders were historically called "fringe banks" because they specialized in high-risk loans that traditional banks rejected. Eventually, more-traditional lenders were enticed into the subprime market because of key developments in the financial sector. After buying only relatively secure mortgages from banks, bundling them into mortgage-backed securities, and then selling them to investors, investment banking firms began applying the securitization process to subprime loans in the early 1990s.[9] This occurred because of the willingness of Wall Street and Fannie Mae (the Federal National Mortgage Association, a privately held corporation operating under a federal charter) to finance and insure higher-risk mortgages. Since securitization eliminates part of a lender's risk, more financial institutions began making loans to troubled borrowers.

As a result of more liberal lending policies, subprime mortgages rose by a whopping 25% a year from 1994 to 2003, nearly a tenfold increase in just nine years. Nationally, the number of subprime loans skyrocketed from 100,000 refinancing and home mortgages in 1993 to more than 1 million in 2001.[10] By 2004 subprime home lending reached a staggering $400 billion, up 98% from 2003. In fact, one in five home mortgage or refinancing loans in 2004 was generated by a subprime lender.[11]

According to Thomas Goetz, subprime lenders say their interest rates are high to compensate for the greater risk that accompanies low-income borrowers.[12] Indeed, while only about 1% of prime-rate mortgages are in serious delinquency, the rate is more than 7% for subprime mortgages.[13] Moreover, one in five subprime refinance loans ends up in foreclosure, 10 times the rate for mortgages in the prime market.[14] On the other hand, a welcome side effect for lenders is the profit that traditional banks cannot hope to match. According to *Forbes*, subprime consumer finance companies can enjoy returns up to six times greater than those of the best-run banks.[15]

Subprime Mortgages and the Color of Money

The good news is that nearly 44 million homes were purchased in the 1990s, of which 8 million (19%) were bought by minorities. In 1999, 32% of first-time home buyers were minorities, compared with only 23% in the early 1990s.[16] The bad news is that many of those purchases were financed by subprime or predatory loans.

From 1993 to 1995, there was a substantial increase in prime-rate loans to minorities. However, since then the number of these loans has stagnated, while subprime loans have skyrocketed. From 1995 to 2001, the number of subprime loans to African American home buyers rose 686%, while prime-rate conventional loans to African American home buyers fell 5.7%. Moreover, the vast majority of subprime loans are refinances and home equity loans made to existing homeowners, not new purchase loans. In 2001 more than 65% of the reported home loans made by subprime lenders were for refinances, and an additional 6% were home-improvement loans.[17]

In 2002, 27% of subprime loans went to African Americans, almost 20% to Hispanics, and 16% to Native Americans; by comparison, only 7.4% of subprime loans went to whites.[18] For subprime home refinancing loans, the numbers were similar: almost 21% went to African Americans, 14.5% to Hispanics, and 13.6% to Native Americans. In comparison, only

THE FRINGE SECTORS

5.7% of whites received a subprime home refinancing loan in 2002.[19] These figures help substantiate the charge that the subprime and predatory loan sector targets people of color.

Home Mortgage Loans

For most consumers, home ownership begins with a mortgage application. Borrowers' interest rates are based on their FICO score (see chapter 4), the numeric representation of their financial responsibility. The higher the FICO score, the cheaper the mortgage. Securing a low interest rate, however, is only one part of the loan package. For example, lenders may offer a low interest rate but compensate by imposing high discount points and loan origination fees, increasing the loan term, or introducing prepayment penalties.

FIXED-RATE, ADJUSTABLE-RATE, BALLOON, AND SAM MORTGAGES

Charlene Duvall is a retired 75-year-old school bus driver who lives in Miami, Florida. Because of the stock market crash in 2001, Charlene lost a good portion of her retirement income. She decided to refinance her house after meeting with a mortgage broker. In 2003 she got a five-year balloon mortgage for $75,000 at an 8.5% APR. Her payments are $590 a month, with a final balloon payment of nearly $72,300 due in 2008. At that point, Charlene will be 80 years old, which will make it even more difficult to secure a new loan. In addition, there is a prepayment penalty if she tries to refinance the loan in the first three years.

There are many types of mortgages, the most common being "fixed rate" (FR) and "adjustable rate" (ARM). With an FR mortgage, the interest rate is set prior to closing and is fixed throughout the 15-to-30-year loan term. Sometimes FR mortgages have a fee called "discount points" (one point equals 1% of the loan amount). When a mortgage is linked to the prime rate, discount points can help borrowers lower the interest rate. Predatory lenders may also charge points, but usually there's no corresponding drop in the interest rate. These points function simply as a loan fee that can total 3% to 20% of a loan. In subprime and predatory loans, points are often not paid at closing but rolled into the loan, which then increases the loan balance and therefore generates additional interest income.

ARM mortgages now represent as much as two-thirds of the subprime market. In an ARM loan the interest rate varies during the term of the loan, although it usually contains a maximum interest-rate cap. The frequency of rate changes and the interest cap are based on the loan terms and the borrower's credit. Subprime and predatory ARMs can allow for large or explosive interest-rate hikes.

Another variation is called a "balloon note," in which a lender structures a loan that appears affordable for a family whose income makes it ineligible for a traditional mortgage. The mortgage is written for a short period—five to seven years—and the borrower pays on the interest and the principal. (In a more predatory balloon, the borrower pays only the interest.) At the end of the loan term, the borrower faces a final lump-sum payment for the loan principal. At that point, the borrower must either refinance or lose the home.[20]

Monthly payments on balloon mortgages are attractive to low-income borrowers because they're based on a 30-year amortization schedule. In a typical balloon note for a $100,000 home with a 7-year maturation date at a 6.5% interest rate, the buyer would pay about $616 a month. At the end of the 7-year loan term, the buyer would still owe $90,650, which would have to be refinanced or paid in cash. In some cases a balloon mortgage has a refinance option for when the balance comes due. However, in other contracts the refinance option can be lost or forfeited. Or the buyer must requalify when the balance comes due. In the real estate business, balloon loans are also called "bullet loans," because if the loan comes due during a period of high interest rates, it's like getting a bullet in the heart. In predatory lending, balloon mortgages tend to have high interest rates, and lenders make money each time the loan is financed. According to the Association of Community Organizations for Reform Now (ACORN), about 10% of subprime loans have a balloon payment.[21]

Homeowners who can't afford the final balloon payment either lose their home through foreclosure or are forced to refinance with the same or another lender at additional cost. Regardless, a new loan must be initiated before the balloon payment is due. Lower-income families are attracted to this type of loan because the low monthly payments allow them to purchase a larger home than they could otherwise afford. Balloon mortgages are risky, because some people may forget the maturity date, interest rates may rise, or a homeowner may experience unanticipated financial difficulty when the note matures. Not surprisingly, a balloon-payment requirement increases the odds of foreclosure by 50%.[22]

Balloons may also involve negative amortization. In this type of mortgage, the loan is structured so that monthly payments don't cover the interest, let alone the principal.

Although the borrower regularly makes payments, the loan balance increases every month and the equity is reduced. Many borrowers aren't aware that they have a negative-amortization loan and don't find out until they see their loan balance rising. Predatory lenders use negative amortization to sell the borrower on the low payment, without making it clear that this will cause the principal to rise rather than fall. Another variation is an interest-only loan, in which the borrower pays only the interest and the principal is never reduced. In 2004 about 11% of all subprime originations were interest-only loans.[23]

On February 14, 2003, *CBS Evening News* aired a segment titled "Unaffordable Housing," which highlighted "shared appreciation mortgages" (SAMs). The report focused on Melinda Howell, a single mother, who bought a house in high-priced Pleasanton, California, using a SAM loan. She borrowed $30,000 with low interest payments. When the house Howell bought for $223,000 sold for $385,000 four years later, the lenders received 60% of the appreciation. In effect, they earned $97,000 for lending $30,000 for four years.[24]

SAMs are fixed-rate, fixed-term loans for up to 30 years. These loans have easier credit qualifications and smaller monthly payments than conventional mortgages. In exchange for a lower interest rate, the borrower agrees to relinquish part of the future value of a home to the lender, whether or not the home sells at the end of the loan period. Interest-rate reductions are based on how much appreciation the borrower is willing to give up. Table 7.1 shows what a typical SAM might look like.

SAM loans carry considerable risks. Assuming an average yearly appre-

Table 7.1.

Example of a shared appreciation (SAM) mortgage.

Type of mortgage	Interest rate
Standard 30-year fixed-rate mortgage	8.00%
SAM w/20% of appreciation	7.50%
SAM w/30% of appreciation	7.00%
SAM w/40% of appreciation	6.50%
SAM w/50% of appreciation	6.00%

ciation of 2.5%, a $100,000 house will be worth $204,640 in 30 years. With a 50% SAM, a homeowner must come up with $52,320 when the loan matures. SAM contracts often state that the shared equity is due upon the maturation of the loan, with no extensions. Homeowners who face retirement on a fixed income would therefore be forced to initiate a new mortgage. SAM lenders also claim their equity share if the homeowner refinances, sells the house, or otherwise terminates the loan. The full loan amount, plus any appreciation, may become due immediately if the homeowner fails to live in the house for at least a year. SAMs have a chilling effect on "sweat equity." For instance, if a homeowner adds a room, deck, or other improvement—even if he does the work himself—the lender receives half the appreciation resulting from the remodeling. According to HSH Associates, "What a SAM loan amounts to is a new version of sharecropping. Instead of the landowner taking a portion of the farmer's crops, we have lenders now taking a portion of a homeowner's equity."[25]

Hidden Mortgage Costs and Other Traps

Low-income home buyers face additional obstacles. For instance, predatory and subprime lenders often require credit life insurance (designed to pay off a mortgage in the event of a homeowner's death) to be added to the loan. This insurance is frequently sold by a lender's subsidiary or a company that pays it a commission. Fringe lenders may inflate the cost of credit life by requiring insurance for the total indebtedness, including the principal and interest, rather than just the principal. Conversely, fringe lenders may deliberately underinsure borrowers by requiring insurance for less than the principal balance, thereby increasing the chance of a foreclosure. So if a borrower dies, his or her heirs will have insufficient insurance funds to cover the loan principal. Despite the low payouts, lenders frequently charge high premiums for credit life. Moreover, if home buyers want this type of insurance, they can usually find other policies with similar or better coverage for less money.

Predatory and subprime lenders may inflate closing costs in other ways. For example, some lenders charge outrageous document-preparation fees, arrange for expensive appraisals, and bill for county recording fees in excess of the law. Another tactic involves "unbundling," whereby closing costs are padded with duplicate charges already included in other categories.

Then there's "private mortgage insurance" (PMI). Despite its name, PMI protects only the lender from losses incurred if the borrower defaults. All home buyers must purchase PMI if their down payment is less than 20% of the home's selling price. Although borrowers can drop PMI once they have accumulated 20% or more in home equity, some mortgage contracts forbid discontinuing it.[26] PMI is a significant expense and can cost $75–$100 per month on a $100,000 home.

Up to 80% of subprime loans include prepayment penalties if the borrower tries to pay off or refinance the loan early, costing low-income consumers about $2.3 billion a year. These penalties lock borrowers into a loan by making it difficult to refinance with another company or resell the home. Subprime lenders have defended this policy by claiming that prepayment penalties allow borrowers to get lower interest rates. However, research by the Center for Responsible Lending shows that borrowers get no rate benefits from prepayment penalties—and that residents in minority neighborhoods have much greater odds of receiving such penalties. Extended prepayment penalties increase the odds of foreclosure by 20%.[27] Other predatory lenders include call provisions that permit them to accelerate the loan term, regardless of whether the borrower's payments are current.

A clause attached to many subprime and predatory mortgages requires homeowners to submit to mandatory and binding arbitration in loan disputes. Mandatory arbitration gives an unfair advantage to lenders, because it requires action in an arbitration forum more favorable to them than to borrowers.[28] In arbitration, (1) legal discovery (gathering information in preparation for a trial) is not required; (2) the proceedings are not public; (3) arbitrators don't need to give reasons for their decision, nor are they required to follow the letter of the law; (4) there are no precedents, and a decision in one case is not binding on another; (5) future judicial review is limited; and (6) injunctive relief (an equitable remedy in the form of a court order that either prohibits or compels a party from continuing a particular activity) and punitive damages are unavailable. Moreover, the lender is not required to arbitrate claims against the borrower. In other words, if a borrower defaults, the lender can proceed directly to foreclosure.[29] For most of us, the purchase of a home is the single largest expenditure we will make in our lifetime. For America's poor, it's also the most dangerous.

Refinancing and Home Equity Loans

Ralph Jefferson is a 51-year-old divorced father of three. In 2000 he lost his $80,000-a-year job with a St. Louis aerospace company. Unemployed, Ralph quickly depleted his meager savings, and soon he was so far behind in his mortgage payments that the bank told him he had to pay $6,000 immediately or risk foreclosure. At about the same time, Ralph received a mailing from a mortgage company offering him a "rescue loan."

Ralph was at his wits' end. As he entered his second year of unemployment, the only job he could find was in part-time retail sales. Desperate, Ralph called the mortgage broker and asked for a $20,000 loan to cure the default, pay past-due utility bills, and catch up with overdue child-support payments. Ralph was persuaded to take out a larger loan and sign a blank note and deed of trust. Only after the loan was approved did he realize that the full amount was $50,000 with a 14% APR for 15 years. Ralph also realized that he was paying $8,000 (16 points) in loan fees, and the mortgage company was holding on to $21,000 to cover 30 months of payments. In the end, Ralph got $21,000 in cash for a $50,000 loan. He later learned that the loan also contained a call provision allowing the mortgage company to demand payment in full if he was just one day late in the first 24 months. For Ralph, desperation led to exploitation.

Homeowners refinance their homes to extract all or a portion of its equity. The cash is then used to pay off debts, remodel, pay household bills, or purchase items such as cars and vacations. Some homeowners draw out equity based on the assumption that their property will continue to appreciate. The premise is that housing prices will always rise, even though they've often contracted in the past, sometimes violently. If property values drop, the homeowner is "upside down"—he or she owes more than the value of the home. What some homeowners fail to realize is that real estate, like any other investment, is a gamble.

LOAN-REFINANCING TRAPS

Home equity is a large part of the net household worth of most middle-class families. Despite the rapid rise of housing prices during the 1990s, home equity has actually declined. From 1989 to 1999, the average home equity per homeowner declined (in 1999 inflation-adjusted dollars) from $91,000 to $89,500.[30] One reason for this is increased equity borrowing. According to the Federal Reserve Board, about 40% of the growth in outstanding mortgage debt in the late 1990s was linked to home equity loans and cash-out refinancing. A Freddie Mac study found that from 1995 to 2000, about 20% of homeowners had borrowed on their home equity, with loans averaging $36,000. Twenty-five percent of the borrowers said they were concerned about repaying the new loan.[31] The rapid growth of refinancing has provided a prime opportunity for fringe economy operators to earn fast money.

There are two general types of refinancing. The first is income-based lending, which is determined by the borrower's ability to repay the loan. The second is asset-based lending, whereby a predatory lender provides a loan based on the home's equity, not on the borrower's ability to repay the loan. To close the deal, a predatory lender or mortgage broker may encourage borrowers to pad their income, giving the impression that they can afford the new loan. Or, lenders or brokers may get inflated home appraisals. Predatory lenders typically lend more than the borrower can afford to repay. If there's a large amount of equity in the home when it's foreclosed on, predatory lenders may get the full equity even if the loan was small.

Home refinancing can be tricky, especially given the aggressiveness of mortgage brokers and the hype that any day interest rates will skyrocket. For many borrowers, home equity loans are attractive because the interest is tax deductible, the rates are usually lower than with other types of loans, and they are easy to obtain for those with good credit. The prospect of quick cash is also appealing to families caught in high consumer debt. Homeowners converted about $180 billion of their equity into cash from 2001 to 2002, and 60% of the 3.7 million homeowners who refinanced in 1999 reported higher payments.[32]

The impact of predatory home refinancing becomes clearer when comparing such financing with loans made to creditworthy borrowers. With a traditional home equity loan or line of credit, a homeowner can borrow up to 80% of the home's equity. The home equity lines of credit (HELOCs) offered to homeowners with good credit contain no closing costs or points, the interest is close to the prime rate, credit life insurance is not required, and borrowers can often access equity through a line of credit without initiating a new mortgage. In contrast, homeowners with poor credit but the same amount of home equity are often steered into subprime or predatory loans that contain high interest rates; points and fees; expensive credit life insurance; and other exploitive terms. These loans are often refinanced several times, resulting in additional costs.

A subprime or predatory lender that is refinancing a home may insist that the original mortgage be paid off and a new one initiated. The homeowner may, therefore, lose the lower interest rate of the original mortgage and be left with a higher interest rate plus a higher principal balance if he took out extra cash. Moreover, when the homeowner initiated the mortgage, he may have qualified for a low-interest mortgage, but he might now be forced into a subprime lending category. This problem is particularly acute for low-income homeowners who obtained down-payment assistance from federal, state, or local sources, which is often forgiven if they remain in the dwelling for some number of years. When predatory mortgage lenders make loans to these homeowners, they often insist that forgivable loans be paid off, which increases the amount borrowed.

THE FRINGE SECTORS

BROKERS, LOAN SOLICITATION, AND DOWNSTREAMING

Mortgage brokers live off of loan fees. Because they are independent contractors rather than employees of large financial institutions, government regulators have limited oversight over their activities. Many subprime or predatory loans originate through local mortgage brokers who act as finders, or "bird dogs," for lenders. Some predatory and subprime lenders have also downsized their operations by shifting their loan originations to independent brokers.

There's often considerable collaboration between fringe economy operators. For example, borrowers pay mortgage brokers a fee (sometimes hidden in the closing costs) to help them secure a favorable loan. A broker working for a mortgage lender may also receive kickbacks for referring the borrower. Consequently, many brokers will steer borrowers to lenders that pay the highest kickbacks rather than those that offer the lowest interest rates and fees. Lenders may also charge borrowers a higher interest rate to cover the cost of the kickback. Closing documents use arcane language to hide these kickbacks, such as "yield spread premiums" (YSP) or "service release fees" (SRF). Passing on the broker fee is called "bonus upselling" or "par-plus premium pricing."[33] In addition, some bank loan officers may receive kickbacks for steering clients to subprime lenders after denying them a conventional mortgage.

Several major banks and mortgage companies practice "downstreaming," whereby they refer customers with problematic credit to subprime lenders that are subsidiaries or company affiliates.[34] (Creditworthy customers are rarely sent upstream from subprime lenders.) Still other financial institutions routinely steer creditworthy minority customers who are eligible for a conventional loan to subprime lenders.[35]

EQUITY STRIPPING

Larry and Erica Huffman are in their mid-40s and have two school-age children. They live in Des Moines, Iowa, in a house they bought for $120,000 in 1995. The house is now worth $175,000 and climbing.

Larry is a shipping clerk and Erica works as a bank teller. Neither of them has had a significant pay raise in years. Over the last decade, Larry and Erica have seen the real value of their incomes stagnate while their expenses have soared. Larry could compensate for this by working longer hours, but his company has cut back on overtime. Erica never had that option. The Huffmans made up their financial shortfall by shifting some of their expenses to credit cards and high-interest consumer loans. Over the years, their credit card balances grew, and they resorted to taking out new cards to pay the interest on their old ones. By 2002 the couple faced a credit card debt of almost $35,000, much of it in high-interest cash advances. Their savings account was long depleted, their cars were financed, and they had no assets except their home. The sole remaining option was to refinance.

The Huffmans had saved enough for a 20% down payment when they bought their home. Since their credit was good at that time, they got an 8% mortgage. However, in the intervening years their income-to-debt ratio increased, they had several late credit card and utility payments, and a few mortgage payments were more than 30 days late. This was enough to push them into a higher risk category.

Although the Huffmans initially wanted a home equity loan, the mortgage broker convinced them that refinancing was a better option. The new appraisal came in at $175,000, and they owed $84,000 on the mortgage. Using an 80% loan-to-value (LTV) ratio, the new appraisal meant that the Huffmans could get $56,000 in cash. However, that amount was reduced to $50,000 after adding in points, origination fees, and other sundry closing costs. The interest rate was 9.5% because the couple was now in a higher risk category.

After paying off their debts, the Huffmans were left with $15,000 in cash. However, they were now stuck with a monthly mortgage payment of $1,177, compared with the $704 they previously paid. This increase hit the Huffmans hard, because they could barely afford $704 a month, no less an additional $473. Their property taxes also went up by $900, since their home was now valued higher. If the Huffmans live within their means and use the remaining $15,000 to pay the difference between the old and new mortgages, they will exhaust the cash in less than three years. After that, they will either lose their home or be forced to refinance again, assuming that their house has appreciated. Since they're in their mid-40s, the new

THE FRINGE SECTORS

30-year mortgage will last until their mid-70s, thus precluding the possibility of retiring at age 67. Without the safety net of home equity, and no other viable resources, the Huffmans are now at the mercy of subprime or predatory lenders.

One of the more damaging practices in home refinancing is "equity stripping," which works in the following way: A homeowner's bills exceed his monthly income. He has accrued home equity and is assured by a broker or lender that he's eligible for a new loan, even though his monthly income isn't enough to meet his current obligations. The lender may fund the loan for two reasons: (1) it deliberately structures an unaffordable loan so that a borrower will be forced to continually refinance (thereby ensuring more fees as equity is systematically stripped away); or (2) it anticipates a default, which will allow it to acquire the property cheaply through foreclosure.

Although outlawed by the Department of Housing and Urban Development (HUD) in the 1990s, loan flipping is still widely practiced and is employed if a home has appreciated or if the homeowner didn't borrow the maximum amount of equity in an earlier loan. Each time a loan is flipped, more equity is stripped away as new appraisals are required, new loan fees are assessed, points and closing costs are added, and the interest rate climbs. Higher interest rates on multiple refinancing loans are virtually certain because a homeowner's FICO score drops with each new loan, and her debt-to-asset ratio is greater due to the additional loans. After several refinancing cycles, a homeowner becomes ineligible for another loan, while her mortgage payments and property taxes rise to the point where the house is unaffordable. In the end, the homeowner loses both her home and her credit rating. A classic case of loan flipping involves Bennett Roberts, who secured 10 loans from a high-cost mortgage lender in four years. He paid more than $29,000 in fees and charges on a $26,000 loan, including 10 points on every refinancing, plus interest.[36]

Some subprime lenders sell their loans to private investors or to Fannie Mae or Freddie Mac. Since these sales are scrutinized, the lender must prove two things: (1) the home contains enough equity to justify the loan, and (2) the borrower's income is adequate to repay it. In the first case, a lender may arrange for an appraisal that inflates the home's value. The borrower receives the loan but is stuck with a home he cannot refinance or resell because the new loan exceeds the real value of the property. To meet the latter term, a lender may encourage the homeowner to pad his income. Or it may require a cosigner, to create the impression that monthly payments will be made, even though the lender knows that the cosigner will not help. In other cases, a borrower may be required to sign a blank loan application into which the lender inserts false information, such as a nonexistent job. In more extreme cases, predatory lenders have forged loan documents.[37]

NEGATIVE EQUITY

"Negative equity" is a relatively new financial ploy that allows homeowners to borrow up to 125% of the loan value of their home. For example, if a property is appraised at $100,000, the homeowner can borrow 125% of the value of the home, giving him a mortgage balance of $125,000, or $25,000 more than the property is worth. If a homeowner is forced to move because of a job, health problems, or other reasons, he won't be able to sell the home without adding money to pay off the existing loan.

In a typical foreclosure, the sale price of the home often equals the debt. However, the foreclosure of a 125% LTV home will not generate sufficient funds to pay off the loan, and the homeowner will remain legally liable for the shortfall. For example, if a home sells for $100,000, the seller's costs at closing might include $7,000 for real estate broker fees (calculated at 7%); approximately $3,000 in sundry closing costs; and an unknown amount for repairs resulting from a home inspection. At most, the seller's proceeds will total $90,000. If the seller has a negative-equity loan of $125,000, he will be forced to pay the extra $35,000 out of pocket.

A HUD-endorsed variation of refinancing is a reverse mortgage for senior citizens, called a Home Equity Conversion Mortgage (HECM). This option allows the elderly to unlock the equity they have in their property by borrowing against it. Elderly homeowners receive payments from lenders monthly, all at once in a lump sum, or as a line of credit. The size of the reverse mortgage is determined by the borrower's age, the interest rate, and the value of the home. The older the homeowner, the greater the percentage of a home's value he or she can borrow. Although the amount owed increases over time, no payments are due until the end of the loan term. When the loan expires, the total loan amount plus interest is due in full. This lump sum payment is usually made through the sale of the property. No repayments are required while the borrower lives in the home, and the monthly income is tax free. While this HUD-endorsed option allows the elderly to stay in their homes and rely less on governmental assistance, it also impedes heirs from inheriting a free and clear property, and thus hampers the intergenerational transfer of wealth, something that is critical for both high- and low-income people.

For many homeowners, refinancing is a shell game in which debt is moved from one shell to another, growing larger as more fees are assessed, more commissions are paid, and more home equity is stripped away. In the end, the homeowner becomes asset-poor and debt-rich. The extent of this indebtedness often becomes apparent only when selling a home or facing retirement. In that sense, instead of generating wealth, home ownership is fast becoming an albatross of debt around the necks of over-leveraged families.

The growing phenomenon of home ownership as crushing debt rather than asset formation is based partly on the disparity between soaring housing prices and the stagnant incomes of millions of working-class Americans. While housing prices since the late 1990s have increased by 30% or more in many parts of the nation, incomes have not kept pace. Family income for many households is maxed out, since both spouses are already in the workforce. Even the well-publicized drop in mortgage rates has been largely neutralized by higher property taxes based on reassessed home values, higher insurance premiums, and rising utility costs.

The challenge for the mortgage industry was to devise ways to get more buyers into houses they couldn't afford, with little or no cash down. Accomplishing this goal required "creative financing," such as shared equity, balloon mortgages, negative amortization, dual loans (one for the mortgage and a second for the down payment), and other options that reduce home equity and increase monthly payments. Creative financing and the growing gap between rising house prices and static incomes also created an environment conducive to large-scale housing speculation, covered in the next chapter.

Who would ever believe that the best way to sell a
house fast is to call a caveman? You heard right!
Introducing Ug, a caveman that buys houses in any
condition. And Ug has experience. He's been buying
caves, I mean houses, for a million years.

–HomeVestors radio commercial, 2005

8

Real Estate Speculation and Foreclosure

We are bombarded with television, radio, and print ads telling us that real estate speculation is the easiest way to get rich. Testimonials like "I've gone from a negative net worth to $1,500,000—our cash flow is over $300,000 a year" abound. Remarkably, these people were able to get rich with "no money down" and using the creed of the savvy investor: buying with OPM ("other people's money").

As with most entrepreneurial activities, the key to successful real estate speculation is to buy low, and sell high and fast. We're told that smart investors buy properties at a minimum of 20% below market value and then flip (resell) them at closing or soon after. Real estate speculation is a seductively simple idea: find a desperate seller who has to dispose of a property quickly and then offer a cash price well below market value. Spice up the deal by promising to close right away and pay cash. Then find a desperate buyer who is willing to pay the full market price or above. In the process, find out how much the buyer can pay each month, and then manipulate the terms so that they appear affordable. In the meantime, plan on getting the property back.

The human cost is rarely factored into the equation. Foreclosure is often the result of speculation and is the final stage for homeowners trapped in the fringe economy. This chapter examines how the poor are separated from their money or assets by rent-to-own housing schemes, by housing speculators, and through foreclosure scams. It also suggests ways to reform the fringe housing economy.

Javier and Ana Trevino migrated to the United States from Honduras in 1990 and settled in Albuquerque, New Mexico. They have four children. In 1996 they brought Ana's parents to live with them. Ana did home child care and Javier owned a mobile food cart. Although Javier's business was good, most of his income was in cash and therefore not reported. Ana was also paid in cash. In fact, the family never filed a tax return. Nor did they have credit cards, since their purchases were in cash. The Trevinos didn't have a bank account; instead, they kept their money in a safe place. Consequently, the family didn't meet the eligibility criteria for a conventional loan. Finding a rental house large enough to accommodate them was almost impossible, and they knew they needed to buy a house. In 1998 the Trevinos believed they had found the perfect home to buy.

Mountaintop Investments bought a residential property in central Albuquerque for $80,000 in a foreclosure sale. It was a larger home located in a low- and moderate-income neighborhood with average home prices of $95,000, and Mountaintop priced it at $150,000.

Mountaintop sold the house to the Trevino family for $150,000, with $7,500 down and a three-year balloon note at a 13% APR. It was essentially a lease or rent-to-own option since Mountaintop still retained deed to the property. Javier and Ana came up with the down payment by using their savings and borrowing from friends. They were excited about their first real home and decorated it with loving care. Javier and his friends also did some remodeling and structural repairs. By the time the balloon note came due in 2001, Javier had sold his food cart and opened a small restaurant. He was doing well. Ana found a job in a day-care center. They also began paying taxes and opened a bank account.

The Trevinos were in for a rude awakening when the balloon note came due. For one thing, the bank appraised their house at only $115,000 rather than the $140,000 they still owed to Mountaintop. Second, the bank would finance only 80% of that amount, or $92,000. Plus, they would have to pay $3,000 in closing costs. To pay off Mountaintop, the Trevinos would need $43,500 in cash. Although they tried subprime lenders, none would finance the home for more than 80% of its appraised value. The Trevino family ended up losing their $7,500 down payment, 36 months of payments, the sweat equity they had in the house, and, perhaps more important, their dream of home ownership. It would take years for the Trevinos to save enough money for another down payment.

Mountaintop came out well. Had the company taken an 8% loan for the $80,000, its monthly payment would have been $600. Since the Trevinos were paying $1,575 a month, the $975 difference over 36 months totaled $35,100. With the $7,500 down payment for the lease option, Mountaintop made $42,500, or half the cost of the house, in just three years, excluding the appreciation. Had Mountaintop used the $42,500 to refinance the house again at 8%, its new monthly payment would have been $275, allowing it to make $1,300 a month from the next buyer, plus another $7,500 for the down payment. In the second three-year go-round, Mountaintop would make $54,300, enough to pay off the property. Not surprisingly, the company immediately put the house back on the market.

Rent-to-Own Housing

Real estate speculators employ various strategies to make money. One way is by owner financing, which is becoming increasingly popular as more lenders start to tighten credit guidelines. Owner financing is attractive to potential buyers who can't qualify for a conventional mortgage because of excessive debt, insufficient income, lack of time on the job, a poor credit score, little or no credit history, or bankruptcy. Some home buyers choose to forgo conventional financing because of privacy issues, such as having income from the nontaxed gray or black markets or from illegal activities. Buyers who cannot or choose not to qualify for a conventional loan have two alternatives: a lease option or non-qualifying financing.

The fringe housing sector's answer to the furniture and appliance rent-to-own industry is a lease option, whereby a renter theoretically moves toward home ownership. In this arrangement, the "buyer" chooses a property from a list of houses owned by an investor or investment company. The list is small, usually 5–10 homes for a medium to large city. For instance, one Kansas City company specializing in owner-financed houses listed 35 homes in the area, but only 10 were available.[1] This was out of a total housing stock of roughly 10,000 broker-listed homes.

After the buyer chooses the property, he or she provides a nonrefundable "option consideration"—similar to a down payment—which is usually 5% of the purchase price. This option locks in the price of the property during the lease term and gives a buyer the exclusive right of purchase. Buyers are not required to purchase the property. If they exercise the purchase option, the down payment or "option consideration" is applied toward the sales price. If they walk away, the money is used to compensate the investor or owner for having removed the property from the market.

Lease options are generally short-term (lasting from one to three years), and after they expire, the prospective buyer must find financing or relinquish the home. Although some lease options are renewable, this typically involves a new down payment and a higher purchase price. The investor usually pays the property taxes and insurance until the closing. The tenant/buyer is responsible for upkeep and repairs. Monthly payments are referred to as rent rather than mortgage payments. Since the lessee is technically a tenant, he or she receives no financial benefits of owning a home, such as tax deductions and other perks that can translate into $3,000–$6,000 a year.[2] According to real estate investment guru John Reed, lease options have failure rates as high as 90%.[3]

The second option is "no-documents" owner financing, which may involve little or no criteria for qualifying. In this scenario, the home buyer purchases the property directly from the investor or company through a short-term loan. The seller is the bank, and the buyer pays it monthly. Loans are usually short-term (one to three years), and the financing agreement explains the length of the loan, the interest rate, the monthly payments, and other terms. Required down payments are higher than with the leasing option, often about 10% of the sales price. Buyers lacking the necessary down payment can sometimes negotiate an arrangement whereby the seller folds it into the loan, which thereby entails separate monthly payments.[4]

Lease option and no-documents buyers are often young couples who can't afford to purchase a house through conventional channels and are convinced that this is the backdoor to home ownership. Unfortunately, the vast majority lose thousands of dollars, and when the lease option expires, they are less able to afford a home than when they started. In fact, losses associated with lease options may permanently prohibit some people from ever owning their own homes.[5]

Lease options and owner financing are dangerous in other ways. First, conventional lenders require an independent appraisal to determine the fair market value of a property. While this appraisal safeguards a lender's interest in the property, it also assures home buyers that they are not overpaying. For example, in 1998 there was a large home for sale in my neighborhood. Strapped for room, we looked at the house. While it was in decent shape, the owner wanted $165,000, which at the time was too high for the neighborhood. After six months the sign went down, and the house lay vacant for almost a year. We later found out that it had gone into foreclosure. Six months later a new "For sale or lease" sign was on the lawn.

Curious, I called and asked about the price. Now the house was owned by an investment company, and the manager told me the asking price was $320,000. There was a brief silence as I caught my breath. Sensing my disbelief, she added "But we finance it."

Some mainstream lenders require a home inspection, by a licensed independent inspector (most home buyers opt for this even if it's not required), that's designed to uncover costly structural and mechanical problems. The results of the inspection are often used to lower the price or to compel the seller to make the necessary repairs. Lenders also require a property survey to determine that the house and other buildings lie within the property boundaries and that all easements are respected. Finally, lenders require the purchase of title insurance, guaranteeing that the property has a free and clear title with no liens against it.

Fringe economy home buyers are often denied these safeguards. For one, an independent appraisal is not required in a non-conventional sale, because the price is determined solely by the buyer and seller. A home buyer may be unaware of the fair market price in a neighborhood and can find herself with an overpriced home that's impossible to sell or refinance. Second, some investors may not inform buyers that they can hire an independent inspector, while others may not even permit a home inspection. A home buyer might therefore end up with a property that has chronic and costly problems. Third, non-conventional home sales don't require a property survey, and a buyer may face serious problems costing thousands of dollars to correct, if they are correctable at all. Private home sales are legal and are at the buyer's risk.

HomeVestors: Bringing Real Estate Speculation to a New Level

While small companies and mom-and-pop operations have been involved in owner-financed housing for years, the late Ken D'Angelo elevated this to a new level when he founded HomeVestors of America (HVA) in the 1990s. HVA is a Dallas-based franchise system that trains and supports its franchisees, who purchase distressed properties in need of repair. By 2005, HVA had more than 200 franchisees in almost 20 states; by 2007

THE FRINGE SECTORS

it plans to have at least 500 offices across the United States. In 2005, *Entrepreneur* ranked HVA 138th among the nation's top 500 franchises.[6]

HVA is a privately held company that chooses to not release its financial information. It's also a corporation that plays its cards close to its vest. For example, when I contacted HVA to acquire brochures, I was told that there weren't any and I should go to the company's Web site. In turn, the HVA Web site was remarkably general and provided little information about the company or how it does business. The only other way to get information about HVA is to express interest in a franchise. When I inquired about that, I received a terse e-mail informing me that there were no franchises available in my area. No other information was offered. Eighteen months later I received another e-mail, inviting me to inquire about opening a franchise.

Getting into real estate speculation the HomeVestors way isn't cheap. The initial franchise fee is $46,000. Franchisees must buy another $5,000 worth of computer equipment and pay an ongoing monthly fee of $495. Plus, franchisees pay a royalty fee for each piece of property sold. In the first two years, this fee is $775 per property acquired; in the third year the fee drops down to $675. HomeVestors franchisees are also expected to have enough working capital to cover operating expenses for six months. The company's estimates for starting a franchise range from a low of $139,150 to a high of $219,450.

In return for their money, franchisees receive an intensive 10-day training program consisting of class and field training directed at learning how to buy, repair, and sell properties; a lead-generating software program; a list of remodelers who work cheaply; discounted ad rates; and so forth. HVA franchisees bought about 3,500 homes in 2002 using the same training, software, and advertising strategy.[7] Perhaps most important, franchisees get the brand-name recognition of the company's high-impact "We Buy Ugly Houses" billboard campaign, giving them increased respectability in the eyes of sellers and buyers. In fact, HomeVestors spends about $18 million annually on billboard advertising and some radio and television spots, which initiate roughly 70% of its business.[8]

HVA franchisees target older, economically stable middle-class neighborhoods, often buying the most run-down house on a block. The company offers subprime financing, since the typical buyer is a first-time home-owner who can't secure conventional financing.[9] In effect, HVA franchisees buy houses from people who can't easily sell them and sell them to people who can't easily buy them.

In addition to buying and selling houses, HVA has also entered the rent-to-own market. One Dallas-based HVA franchisee listed a house for $72,900 with a rent-to-own option. To close the deal, the buyer had to come up with a $2,500 down payment and pay $995 a month on a two-year lease. Of that $995, $100 was applied to the sales price. After two years the tenant/buyer could buy the house for $68,700, assuming he could find financing. If not, he lost the $2,500 down payment plus the $2,400 in lease payments. As the listing agent explained, "This is for people who can't get credit." But the chances aren't good that a credit-challenged buyer will be able to build or rebuild his credit in only two years.

HVA's success is related to the increase in used-housing stock due to an aging population, a growing pool of indebted homeowners desperate to sell, and families unable to qualify for conventional mortgages.[10] Other targets include the elderly who need quick cash or can't manage the upkeep on their property, divorced couples who must sell quickly, and those who inherited a home they don't want.

Like most real estate speculators, HVA is interested only in undervalued properties. It warns buyers that "HomeVestors offers you the option of selling your property to us at a DISCOUNT PRICE. . . . Therefore, please DO NOT SUBMIT INFORMATION about your property if you are NOT INTERESTED in receiving a DISCOUNT PRICE OFFER." True to its word, franchisees generally buy homes at roughly 65% of their fixed-up market value.[11]

The HVA concept represents a sea change in real estate speculation. Specifically, the company is attempting to "McDonaldize" speculative real estate in much the same way as other large and well-financed fringe market corporations have revolutionized the used-car industry, pawnshops, and rental furniture and appliances. It's also following the lead of other fringe economy corporations by legitimizing predatory real estate speculation through intensive advertising coupled with a large network of franchisees.

The Wannabe Millionaires

Real estate speculation is big business, but coaching wannabe millionaires is potentially even more profitable. John Reed runs a Web site that rates and investigates real estate gurus. Reed notes, "If you go to a live presentation . . . you can see . . . the customers of the guru in question. B.S. artist gurus have audiences that look sleazy, unkempt, the bottom of the socioeconomic barrel."[12] The "bottom of the socioeconomic barrel" that Reed criticizes is made up of the targets for real estate hucksters who help exploit the near-poor.

Trusting "get-rich-quick" real estate gurus, wannabe millionaires get ripped off as their bank accounts are depleted by expensive seminars, overpriced course materials, and "boot camp" training sessions costing thousands of dollars. Best-selling guru Robert Kiyosaki's three-day real estate seminar costs $4,750, excluding travel and accommodations. The lesser-known "wealth trainer" Vena Jones-Cox charges $600 for a real estate training package.[13] Robert Leonetti charges almost $10,000 for a package that includes coaching. Carleton Sheets, probably the most recognized real estate guru after his 20-year stint with infomercials, charges $400 for his *initial* training program. The rest of the money is bilked from customers through personal coaching (with one of his associates), $3,000 seminars, newsletters, and other necessities. As with most "coaches," there's little evidence that Sheets has ever sold much real estate by himself.[14]

Foreclosures

Helen Wisankowski is a disabled middle-aged woman who lives in Chicago with her two older children on a modest income generated by a small trust fund. In 1998 she found herself in default for $10,000 on the mortgage on the home she had lived in for 15 years. Helen was approached by an investor specializing in "foreclosure rescue," who promised to save the home and keep her and the children from being homeless. The investor covered Helen's overdue payments in return for the title. In turn, she would pay off the loan in payments. Helen signed the papers despite being confused by the legal mumbo-jumbo. In early 1999 she received a foreclosure notice from a bank she'd never heard of. Helen later discovered that the investor had sold her house to someone else and that the buyer had taken out a $50,000 loan on the property and defaulted. She had unwittingly deeded the property to the investor.

Keeping a roof over one's head is becoming increasingly difficult in the United States. A 2002 study by the Mortgage Bankers Association found that foreclosures in every category were the highest since these numbers were first tabulated in 1972.[15] From 1999 to 2002, foreclosures among the 26.4 million conventional loans climbed 45%, the highest number in more than a decade.[16] In late 2004, about 435,000 mortgages nationally were in the foreclosure process and 1.7 million were delinquent. Moreover, about 60% of all loans that enter the foreclosure process will eventually result in the loss of a home.[17]

According to foreclosure expert Alexis McGee, there are 1,300–1,500 homes in foreclosure in any given week in the six Chicago-area counties.[18] McGee's observation is borne out by a National Training and Information Center study showing that Chicago foreclosures doubled from 2,074 in 1993 to 3,964 in 1998.[19] Not coincidentally, the rise in foreclosures corresponds to the increase in subprime loans.

A wide range of foreclosure scams are foisted upon vulnerable homeowners. For example, homeowners behind in their mortgage payments will have notices of default entered against them by the lender, which then become a matter of public record in the county recorder's offices. While foreclosure notices have been public record for years and could be found by investors who checked newspapers ads or government offices, records are now computerized, and firms are set up to sell the lists. Real estate speculators comb these files to target people for "foreclosure rescue" services. These homeowners are then inundated with unsolicited visits, phone calls, mailings, and flyers. Street corners and telephone poles in low-income neighborhoods are plastered with signs promising to "stop foreclosures" or "save your house." Those preyed upon are the most vulnerable, such as the elderly, who are often house-rich but cash-poor and desperate to stave off foreclosure. This vulnerable group also has the fewest legal resources to fight scams.

In a *Washington Post* article, Sandra Fleischman told the story of Idriis Bilaal, 77, who got a foreclosure notice in 2003 on his run-down row house in northeast Washington. [20] Bilaal accepted an offer from one of the many "foreclosure rescue specialists" who had contacted him after his foreclosure notice was published. After signing papers provided by Calvin Baltimore, an ex-con and former minister, Bilaal realized that this wasn't a loan. In fact, he had signed away the title to his 100-year-old house to Vincent Abell, who had been convicted of real estate fraud in the 1980s.

Although the house had appraised for $255,000, Bilaal received only $17,000—the $7,000 he owed in mortgage payments plus $10,000 in cash. Because Abell's company hadn't agreed to pay off or assume Bilaal's mortgage, he remained responsible for the $714 monthly mortgage payments. But now Bilaal was also responsible for monthly rent payments of $500 to Abell's company. According to the contract, Bilaal would rent his home and have the option to repurchase it for $110,000 after a year. However, he would have to initiate a new loan on top of his existing mortgage. Even if Bilaal understood the terms of the buy-back option (which he claimed he didn't), it would be impossible for him to qualify for a $100,000 loan on top of his current loan. Why did Bilaal sign the contract? "I was under duress when Baltimore walked through my gate and said he could save my house. Every time I saw people's stuff on the street, I would say that was me next."[21]

Predatory activity around foreclosures can take several forms. For example, "We'll save your credit—just pay a fee and sign the house over to us. The foreclosure will be recorded against us, not you." In reality, a foreclosure is reported against the original borrower regardless of any subsequent purchasers. Another scam goes like this: "We'll give you money; just sign the house over and we'll pay off the debt." In that scam, the seller often doesn't know how much equity she is selling. Homeowners face other risks in foreclosure scams. Will the speculator really cure the debt? Will he make the payments knowing the homeowner is still responsible for the loan? Once a speculator has the deed to a property, he can treat it as his own. He may borrow against it or even sell it to someone else. Because the homeowner has released the title, she will not realize any money if the property is sold. Moreover, the speculator treats the homeowner as a tenant and the mortgage payments as rent. Hence, she can be evicted if payments are late.

Still another scam is "We'll buy the property and lease it to you. You can then buy it back." To repurchase the home, the homeowner will need another loan, larger than the original. Mortgage payments will be greater, qualifying will be more difficult, and the interest rate will be high. And then there's "We'll get you a new loan that will solve your problems." Almost every instance of refinancing involves a higher loan balance and higher monthly payments. Another scam involves a speculator's giving an owner facing foreclosure a cash amount for the equity in the home. With this small cash payment the speculator gains control of the property, which is then rented out with no payments made to the homeowner. The speculator pockets the rent while delaying the foreclosure as long as possible.

Several cases cited by Robert Heady in a *St. Paul Pioneer Press* article help explain how mortgage foreclosure scams work.[22] Heady outlined the case of Ruth B., an 85-year-old Minneapolis woman who fell behind on her $41,000 mortgage and was facing foreclosure. Ruth was contacted by a lender who promised to help her keep the house. The speculator purchased her $125,000 house for $50,000, then rented it back to Ruth for $800 a month, knowing that she couldn't afford the payments on her $818 monthly pension. When Ruth was unable to pay, the lender began eviction procedures. Ruth eventually secured a reverse mortgage and bought the house back from the lender for $96,000. In another case, Denise B. bought a house for $88,000 with a 6.5% mortgage. Shortly afterward, she suffered a heart attack and was facing foreclosure. Denise got a call from a lender who explained that he could find a buyer for the house and then sell it back to her, thereby allowing her to remain there. In addition, she would get $10,000 at closing. The company appraiser, a private investor, valued her house at $135,000 and explained that with an outright sale Denise would see a net gain of $40,000. The investor bought the home for $135,000, but the proceeds were divided as follows: an $85,000 payoff on Denise's mortgage; $5,300 in closing costs ($4,000 went for sales commission); $15,000 for other closing costs, management fees, and other items; and $26,000 for a down payment so that she could repurchase the house. Denise received only $4,000 in cash.

Refinancing loans and other shenanigans might be presented as a "rescue," but they only postpone the inevitable loss of a home while draining the remaining equity. The essential fraud is that these companies are not really making loans, but rather expropriating houses at discounted prices and then pocketing the difference. Although speculators may promise to let an owner stay in his home, once the door is opened, they usually find legal ways to evict him.

Reforming the Fringe Housing Market

Despite mountains of federal and state laws designed to protect home buyers, U.S. housing policy exists in the gray area between an unregulated market commodity and one containing more consumer protections than most. For fringe economy operators the stakes are great, because housing is a $10 trillion industry in which stunning profits can be made at every stage in the process. Consequently, many homeowners risk losing their property through predatory lending practices employing a variety of tactics that strip home equity, artificially inflate the costs of monthly payments, and make claims on future equity.

The lifeblood of the mortgage industry is the initiation of new loans and the refinancing of existing ones. To that end, young families are pressured into overbuying through "creative financing"; financially stressed homeowners are coerced into refinancing; and the more affluent are lured into second mortgages to pay for new cars, pay off mounting credit card debt, or purchase expensive vacations. While predatory lending practices are not novel, they are becoming more widespread in the wake of soaring housing prices, the growth of the subprime lending industry, and rising consumer household debt.

One of the most troubling long-term implications of the fringe housing economy is its impact on the intergenerational transfer of assets and wealth. Property and home ownership have always been important means for transferring wealth and assets. A free and clear home valued at

$300,000 and divided among three heirs may provide enough capital for getting an education, setting up a small business, or purchasing a home with a substantial down payment. But instead of being a vehicle for transferring wealth, home ownership is quickly becoming a means for the intergenerational transfer of debt. The Joint Center for Housing Studies of Harvard University notes that the present generation of Americans is wealthier than the preceding one. However, if current housing trends continue, subsequent generations won't be able to lay claim to the same honor.

Problems in the fringe housing economy cannot be solved through a piecemeal approach aimed at ending one or more inequities. Even if the worst features of this economy were legislated away, they would be likely to resurface in other forms. Simply put, the fringe housing economy exists because it addresses needs not being met in the conventional marketplace. The following are a few general recommendations for reforming this fringe sector.

First, mandatory nonessential insurance, such as credit life, should be prohibited. Second, predatory lenders routinely charge home buyers a variety of loan fees, such as mortgage broker fees, origination fees, service release fees, processing fees, and discount points, that have a negative impact on home equity. These fees should be regulated and capped at the state and federal levels. Third, prepayment-penalty-fee clauses should be abolished, since their sole function is to keep borrowers enmeshed in high-interest loans. Besides, no prime-rate mortgages contain these clauses, and there's little justification to include them in subprime loans. Fourth, all forms of financing designed to systematically strip home equity, such as SAM loans, 125% LTV loans, and negative amortization, should be outlawed. According to the U.S. Department of Housing and Urban Development, alternative-financing schemes make it more likely that borrowers will go deeper into debt or lose their homes through foreclosure.[23] Fifth, balloon loans should be prohibited. In fact, any loans that jeopardize home ownership and equity formation should be disallowed. Sixth, scams such as nonrefundable lease options on home purchases should be outlawed. Tricky lease options function as down-payment traps, since 50%–90% of lessees are unable to exercise the purchase option.[24] Seventh, federal and state regulators must develop a clearer definition of the difference between predatory and subprime lending. Without a firm definition, it is harder to promulgate and enforce federal and state regulatory policies.

Federal housing policy should focus on core issues that are driving up housing prices and making home ownership increasingly unaffordable for middle-income families, let alone poor ones. Housing prices should be stabilized through governmental intervention, and "creative financing" should be regulated to where it doesn't inevitably lead to foreclosure. But this must occur in a way that doesn't harm the poor, who would be bereft without fringe housing services. To implement this delicate balance, the federal government must initiate new and robust loan programs that are complemented by a large increase in governmentally subsidized low- and moderate-income housing stock, which may require aggressive new construction goals.

Credit, the problem and solution to all of life's problems.

−Vista Cars & Trucks, Houston, Texas

9

The Fringe Auto Industry

Owning a car has become a necessity in many American cities. In particular, many of the post–World War II car-based cities of the Midwest, Southwest, South, and West Coast have notoriously poor public transportation—fewer than 5% of U.S. roadways are served by public transportation. Having a reliable vehicle is important for getting to work on time, for picking up children in day care, for shopping at the lowest-priced stores, for visiting friends and family, and for finding employment. Vehicle ownership is also fertile ground for all types of fraud, from used-car purchases to auto title pawns, and even to tire rentals.

This chapter explores some of the hurdles that the poor encounter when trying to find and keep basic transportation. In particular, it examines how the used-car industry is organized, the difficulties that the poor face when trying to find affordable used cars, the ins and outs of used-car financing, and subprime financing. It also looks at loosely regulated fringe auto insurers and auto title pawns. Finally, the chapter offers some solutions to help rein in the fringe auto economy.

Buying a Used Car

When I started this book, I was certain that salespeople in seedy used-car lots were more aggressive and avaricious than their brethren in upscale car dealerships. To my surprise, most salespeople I encountered at fringe car lots were actually more laid-back than those in mainstream auto dealerships. Most didn't pounce on me, and grab my hand and vigorously shake it. Nor did they circle like hungry predators, stalking me as I went from one used car to another. These street-savvy salespeople appeared to understand that longstanding economic abuse made the poor sensitive to respect in financial transactions. In fact, many seemed to empathize with the financial plight of their customers, earnestly believing they were doing the customers a service, since no one else was willing to serve the poor. They were probably right. Perhaps they understood their own proximity to their customers' plight, since no doubt more than a few had emerged from the ranks of the poor. On the other hand, maybe they were just talented sociopaths able to spin a good yarn.

The path to car ownership for the poor is mined with old high-mileage cars, high down payments, extortionate interest rates, and overpriced insurance. However, before we examine the obstacles faced by the poor in finding and keeping reliable transportation, we'll take a look at the organization of the used-car industry.

In 2000 about 40 million used vehicles were sold annually in the United States—11 million by franchised new-car dealers and the remaining 29 million by independent used-car lots.[1] Used-car lots fall into two categories: independent lots and franchised dealerships. Independent, or non-franchised, lots sell only used cars. Franchised used-car lots, on the other hand, are part of new-car dealerships authorized by a car maker to sell its vehicles. Used cars at these dealerships are generally newer, cleaner, and more expensive than those in independent lots. Financing on newer used cars is often available only to relatively creditworthy buyers.

Independent used-car lots generally sell older, less expensive, and higher-mileage vehicles. For example, the typical used car in a franchised dealership is three years old, while the typical car or truck in an independent lot is eight years old. In the independent lots I visited, I rarely found a vehicle with fewer than 50,000 miles on the odometer. In fact, any car with under 80,000 miles was considered "low mileage," and many had 150,000–200,000 miles on them. Independent car lots often sell vehicles rejected by franchise dealerships, and about 5 million flow from franchised dealers to independents through auctions or other forms of wholesaling.[2] Because of this market segmentation, most poor buyers end up in independent car lots, some of which are "here today and gone tomorrow." The used-car business is profitable, and new-car dealers earned 22% of their total profits from used-car sales in 2000. In fact, since the early 1990s, used-car profits have outstripped new-car profits.[3]

There are important differences between buyers who use franchised dealers and those who go to independent lots. For instance, many buyers who visit franchised lots *want* to upgrade their vehicle or swap it for another model. Since most already have transportation, they can take their time to find the right car at the right price. Buyers in independent lots often look for a vehicle because they *need* one, and many are so desperate that they'll purchase almost anything that fits their budget.

Too often, low-income buyers end up with vehicles that have salvage or junk titles, called "branded titles." State motor vehicle departments assign these titles to stolen vehicles that have been retrieved after being declared a loss by an insurance company; were in an accident and deemed non-repairable; or were declared a total loss due to flooding or some other natural mishap. Vehicles with branded titles are ineligible for traditional financing and extended warranties, are more expensive to insure, and are not eligible for manufacturer warranties or recalls. Regardless of their condition, branded-title vehicles are considered "junk" by insurers, state motor vehicle bureaus, and car manufacturers. As a result, they're worth only a fraction of their book value.

In one independent car lot I came across a six-year-old Acura with 70,000 miles on it. The retail blue book value (in excellent condition with a *clean* title) of the car was $8,000, or what the dealer was asking for it. When I inquired about the title, the salesperson said he didn't have it but he could get it. The car was in good shape and drove well. In fact, I was even tempted to buy it. Being cautious, I wrote down the vehicle identification number (VIN) and ran it through Carfax.[4] As it turned out, the car had been wrecked and had a salvage title. Angry, I went back to the dealer and demanded to know how he could sell a branded-title vehicle for full retail price. He nonchalantly shrugged his shoulders, turned, and walked away. Just another day in the fringe auto economy.

The salary structure in the used-car industry contributes to the shortage of affordable vehicles. Because salaries are based on commission, salespeople in franchised lots have little incentive to sell a $5,000 vehicle when they can earn twice that on one costing $10,000. They're also reluctant to spend hours trying to find financing for a credit-challenged buyer who wants a $5,000 vehicle, only to be turned down by one lender after another. As one salesman in an independent lot put it, "Those guys at the Ford place don't want to hassle with poor folk, so they send them my way." Not coincidentally, his lot specializes in credit-challenged buyers, and the loan rate ranges from 23% to 28%.

Financing Used Cars

The lending practices of financial institutions in regard to the $370 billion used-car industry contribute to many of the transportation obstacles faced by the poor. The good news for used-car buyers is that the interest-rate gap between new and newer used cars has narrowed, and in some cases it is only a fraction of a point. Lenders have come to realize that used-car loans are less risky, since the vehicles have already experienced the largest drop in depreciation. The bad news is that mainstream lenders like Bank of America, Wells Fargo, and Chase refuse to lend money on high-mileage vehicles (over 100,000 miles) or those more than 4–6 years old. This bias limits options for the poor, because 128 million of the 213 million vehicles on the road today are over 7 years old, and 30% are at least 10 years old.[5] In addition, many lenders only finance vehicles purchased through more expensive franchised dealerships.

There are several financing tiers available to used-car buyers. The first is prime auto loans, which are offered to borrowers with an excellent credit rating. Interest rates are low, since these loans are tied to the prime rate. In fall 2004 the interest rate for new and newer used cars was about 4.75%, with a higher rate for those who have lower credit scores but are still in the higher tier.

The next tiers involve various forms of subprime lending. In particular, the second tier includes higher-interest loans that are geared toward buyers who have moderate credit problems but still have sufficient credit-worthiness to secure a loan. The third tier, called "third-chance financing," has considerably higher interest rates than the second tier, and the loan terms and conditions are usually more severe. For example, third-chance lenders often require a higher down payment and have harsher late penalty fees. In some instances, interest rates charged by third-chance lenders may be similar to those of other subprime lenders, but these lenders are more aggressive in pursuing loans, and they require deeper loan discounts, thereby increasing the price of the vehicle. For example, while second-chance lenders will wait 30–60 days to repossess a vehicle, third-chance lenders often repo within a few days after a payment due date. All subprime loans include high interest rates, involve a substantial down payment, and, in some cases, may require the vehicle to be purchased from a franchised dealership.

The fourth tier is nonprime lending, or dealer financing, whereby vehicles are financed in-house through a "buy here, pay here" (BHPH) trans-

Table 9.1.

Monthly payments and interest charges on a $10,000 vehicle with a two-year loan.

Interest rate	Monthly payment	Interest cost	Total cost of vehicle
5%	$438.71	$529.13	$10,529.13
9%	$456.84	$964.33	$10,964.33
15%	$484.86	$1,639.79	$11,639.79
19%	$504.08	$2,098.06	$12,098.06
25%	$533.71	$2,809.16	$12,809.16
35%	$585.16	$4,044.47	$14,044.47

action. This kind of financing often carries the highest interest rates and is totally removed from any linkage to the prime rate. As Table 9.1 illustrates, those who can least afford it pay considerably more in monthly payments and interest charges than creditworthy buyers.

The heart of the loan decision is the credit scores that are used to set interest rates and loan terms. Once a loan is made, companies then use behavioral scores—including the borrower's payment history with the loan company and other creditors—to target customers most likely to default. Phone clerks call customers almost immediately after a payment is due and follow up until the customer agrees to pay or agrees to a repossession. Surprisingly, only 5% of subprime car loans are charged off as unrecoverable debt, a low number given the problematic credit histories of some borrowers.[6]

Kim Landry is a 23-year-old data-entry specialist. After graduating from high school, she found a job that paid $14 an hour with full benefits. Her first purchase was her dream car—a red Camaro. When Kim started working, she was deluged with credit card offers. Never having had credit, she was flattered and applied for several credit cards. Things were going well until Kim went into a depression. Although able to work, she began spending with abandon, which was reflected in her high credit card bills. Kim's overspending also resulted in several late payments.

Her auto insurance skyrocketed to almost $4,000 a year after her second accident. The dream Camaro suddenly became a nightmare, and she wanted to find a car that was cheaper to insure. Kim ended up in a no-haggle used-car superstore. According to CNW Marketing Research, her choice of a no-haggle lot cost her $500 more than if she had gone to a traditional used-car lot.[7] Although Kim had never defaulted on a loan, her short and blemished credit history meant that she was ineligible for a prime-rate auto loan. She ended up with a 2000 Honda Civic for $13,000 that she was able to finance with $2,000 down on a four-year loan at a 12% APR. Her monthly payments were $290, and her total interest charges were $3,000, or double what she would have paid with a 6% loan.

Subprime financing is a large industry (nationwide estimates range from $75 million to $194 billion a year) and includes lenders like Ford Motor Credit and General Motors Acceptance Corporation.[8] These auto lenders extend credit to borrowers with poor or unstable credit histories. Depending upon the customer's credit risk, interest rates can vary from 10% to 35%, or the state usury limit. In states with strict usury laws, subprime lenders often set high loan fees or use other means to boost profits. Although some companies lend directly to consumers, most subprime lending occurs through dealer-originated loans.

Despite the potential profitability, mainstream banks are reluctant to become directly involved in subprime lending because of their conservative lending culture and the stigma associated with these kinds of loans. Lending money at a 25% interest rate and then repossessing a car doesn't make for good public relations. Besides, it's safer for banks to lend to the lenders.

Although potentially profitable, subprime loans also pose considerable risks for lenders. For example, the average subprime auto borrower has a 25% chance of being 60 days past due on a payment, at which point the car is likely to be repossessed. According to the Federal Reserve, a prominent credit-scoring vendor reports that 90% of prospective subprime borrowers have at least one significant negative credit event, 20% have gone through bankruptcy, and about 10% have had at least one car repossessed.[9]

Subprime auto lenders control losses by demanding loan terms that offset the credit risk. Lenders catering to the riskiest borrowers purchase loans from dealers at a discount to the principal value (for example, they buy a $7,000 loan for $5,000). The riskier the borrower, the greater the loan discount. Third-chance lenders—those who serve the riskiest borrowers—purchase loans at 50%–66% of the principal loan amount.

This financing structure explains why many used-car dealers refuse to negotiate a final price until after the buyer undergoes a credit check. Because dealers know they will have to discount loans, used-car prices are inflated to make up the difference. This works like a shell game. An independent dealer sells a car for $7,000 that cost it $4,000. If the car is financed through a prime lender, the dealer's profit will be $3,000. But if it sells the loan to a subprime lender at a $2,500 discount, its profit drops to $500. To realize a $3,000 profit, the dealer prices the car well above its actual value. Because of discounting, subprime borrowers are hard-hit by sky-high interest rates *and* high vehicle prices. Borrowers are also subject to deceptive practices, since higher vehicle prices are actually a hidden finance charge to the buyer for the discounted loan. This is one reason why the poor rarely find good deals in independent car lots that cater to subprime buyers.

Subprime lending can cause conflicts between lenders and dealers. Loans underwritten on terms favorable to dealers mean greater losses for lenders, since the dealer has an incentive to sell the buyer the most expensive car that he can, thereby maximizing his profit. More-expensive cars result in higher monthly payments for borrowers and a greater chance for a loan default. The dealer can also extend the loan term or lower the down payment to make the car more affordable, which diminishes the buyer's incentive to repay the cost of a vehicle in which he or she has little equity.

Subprime lenders protect themselves in several ways. First, they try to screen dealers to ensure loan quality and minimize dealer fraud such as misrepresenting car titles, coaching borrowers to fill out applications fraudulently, and inflating car values by underreporting mileage or claiming standard features as options. Consequently, many large prime and subprime lenders refuse to purchase loans from independent car lots; instead, they rely on franchised dealers that are less likely to be duplicitous because of manufacturer screening and inspection processes. The other way they protect themselves is to repossess a car quickly.

Ralph Christianson lives in a moderate-income Houston suburb and earns $21 an hour as a machinist, which puts him—at least theoretically—above the poverty line. Five years ago his wife left him. In the divorce settlement, she got the house, most of the furniture, and the newer of the two vehicles. By the end of the bitterly contested divorce, Ralph was heavily indebted to his attorney, complete with a stiff monthly repayment schedule.

Ralph used his Visa card mainly for cash advances that carried a hefty 19.9% APR. When he maxed out his cards, he secured new ones to pay the monthly payments he owed on his old cards. In the end, he declared bankruptcy. In fact, Ralph's credit history put him in the lowest lending bracket, and he was forced to resort to a third-chance lender when his car gave out.

Ralph bought a 1999 Chevrolet Cavalier for $5,000 at Excelsior Motors, an independent used-car lot. Although the car had been in an accident, it was rebuilt, had a good title, was less than six years old, and had just under 100,000 miles on it. Ralph's down payment was $1,000, and he financed $4,000 at a 28% interest rate for 24 months. His monthly payment was $229, reflecting an interest cost of $1,275. Because of Ralph's credit history, Excelsior Motors used a third-chance lender, which discounted the loan by 50%. Since Excelsior had paid $1,000 for the car and invested $300 in refurbishing it, even after the loan discount, its profit was still $1,200. If Ralph repays the loan, it will cost him almost $6,300 for a car with a trade-in value of $1,440. Like many fringe economy customers, Ralph knew he was getting ripped off, but he just couldn't see any other alternative.

The profit in subprime lending can be a powerful temptation even for franchised car dealerships. Katia Williams is a 28-year-old African American woman who is employed as a math teacher in a suburban high school. She makes a comfortable living and has a frugal lifestyle. She pays her bills on time, and her credit card debt is small in relation to her income. When Katia went shopping for a new Toyota, the salesman told her that, based on her income, she would qualify for a prime rate loan at 6%. After completing some paperwork, he disappeared into the finance office and returned an hour later with a worried look on his face. "Katia, you have credit problems, and the best rate I can get you is 11%." She was stunned. After composing herself, Katia asked, "What problems are you talking about?" His response was, "I can't talk about it. You'll have to ask the credit bureau. But I've got a special lender that will approve you right now." Katia left the showroom angry and confused. At the next Toyota dealer she was approved for a 6% car loan.

Was racial stereotyping behind Katia's "credit problems" (even though the salesman and finance manager at the first dealer were both African American)? A well-kept secret in the auto industry is the practice of lender kickbacks to dealers who charge higher interest rates. For example, if a lender's current loan rate is 8%, but the dealer charges the customer 10%, the dealer usually gets to keep a portion of the additional finance charge. On a five-year loan for $20,000, that extra 2% adds $20 to the monthly payment and $1,200 to the total interest costs. The higher the interest rate, the higher the dealer kickback.[10]

Alternatively, the salesman could have duped Katia into "packed" or "loaded" payments. In this scheme, when Katia asked about the monthly payment, the salesman would quote her an inflated figure. For example, if the real monthly payment was $345, Katia might have been quoted $385. If Katia had agreed to the $385 monthly payment, the salesman might have gotten the extra money by pushing high-profit items like an extended service warranty, anti-theft window etching, undercoating, a car alarm, or credit life insurance. On a five-year loan, this would add $2,400.

Virtually all subprime auto loans include extremely high interest rates. According to the Federal Reserve, a first-time home mortgage is considered high interest if it is eight points above the yield on a 30-year Treasury note. In 2004 the prime rate was roughly 5%, and a subprime car loan at 13% would have been considered high interest. In comparison, a second- or third-tier subprime auto loan at a 26% APR rate is twice the Federal Reserve's classification for a high-interest loan.[11]

There are several reasons why subprime lenders can get away with charging such high interest rates. First, the lack of competition among subprime lenders and the limited finance options for those with problematic credit allow lenders considerable freedom in setting rates. Second, the refusal of the federal government and most state governments to enact and enforce stringent protective legislation against predatory lending allows subprime lenders to do business almost with impunity. Third, a bad economy is a good economy for subprime lenders, because their customer base increases and they can borrow cheap money and resell it (in the form of loans) for much more to low-income consumers.

Buy-Here, Pay-Here Lots

Like many fringe economy businesses, BHPH lots (sometimes called "note lots") often appear to be minor storefronts relegated to low-income neighborhoods. But looks can be deceiving. According to journalist Terry Box, these 19,000 BHPH lots account for 22% of the used-car business nationally. They're also one of the industry's fastest-growing areas and could be responsible for 30%–40% of used-car sales in the next decade.[12]

BHPH lots are at the bottom of the subprime feeding chain: they provide in-house financing for their used cars; they don't require credit checks; and they don't forward payment information to credit bureaus. In-house financing usually requires a hefty down payment (about $1,000 on a $5,000 vehicle), and buyers pay weekly. Late payments can result in immediate repossession. As Table 9.2 illustrates, BHPH lots can be very profitable.

Like many fringe businesses, the BHPH industry can be risky, and about 30% of all cars are repossessed.[13] On the other hand, these lots are more profitable than franchised car dealerships.[14] By 2002 the average retail price of a used car in a franchised lot had risen to $11,793, with a

Table 9.2.
Costs and profitability of a typical buy here, pay here used-car dealer in 2000.[15]

	Per month	Average annual
Retail units sold	77	924
Total sales	$659,836	$7,918,032
Total operating gross	$243,115	$2,917,380
Total expenses	$187,399	$2,248,788
Total net profit (pretax)	$ 55,716	$ 668,592
Net profit as a percentage of gross	22.9%	22.9%

Average weekly payment:	$58.96
Average down payment:	$633
Average cost of unit sold:	$2,957
Average contract term:	102 weeks

gross profit of $1,741. In comparison, the average retail price of a BHPH used car had gone up to $7,810, with a gross profit of $3,772. Sales expenses in every category—vehicle reconditioning, advertising, sales commissions, and floor-plan costs—were lower for BHPH lots.[16] Table 9.3 illustrates the profitability of BHPH lots.

BHPH lots are so profitable that even traditional car dealerships are getting in on the action. Chris Leedom, a guru of the BHPH industry who has coached more than 1,500 dealers, observes that "many of the participants in our Buy-Here, Pay-Here Training School are rookies. These dealers are savvy, have capital, and are looking for attractive returns. Buy-here, pay-here certainly offers attractive returns when executed properly."[17] Many of the rookies that Leedom is talking about are franchised dealers wanting to cash in on this high-profit industry.

Large BHPH dealerships are generally not marginal fly-by-night operations. For example, in 2004 the National Association of BHPH dealers hosted its annual convention at Caesars Palace. More than 1,500 people

Table 9.3.
Profitability of selling cars and trucks in buy here, pay here dealerships, 2000.[18]

Retail price category	Percentage of total sales	Average gross profit per unit
Cars		
Under $2,000	1.4%	$798
$2,001–$4,000	10.3%	$2,229
$4,001–$6,000	20.9%	$2,896
$6,001–$8,000	29.8%	$3,759
$8,001–$10,000	33.3%	$4,966
Over $10,000	4.4%	$4,578
Total	**100%**	**$3,387**
Trucks		
Under $2,000	0.4%	$204
$2,001–$4,000	3.5%	$1,700
$4,001–$6,000	17.0%	$2,767
$6,001–$8,000	30.9%	$3,599
$8,001–$10,000	29.5%	$4,297
Over $10,000	18.7%	$4,776
Total	**100%**	**$2,890**

attended the conference from the United States and Canada, plus 60 sponsors, including Wells Fargo Financial, SeaWest, CarMax, and Auto Trader.

Like other parts of the fringe economy, the BHPH sector is undergoing financial consolidation. DriveTime (formerly Ugly Duckling) is a BHPH chain, owned by Ernest Garcia, that operates 76 dealerships in eight states and 11 metropolitan areas. The company sells more than 50,000 cars a year, with interest rates ranging from 20% to 30%. DriveTime's gross sales in 2003 were $729 million, and its one-year sales growth was 82.2%.[19]

America's Car-Mart (formerly Crown Group) is a NASDAQ-traded company with 76 dealerships in seven states. Located in Bentonville, Arkansas (the home of Wal-Mart), Car-Mart sells more than 24,000 vehicles a year and has maintained profitability in every year since it began in 1981. Company revenues grew from $128 million in 2001 to $176 million by 2004.[20] Car-Mart proudly claims to honor its customers—every 5-, 10-, and 15-time repeat customer is placed in the company's exclusive Silver, Gold, or Platinum Club. The ostensible honor is to have your name engraved on a plaque in the front of the store. That's probably the least Car-Mart can do to honor customers who pay 20%–30% interest on their vehicles.

The J.D. Byrider network is a unique franchise with 124 locations in 30 states and Canada. Byrider specializes in 5-to-10-year-old cars that sell for about $7,000. All of Byrider's franchises are composed of two companies: a used-car company (J.D. Byrider) and a subprime auto finance company (CarNow).[21]

In 2004 the Kentucky attorney general filed a lawsuit against Byrider and its franchisees. The charges included failing to repair vehicle defects under an implied warranty; making unfair, false, misleading, and deceptive statements about warranties; refusing to recognize a customer's lawful right to revoke his or her contract; making false, misleading, and deceptive statements about vehicles' being "certified" or "inspected"; and requiring buyers to purchase credit life insurance and service contracts, and failing to disclose those as a credit cost (that is, violating the federal Truth in Lending Act). The complaint also alleged that Byrider's business model is unlawful, since it unfairly makes consumers vulnerable to abusive sales tactics. Finally, the complaints included Byrider's discouraging customers from purchasing certain cars; hiding or failing to reveal the real purchase price; and requiring detailed financial information and a credit check before disclosing a vehicle's price.[22] It seems that Byrider's mission to "Deliver dependable cars and provide affordable financing in a friendly and professional atmosphere" may need some fine-tuning.

BHPH dealers foresee a brisk future as more middle-class families face increased debt and blemished credit. In fact, the BHPH sector is beginning to stratify, with middle- and higher-end lots selling vehicles costing $10,000 or more. Some are even selling newer cars and trucks for $20,000 and up. According to Michael Linn, CEO of the National Independent Automobile Dealers Association (NIADA), "We're no longer just talking blue-collar working people. . . . We're talking doctors, lawyers. It's a growing industry because of what is going on economically, and the influx of immigrants. The common denominator is no credit or damaged credit."[23]

Like much of the fringe economy, the BHPH industry is driven by the profitability of financing rather than the profitability in selling a product. As one BHPH customer described, "They wanted $1,900 for that car. . . . These people wouldn't take cash; they wouldn't take cash for any of their vehicles. I asked, and he said that they wouldn't let us buy the car. They wanted us to put $1000 down and pay $89 a week for two years, which totals much more than the car's actual worth. If it broke down, you couldn't get your down payment back." BHPH dealer Ingram Walters observes, "The BHPH business is not the car business. It is the collections business."[24] BHPH industry analyst Chuck Bonanno has a similar message: "If you repossess cars when they fail mechanically, repair them only to sell it to another customer, you miss the point of buy-here, pay-here. We want $70/week from everyone and forever!"[25]

Carlotta and Sunshine Motors

Sunshine Motors is a typical small BHPH car lot. It has 30–40 cars at any given time, it's located on a wide Texas highway, and its sales office is in a small prefab building. Its stock consists mainly of high-mileage vehicles bought at auction, at least six years old, and of little interest to most franchised car dealers. Sunshine purchases its vehicles well below book value, rarely paying more than $2,000 for any car. The minor reconditioning generally costs less than $300. Sunshine's strategy is to sell a lot of $5,000–$8,000 cars fast.

A big sign painted with a cheery sun sits in front of its lot. In prominent letters the sign advertises that Sunshine will "tote-the-note" and provide in-house financing. As in many of these car lots, salespeople and apparent hangers-on mill around in dense clouds of cigarette smoke and overflowing ashtrays. The tops of their desks are empty, and calculators are nowhere in sight. When I asked a salesman why he didn't have a calculator on his desk, his response was, "The computer figures everything out." This isn't surprising, since the last thing a fringe economy salesperson wants is for the customer to add up the numbers. Sunshine's salespeople are so laid-back that they almost seem uninterested in selling cars. On the other hand, they may just have good instincts about who will buy, reserving the heavy come-on for real customers.

Carlotta Hernandez is a 35-year-old Guatemalan who has lived in the United States for 15 years. Her husband, Raul, works for a lawn service and earns minimum wage. Only her children speak fluent English. Carlotta has built up a small housecleaning business that provides the lion's share of the household income. She has also built a loyal clientele, who, at her request, pay in cash. Raul is also paid in cash. Although the combined family income provides a modicum of comfort, the Hernandezes don't have a bank account or credit cards. They pay their bills in cash or money orders that they purchase from a local check-cashing outlet.

Carlotta had just had their fourth child, and their car was too small for the family. Although the Hernandez family had always paid for cars in cash, the new baby left them short of money. Without established credit, a bank account, pay stubs, and employer verification, they were forced to turn to a BHPH lot.

Sunshine Motors was designed for customers like Carlotta. There are no complicated forms to fill out, since there's no credit check or subprime lender to satisfy. Carlotta put $1,000 down and would pay weekly until her loan was paid off in two years. Her interest rate would range from 23% to 28%, depending on the deal she could strike with the salesperson.

Carlotta bought a 1991 Chrysler minivan with 132,000 miles for $7,000. If the minivan had been in excellent condition (which it was not), the retail price would have been $5,000. Carlotta overpaid by at least $2,000 but was able to negotiate a two-year 23% APR loan, for a payment of $80 a week. Like many fringe economy buyers, Carlotta was more concerned with the amount of the weekly payments than with the interest rate. If she had calculated the total cost, Carlotta would have found that the loan interest was $1,500, which increased the minivan's cost to $8,500. If Sunshine Motors had purchased the minivan at trade-in value, it would have paid only $1,900 for a vehicle costing Carlotta $8,500. Her $1,000 down payment alone paid for half of Sunshine's investment, and in only three months its entire costs would be paid off. The remaining 21 months would be almost pure profit for the dealer.

If Carlotta's minivan needed expensive repairs (likely for an older, high-mileage vehicle), she would be forced to choose between paying off the loan, having the vehicle repossessed, and losing the down payment (plus the monthly payments she'd made), or selling the minivan and adding money to close the deal. Chuck Bonanno details the dilemma: "Our customers typically don't pay for repairs because they can't afford the repairs and not because they refuse to make the repairs. Remember that when vehicle repair estimates inch toward down payment requirements in your market, it only makes economical sense to consider the options: fix the one I got or get a new one. The fear of bad credit is not a factor to our customer and will typically not influence their decisions."[26] To keep customers in the financing loop, some BHPH dealers offer service plans. Sunshine Motors does not.

BHPH lots also make money on repairs. As one BHPH dealer put it, "When their battery dies, they call us. I send a wrecker and pick it up. Now I got a $45 wrecker bill. If it's the battery, it's $45 for the battery plus $20 to put it in. But they don't even have the money to do that. So I say, 'Can you give me $30 down and I'll finance the other $70?' Now they're $100 in the hole plus interest." Another BHPH customer observed, "If your car breaks down, you can take it there and they just keep tacking on the repairs to your bill. Some people have this old car, and they're having this six-year, seven-year bill from them."

Given the age and high mileage of Sunshine's cars, it's no surprise that when I asked the salesman about the length of its loans, he said, "Don't worry, no one pays off a loan. We have repeat customers. People just keep on trading in cars and buying more expensive ones. Most of our customers don't keep their cars for more than a year." In any case, Sunshine Motors can't lose. If Carlotta's minivan were to be repossessed, the dealer would resell it to the next customer for roughly the same price. Since Carlotta would have repaid Sunshine's initial investment in only three months, any subsequent sale would be almost pure profit.

Repossession looms large for BHPH customers. When I asked the Sunshine salesman about this, his response was, "We don't repossess much. We want the customer to be happy and to come back and buy more cars. Hell, I can show you customers that owe us $600 and we still haven't repoed them." I felt reassured until I drove down the road to Small City Auto Sales. The salesman there had a different take on the issue: "I don't like to do in-house financing unless I have to. If I finance a vehicle, I'll repo it the day after a payment is late. Just like Sunshine."

Although the fear of repossession is real for Sunshine's customers, it may be the last resort for dealers, because it signals the end of the relationship. The key to profit in the fringe economy is keeping borrowers firmly ensconced in the financing loop. In fact, the most invidious part of the BHPH system is that it locks the consumer into its system in two ways. First, even if Carlotta makes timely payments and pays off the loan, her credit will not be enhanced, since Sunshine doesn't report transactions to a credit bureau. Carlotta's responsible behavior will go unrewarded, and she won't be building a positive credit history. The next time Carlotta needs a vehicle, she'll again be forced into the fringe auto economy. While many fringe economy consumers are keen on avoiding a credit check—or are misled by salespeople into believing that they will never qualify for a loan—in-house financing diminishes the possibility that a responsible borrower can rectify his or her bad credit. Captive buyers are therefore forced to remain dependent on the largesse of Sunshine Motors' "good deals." This cycle continues indefinitely, and with each trade, Sunshine's profits grow while people like Carlotta go deeper into debt. Once the economic hook is set, it goes deep.

Second, having bought a grossly overpriced vehicle, Carlotta can't resell it until after the loan is paid off. If she's lucky, she can get back her

$1,000 down payment, but she'll have lost $7,500 in 24 months of high-interest payments. She'll also be back to square one. Carlotta's other option is to trade the minivan back to Sunshine Motors for yet another overpriced vehicle. Since Sunshine has already recouped its initial investment several times over, it can offer Carlotta more than her minivan is worth. In turn, she can buy a $12,000 vehicle (worth maybe $6,000) with her $2,000 trade-in.

High-Cost Auto Insurance

The poor are also hard-hit by auto insurance. For example, many people with older cars only insure them for state-mandated liability coverage rather than for collision (damage to *their* vehicle). It makes little sense to spend $600 a year for collision coverage on a car worth $1,000, especially after a $500 deductible. To protect their loan, BHPH dealers and subprime lenders require borrowers to insure their vehicles for liability *and* collision, regardless of its cost-effectiveness.

According to a Conning and Co. study, 92% of large insurance companies run credit checks on potential customers.[27] These checks translate into insurance scores that are used to determine if the carrier will insure an applicant and for how much. Those with poor or no credit, like Carlotta and Ralph, are denied coverage, while those like Kim, with limited credit, pay high premiums.

Insurance companies argue that credit scoring helps prevent low-risk policyholders from subsidizing higher-risk policyholders, thereby lowering their premiums by 60%–80%.[28] Despite the industry's reliance on insurance scoring, it has provided no hard evidence to support its claim that credit-impaired or low-income drivers are any less safe or more prone to file claims than creditworthy ones.[29] What is clear, though, is that insurance scoring is a form of redlining that punishes those with poor credit, minorities, and the young. State and federal government agencies should enforce existing anti-redlining statutes by taking action against insurers who violate the law. Government should force insurers to offer drivers with no moving violations or at-fault accidents policies at their standard or preferred rates. This would ensure that everyone has an equal opportunity to buy affordable insurance.

Because Carlotta and Ralph would likely be refused coverage by first-tier insurance companies, they would end up in the fringe auto insurance market. The A.M. Best Company has two categories for ranking the financial strength of insurance companies: Secure Ratings and Vulnerable Ratings. Most large auto insurers are rated as secure, and most fringe insurers are rated as vulnerable.[30] These categories reflect the ability of insurers to pay out claims and protect the interests of their customers. For example, large auto insurers will pay out claims even if faced with huge losses resulting from floods, hurricanes, or other natural catastrophes. Facing similar losses, marginally capitalized insurance companies may declare bankruptcy to avoid honoring claims. While most states have guaranty funds to pay claims if an insurance company fails, those funds can be quickly exhausted in an emergency. About 17 U.S. insurance companies are liquidated, dissolved, or placed in receivership each year.[31] Fringe or second-tier auto insurers are a big risk for low-income auto buyers, who are responsible for repaying their loans even if the insurer becomes insolvent.

Mainstream auto insurers calculate premiums based on six-month or one-year periods. On the other hand, fringe auto insurers typically provide only monthly quotes, and, not surprisingly, these are outrageous compared with rates from large auto insurers. If Ralph and Carlotta had excellent driving records and were accepted by a mainstream insurer like State Farm or GEICO, their annual full-coverage premiums would range from $700 (GEICO) to $900 (State Farm) for the Chrysler minivan and from $800 (GEICO) to $1,100 (State Farm) for the Chevy Cavalier. If they chose only liability coverage, their premiums would drop to $500 a year.

Because of the lenders' requirement for full coverage, Carlotta and Ralph would pay double the insurance premiums necessary for an older vehicle with little trade-in value. Moreover, since they overpaid for their vehicles, even full insurance coverage would leave a huge gap between what they would receive for a total loss and what they actually owed. Borrowers are responsible for the difference between insurance compensation and loan repayment, a difference that could cost thousands of dollars. To protect themselves, some buyers buy expensive "gap" coverage to supplement their regular auto insurance.

Carlotta and Ralph ended up with a minimally regulated, high-rate local insurance agency. If Carlotta chose Houston's Alamo Insurance, full coverage for the Chrysler would be $2,100 a year, or three times the $700 quoted by GEICO. Ralph would pay an astounding $2,800 a year, or more than three times the $800 quoted by GEICO. In only one year, Carlotta and Ralph would pay more in car insurance than the wholesale value of their vehicles. If they shopped carefully, they could find slightly cheaper insurance at AAA Insurance (not related to the American Automobile Association), a local Houston company. At AAA they'd pay $1,400 and $1,800, respectively. But full insurance coverage even at the lowest rate would raise Carlotta's monthly auto payments to $380, while Ralph's would jump to $365.

Fringe auto insurers can charge outrageous premiums for several reasons. For one, they have a captive consumer who has already been rejected by large insurance carriers. Second, the loan terms of BHPH dealers and subprime lenders create a steady stream of car owners desperate for insurance. Third, many fringe auto insurers are minimally regulated, and state insurance regulators are lax in rooting out predatory insurers, especially those serving the poor. Not coincidentally, fringe auto insurers take the pressure off mainstream carriers to provide coverage for the poor. Finally, many state vehicle inspections require a proof-of-insurance card before a vehicle can pass inspection. Some car owners pay the high monthly premium to get the insurance card, pass the inspection, and then drop the coverage. This may be one reason why fringe auto insurance rates are quoted monthly rather than biannually.

Carlotta, Ralph, and tens of thousands of other poor car buyers are victimized thrice: once by predatory fringe auto dealers with inflated car prices; again by finance companies charging scandalous interest rates; and finally by avaricious auto insurers. Each year Carlotta and Ralph will pay about $4,500 for the privilege of driving a battered old car. In fact, they will spend almost as much each month on junk cars as the middle class spends on newer, sound vehicles.

Vehicle Inspections and the Poor

The effects of insurance scoring, coupled with greedy fringe market auto insurers, result in vast numbers of uninsured motorists—400,000 in

Philadelphia, 500,000 in Los Angeles, 10% of St. Louis drivers; and 21% of Texas drivers.[32] About 14% of U.S. drivers carry no auto insurance whatsoever.[33]

The rising cost of state vehicle inspections also helps to discourage drivers from making their vehicles legal. Mandatory New York State vehicle inspections cost $35; Texans pay $40. Moreover, whether vehicle inspections actually protect public safety is open to question. As one vehicle inspector put it, "I think these things are a waste of money. I fail about two cars a week. The other inspectors I know fail about the same." One of the major causes of inspection failures is worn tires. Luckily, the fringe economy has come to the rescue.

Rent-A-Tire and Rent-A-Wheel are the nation's largest tire-rental outlets, with more than 30 stores in California, Texas, and Arizona. Rent-A-Tire was started by Cash America International, although it divested itself of the company when it merged with Rent-A-Wheel in 2002.

Roberta Goldstein is a nursing assistant and a single mother of two teenagers. Although she tries to maintain her 1998 Ford Explorer on limited finances, it failed Texas's vehicle inspection because of worn tires. Cash was tight for Roberta, and she was at the limit of her Visa card. Never a scofflaw, she feared driving illegally. When Roberta checked Discount Tire, the cheapest tires she could find cost $400. Driving around, Roberta discovered Rent-A-Tire. At her wits' end, she had little choice. In only two hours, Roberta was out of Rent-A-Tire and had the Explorer successfully reinspected.

Rent-A-Tire's application form is straightforward, and Roberta was relieved that there was no credit check, because she had had several late Visa and utility payments. To close the deal, Roberta needed $108. Although the salesperson explained how the rent-to-own agreement worked, Roberta only partially paid attention, since all she could think about was making her only transportation legal again. After signing the agreement, she drove off with four *possibly* new tires (Rent-A-Tire resells its repossessed tires).

Roberta's tires came with a high price tag. Her weekly payment was $45, or $180 a month (almost half the cost of new tires) for 26 weeks. At the end of the six-month rental, Roberta would have paid $1,170 for tires worth $400. Although she could purchase the tires anytime and receive a 50% discount off her balance, the cash-out was based on the initial price of $600, which was still $200 higher than the cost of buying new tires at Discount Tire. While Roberta's rental payment included mandatory theft insurance on the tires, it didn't cover road hazards, which meant that she was still responsible if her tires became irreparably damaged. Rent-A-Tire has no grace period. If Roberta were to be one to three days late with her payment, she would be required to pay two weeks in advance. If she were four to six days late, she'd have to pay three weeks in advance. Roberta's tires would be repossessed if her payment were more than seven days late. Mandatory vehicle inspections are a blessing for companies like Rent-A-Tire.

Auto Title Pawns

Although auto title pawns began in the South, by 2000 these outlets were a common sight in many large metropolitan areas. In fact, auto title pawns are legal in 20 states. These loans are fairly straightforward transactions. A consumer needs a short-term loan, but instead of using his television or stereo as collateral, he uses his vehicle title. This substantially increases the amount he can borrow, because cars are generally worth more than appliances or electronics. Vehicles are also easier for lenders to resell at auction. However, unlike pawnshop transactions, auto title pawns don't require the borrower to relinquish the use of his property during the course of the loan, even though the lender owns it.

Auto title loans can have several stipulations. For example, some title pawn companies will not lend on vehicles 12 years or older. Others will not lend when the loan exceeds 25% of the borrower's monthly wages.

An auto title pawn can include a lease-back arrangement, whereby the lender buys the car for the price of the loan and then leases it back to the borrower. Once the interest, fees, and cash advance are paid, the lender resells the vehicle back to the borrower. Lease-back transactions are often used to bypass state usury laws.

Gary Higgins is a 25-year-old lumberyard worker from Alamogordo, New Mexico, a city of 15,000 people. When Gary worked, he earned $6.50

an hour, which was about the average wage in rural New Mexico. Gary lives with his girlfriend, Lettie, and their 2-year-old son in a rented trailer just outside the city limits. Lettie works for Wal-Mart and earns $7.50 an hour. Getting by was hard when Gary and Lettie both worked, but after he broke his leg in an accident, it became even harder. Like many rural New Mexico residents, Gary didn't have health insurance through his job. Without his salary, the family couldn't pay the rent.

Gary inherited his grandmother's 1998 Oldsmobile. The car had only 45,000 miles on it and was in excellent condition. It was the only asset that he and Lettie owned. They couldn't sell their only car outright, because Alamogordo has no public transportation and Lettie would therefore have no way to get to work. Because Gary was unemployed, Alamogordo banks would not consider a personal loan. This couple felt that their only option was to pawn the auto title.

High Desert Title Pawn is located in a small strip mall on Alamogordo's busiest street, which isn't saying much. It's run by Terry Hinojosa, a Charles Bronson look-alike in his mid-40s. Despite his rugged demeanor, Terry displays a warm empathy for his customers: "I'm here to help these people. They're my people. I know where they're coming from, and I know what they're facing. I don't want to repo anybody's car, I just want to help them out of a jam." As is the case with many of the salespeople I've met in the fringe economy, I'm not sure whether to help Terry enroll in a social-work program or nominate him for the Bullshitter of the Year award.

To secure the loan, Gary had to provide a paid-up vehicle title free of any liens and an extra set of keys. He signed over the title to High Desert, which appraised the car based on the lowest possible value (the wholesale price in rough condition). Some auto title pawns lend up to 50% of the vehicle's value in poor condition, while others, such as High Desert, lend only up to one-third. The maximum loan from High Desert was $1,250. If Gary defaulted, High Desert would get a car worth at least $7,000 for $1,250, a sum that wouldn't include Gary's previous payments.

Car title loans are written for 30 days and typically involve an APR of 300% or more. Although loan terms vary between companies, High Desert operates in the following way: Gary's original loan of $1,250 was due in 30 days with a payoff of $1,560 (25% interest). If the loan weren't repaid, the car would be repossessed on the 31st day. Gary could request a 30-day extension after paying $310 in interest charges. In fact, he could get almost endless extensions as long as he paid the interest charges. Gary's interest costs would total more than 50% of the original loan after 60 days. In only five months, his interest charges would exceed the original loan amount. If the loan were extended for a year, Gary would pay $3,800 in interest charges on a $1,250 loan.

If High Desert repossessed Gary's car and sold it at auction or to a car dealer, he'd receive no proceeds from the sale, even though its value was greater than the loan. Should Gary default after four months (when the interest payments equaled the original loan), High Desert's proceeds from the resale would be almost pure profit. Once Gary relinquished the title, he would lose fiscal control of the car until the interest and cash advance were paid. Since Gary no longer owned the title, he couldn't easily resell the car to get out from under High Desert. Not surprisingly, many title loan companies find it more profitable if the borrower defaults.

Other auto title pawn companies operate in a slightly different manner. Car Title Loans of America has 37 outlets in five states. If the company appraises a vehicle at $2,000 (the wholesale value in poor condition), it will give the borrower a 30-day loan for 50% of the car's value. After 30 days the loan payoff is $1,250, or the original amount of the loan plus 25% in interest and fees. After paying $500 in interest payments for the first two loan periods, a borrower can request an extension for a maximum of one year. At that point, the monthly payment rises, because the borrower is now expected to pay $100 a month toward the principal and continue to pay the interest. By the fourth month, the principal will be only $900, and so on, until the loan is paid off or the car is repossessed. In an ironic twist, the company states that "Car Title Loans of America is . . . organized to provide financial help for customers. . . . [The company] . . . offers its customers more than just money. At the time a loan is made, customers are given their choice of 'How to Escape Financial Bondage,' 'The New Testament,' or 'God's Promises'—tools that hopefully will help them get in a financially sound situation."[34] Creating a financially sound situation under a crushing 300%-interest loan isn't easy, even with the help of the Bible.

Reforming the Fringe Auto Sector

It's easy to blame the excesses of the fringe auto economy on BHPH lots, sleazy salespeople, unscrupulous subprime lenders, and rapacious insurance companies. While not blameless, these institutions and actors are symptomatic of larger problems, including the reluctance of mainstream banks to provide financial services to the poor and society's obsession with credit scores. Nowadays, credit ratings have become the benchmark by which moral probity is judged. Bad credit is the equivalent of bad character, and few politicians are willing to stick out their necks for people with bad character. This partly explains why there's so little legislation to protect the poor from predatory economic activity.

The fringe auto economy provides an important, if expensive, service for the poor. Independent used-car lots resell older vehicles that mainstream dealers would otherwise discard or sell for export. Moreover, BHPH lots finance poor credit risks that even many third-tier lenders would run from. Subprime lenders provide the means for the working poor to secure transportation so that they can hold down a job. Although second-tier auto insurers charge extortionate premiums, low-income car owners would be bereft of insurance without them. Even auto title pawns provide an important service by allowing borrowers to drive their cars while owing money on them, something that traditional pawnshops won't do. So it's not surprising that the biggest opponent to auto title loans in Florida has been the pawnshop industry.[35]

Outlawing the fringe auto economy won't solve the problem, because that will punish low-income consumers as much as unscrupulous car dealers, lenders, and insurance companies. Moreover, crafty dealers, lenders, and insurance companies would undoubtedly find other ways to do business. Despite this, there are several ways to exercise some control over the fringe auto economy. For instance, states can enact stricter usury laws with fewer loopholes. There's little economic justification for BHPH lots and subprime lenders to charge five or six times the prime rate for an auto loan, even for a high-risk borrower. Maximum interest rates for all auto financing should be keyed to the prime rate and should not be permitted to exceed it by more than a fixed number of points.

Other reforms are also needed. Mandatory disclosures should be required in all used-car sales, especially for dealer-financed autos. How much a dealer discounts a car note to a subprime lender should be explained to buyers so that they can see how the discount affects the price of the vehicle. In addition, BHPH auto dealerships and auto title pawns should be required to report all transactions to a credit agency, which could help responsible consumers build or rebuild their credit histories. This reporting may also help weaken the reliance of the poor on the fringe economy. Another way to discourage the poor from using the fringe economy is to provide consumer education, which begins with understanding the economics of fringe buying. However, this won't be successful unless disclosure statements and other legal forms are drafted into succinct language that is easily comprehended by non-attorneys.

Several interesting experiments are under way to address transportation problems for the poor. In fact, there are currently 40 nonprofit car-ownership programs in the nation that provide as many as a few hundred cars a year or as little as five. One example is Fannie CLAC, started by auto-industry veteran Robert Chambers. CLAC is a nonprofit car-ownership program in Lebanon, New Hampshire, that helps low-income people buy new cars and thereby avoid the used-car market altogether. Chambers has persuaded auto dealers to offer new base-model cars at $100 over dealer invoice. Fannie CLAC then negotiates with banks to secure loans for clients at favorable rates. In 2004 these loans typically lasted 66 months, carried an interest rate of 4.75%, and cost borrowers only $243 a month. CLAC guarantees the value of each loan, thereby eliminating the lender's risk. So far, the default rate on CLAC-guaranteed loans has been less than 3%—lower than the industry average. In turn, CLAC requires most clients to undergo credit counseling before it will guarantee the loans. To further insure the loans, CLAC clients drive used "bridge cars" that it lends them for $200 a month while they build a credit history and become accustomed to making car payments.[36]

Another example is the Good News Garage, which Hal Colston started in 1996 in Burlington, Vermont, with $35,000 from Lutheran Social Services. Good News solicits donations of used cars, inspects them, and repairs the ones with life left in them. It then sells the cars to needy families for the cost of repairs—usually less than $1,200—and offers a 30-day warranty. In 2003 Good News provided 210 cars to low-income families. Seattle's Working Wheels program furnishes clients with late-model cars donated by government agencies. Detroit's Driven to Succeed program helps low-income buyers purchase previously leased cars. Despite these notable attempts, most nonprofit car programs have hundreds of families on their waiting lists, and the need far exceeds the availability of affordable autos.[37]

Born of people's misfortunes, credit counseling was
a sleepy cottage industry for a long time. Now,
larger and troubled, it may be more in need than its
clients of being set back on the straight and narrow.

–Christopher H. Schmitt with Heather Timmons and
John Cady, "A Debt Trap for the Unwary,"
BusinessWeek, October 29, 2001

10

The Getting-Out-of-Debt Industry

We are besieged by advertising on two fronts: how to get more and cheaper credit, and how to get out of debt. On the one hand, we are lured into taking on more debt through cheap credit; on the other hand, we're warned of being in too much debt.

Federal Reserve chairman Alan Greenspan pointed out in 2004 that because of low interest rates, we could more easily handle high levels of personal debt.[1] In 2003 economics journalist Robert Samuelson argued that Americans were already too heavily in debt and the last thing we needed was more "cheap credit."[2] Despite Greenspan's insouciance, "cheap credit" still mounts up and must be paid off. For instance, since 2001 U.S. households have spent more than 13% of their disposable income on debt, a level not seen since the Fed began collecting this data in 1980.[3] The contradictory messages of "borrow more" and "borrow less" reflect the simultaneous growth of the credit and getting-out-of-debt industries. This chapter examines the consumer credit counseling industry, debt settlement, and ways to rein in runaway credit counseling agencies.

Consumer Credit Counseling Agencies

Debt management is a multibillion-dollar industry. Nearly 9 million people a year in financial trouble have some contact with a consumer credit counseling agency (CCA), and 3 million people nationwide have a active debt-management plan (DMP) in any given year. In the early 1990s there were about 200 debt-management agencies; by 2004 that number had jumped to 1,300 or more. By 2004, $5 billion of debt was repaid to creditors through credit counseling agencies.[4]

THE EVOLUTION OF THE CCA INDUSTRY

The CCA industry emerged in the mid-1960s through the efforts of credit card companies to recover overdue debts. The original nonprofit Consumer Credit Counseling Services (CCCSs) were affiliated with the National Foundation for Consumer Credit (NFCC), the earliest and perhaps most reputable trade organization. Early credit counseling agencies used a social service model based on face-to-face counseling. However, as with many underfunded social service–type agencies, consumers endured long waiting periods for assistance, were required to attend counseling sessions, and in some cases had to make on-site payments. On the other hand, early agencies provided credit counseling even for those not enrolled in revenue-generating DMPs, consumer education, budget-management seminars, and financial-advice programs.

The CCA industry is primarily funded through a policy known as Fair Share. Under this arrangement, credit card issuers (CCIs) voluntarily return a percentage of each payment they get through a DMP. Traditionally, CCAs received a 15% reimbursement on each payment they received, which was used to cover operating expenses. Since the kickbacks were higher than actual expenses, the surplus funded non-revenue-generating services such as consumer counseling and public speaking. The CCAs' dependence on creditor funding was rarely disclosed to consumers until the industry reached a settlement with the Federal Trade Commission in 1996.

Entrepreneurs were enticed by the possibilities of the Fair Share plan. For example, a single $15,000 DMP with a 15% kickback could earn $2,250. Unlike other fringe economy businesses, CCAs carried little risk, since reimbursements came from creditors rather than debtors. Entrepreneurs soon realized that they could make even more money if they eliminated expensive non-revenue-generating services, such as face-to-face counseling.

The CCA industry grew rapidly as newer agencies developed competing trade associations, such as the American Association of Debt Management, the American Federation of Independent Credit Counseling Associations, and the Association of Independent Consumer Credit Counseling Agencies.[5] Newer CCAs were less stodgy than traditional agencies and applied more business-oriented practices, such as generating positive net revenues. They adopted more consumer-friendly policies, such as flexible hours, phone and Internet counseling, and electronic payments. In turn, older CCAs were forced to become more responsive to clients.

The newer and more aggressive CCAs also introduced a host of new problems. For example, leaner businesses meant less face-to-face contact with clients and less personalized budgeting advice. Agencies began to focus exclusively on revenue-generating DMPs rather than on non-revenue-generating financial services. Through aggressive marketing, newer CCAs occasionally crossed the line into deceptive practices, such as falsely claiming that involuntary fees were voluntary; providing customer bonuses for referrals; and paying for incentive-based telemarketing and spam e-mail. The newer agencies also charged high fees—typically a full month's DMP payment—to set up an account. In contrast, traditional NFCC member agencies may offer one-on-one budget counseling for $13 a session, and charge a $15-per-month DMP fee plus $25 for setting up a new account.[6]

Because many newer CCAs deal solely with CCIs that pay a Fair Share reimbursement, they place only a portion of customers' unsecured debt into a DMP, leaving them to manage other creditors on their own. (Reputable CCAs work with all creditors, regardless of whether they contribute.) Still other CCAs are DMP mills, where "credit counselors" are paid a commission based on the number of people they sign up.

Although consumers searching for credit counseling services are often advised to look for accredited NFCC or CCCS agencies, this does not guarantee fiscal integrity. In 2004, state investigators searching for missing funds seized the nonprofit CCCS of Utah, a founding and decades-long member of the NFCC. Regulators also ordered its president, nightclub owner Scott McCagno, to turn over his credit cards and a CCCS-owned BMW. McCagno was eventually fined $45,000 and banned from the credit counseling industry. In 2001, just three months after the NFCC withdrew its accreditation from the CCCS of Utah, the president and treasurer of the Hawaii Credit Counseling (HCC) service were convicted of using clients' funds to launder drug money for heroin dealers.[7] Some lenders and creditors represented on the NFCC board have paid hundreds of millions of dollars in Federal Trade Commission fines and other settlements for anti-consumer practices.[8] The main strategy that CCAs use to help consumers exit the debt trap is a DMP.

DEBT-MANAGEMENT PLANS

Legitimate debt management works in the following way: A consumer who is embroiled in revolving debt consults a CCA. His or her total credit obligation is reviewed, and a plan is created for debt reduction, which may call for credit counseling, consumer education, or a self-administered debt-reduction strategy. If the debt is high, the CCA may develop a debt-management plan that consolidates unsecured bills into a monthly payment schedule designed to satisfy creditors. In turn, creditors may lower interest rates and waive certain fees. DMPs can include unsecured debt, such as that from credit cards, personal signature loans, store cards, medical bills, gas cards, and collection accounts. However, DMPs mainly focus on credit card debt. Non-revolving debts, such as mortgages and auto loans, are rarely consolidated.

The proposed DMP is forwarded to the credit company(ies) for approval, which is not necessarily automatic, since they may not easily grant concessions. For instance, creditors may require the CCA to supply a detailed financial snapshot of the borrower, including belt-tightening specifics about where nonessential spending (entertainment, restaurants, magazine subscriptions, and so forth) will be reduced. To prove their sincerity, some borrowers may be put on probation and be required to make three monthly on-time payments before the concessions kick in.[9] If the DMP is accepted, the credit card companies may waive late and other fees and grant a lower interest rate. Although monthly payments are slightly reduced, the full balance is still owed, and interest continues to accrue during the repayment period. A Consolidated Credit Counseling Services advertisement illustrates the hypothetical difference a DMP can make in debt repayment, as shown in Table 10.1.[10]

Once the credit card issuer accepts the DMP, the customer sends a monthly payment to the CCA that is deposited into a trust account and used to pay creditors. Apart from *possibly* receiving lower interest rates and waived fees, customers have the convenience of making only one monthly payment instead of dealing with multiple creditors. In exchange for the concessions, the CCI terminates the borrower's credit card

Table 10.1.
Comparison of repayment methods for $16,000 total debt on six credit cards.[11]

Without consolidation	With consolidation
Average interest rate: 18%	Average interest rate: 6.9%
Total time to pay off: 35 years, 9 months	Total time to pay off: 4 years
Total interest: $23,615	Total interest: $2,355

accounts. Most CCAs also require clients to not apply for any new credit cards while in the program unless they have to for business purposes. The four to five years it takes to repay a debt, high monthly payments, and absence of credit cards or other forms of revolving credit help explain the high failure rate of credit counseling (only 26% of debtors complete their DMPs).[12]

DMPs are sometimes falsely advertised as debt consolidation. Despite advertisements promising, "Consolidate your debts into one monthly payment and get out of debt quicker," only the monthly payments are consolidated in DMPs—the debt remains the same. Moreover, DMPs are not debt-consolidation loans, which are almost impossible to get unless the borrower owns a home from which equity can be withdrawn through some form of refinancing. Even if a debtor manages to find an unsecured debt-consolidation loan, it will usually contain the same high interest rates (or higher) as those on credit cards. While monthly payments may be lower for homeowners who opt to repay their debt through refinancing, they end up paying longer and hence pay more interest. We can't borrow our way out of debt.

The Limits of DMPs

According to attorney David Lander, "The credit counseling agencies were set up for the benefit of the credit industry. . . . They can be looked at as a subtle collection agency. . . . A few also provide good budgeting education."[13] New York University law professor Karen Gross maintains that "many consumers are unaware of the relationship between debt counselors and creditors. It doesn't bother me that credit card companies want someone to help them with debt collection. . . . The problem is that consumers think they are getting an advocate. They don't have a clue they're not operating on a level playing field."[14] In short, consumers fail to understand that the credit counseling agencies' primary customers are the CCIs that participate in Fair Share plans. This conflict of interest is illustrated by the makeup of the NFCC's board of directors, which in 2002 included representatives from Household Credit Services (a well-known subprime lender that has paid millions in restitution to fleeced consumers), Citigroup, Visa,

THE FRINGE SECTORS

Petroleum National Bank, J.C. Penney, and Experian (one of the three national credit reporting agencies).

The conflict of interest between client needs and the revenues that DMPs generate has led to some industry abuses. For instance, CCAs frequently push debt-management plans at the expense of other options and most strongly discourage bankruptcy, an avenue that doesn't generate agency revenues. According to the Consumers for Responsible Credit Solutions, 86% of borrowers who approach NFCC agencies are eligible to file for bankruptcy due to legal insolvency, but only 11% file in the subsequent 18 months.[15] For creditors, a key purpose of credit counseling is to keep their customers from declaring bankruptcy, regardless of their financial situation. At minimum, creditors want to keep customers paying as long as possible before they declare bankruptcy. In reality, almost 42% of DMP dropouts file for bankruptcy, causing credit card companies to lose about $12 billion a year, of which only a fraction is ever repaid.[16]

Unlike secured debt, which can lead to repossession, revolving credit offers creditors limited recourse for repayment, except for garnisheeing wages. When an account is declared uncollectible, the creditor writes it off as a bad debt or a charge-off. Depending upon the creditor, a charge-off can occur 90–180 days after a debt is declared delinquent. Charge-offs are reported to credit bureaus and remain on the borrower's credit record for seven years. While charge-offs are used for internal accounting purposes, creditors can still pursue debtors, and they will often sell bad debts to a third party—usually a collection agency—that keeps any money it collects.

Although often useful, DMPs can aggravate the credit problems of those with high debt and limited financial resources. For instance, money spent on repaying revolving debt increases the risk that secured debt property, such as a house or car, will be repossessed. Consumers saddled with high DMP payments may also have little left over for rent, mortgage payments, or family and household emergencies. Since secured loans generate no DMP revenue, credit counselors may erroneously advise clients to first pay their revolving debt. Clients may also not be advised that bankruptcy can be the best option in a high-debt/low-resource scenario.

There are two types of personal bankruptcy: Chapter 13 and Chapter 7. Chapter 13 bankruptcy requires a plan that outlines how a debtor will repay creditors over a three-to-five-year period. Only Chapter 13 can stop a creditor from foreclosing on a debtor's secured property. If payment plans are not kept current, the court allows the secured property to go into foreclosure.

Chapter 7 bankruptcy is more common and requires that all nonexempt assets be turned over to a bankruptcy trustee, who discharges the debts. Exempt assets vary from state to state but often include basic household furnishings and work-related tools. Since most debtors facing bankruptcy own few possessions, they are generally allowed to keep everything. Bankruptcy typically does not eliminate the responsibility for child support, alimony, fines, taxes, and student loan obligations. Bankruptcies can remain on a credit report for up to 10 years.

In contrast with their aggressive advertising, CCAs have little real control over what they can offer, since CCIs determine the concessions, and they rarely reduce the principal owed. CCAs can generally affect three aspects of the debt: (1) creditors can re-age credit card accounts so that delinquency notations are eliminated on a consumer's credit report;

Table 10.2.
Creditors' DMP interest-rate concessions in 1999.[17]

Creditor	DMP interest rate	Previous interest rate
Citibank	No reduction	–
Bank One Corp./First USA	6.0%	11.0%
MBNA	May be lowered	15.90%
Discover	9.9%	17.99%
Chase Manhattan	6.0%	7.0%
Providian Financial Corp.	8.0%	12.0%
Capital One Financial Corp.	15.9%	19.8%
Fleet Boston Financial Corp.	9.5%	9.99%
Household Credit	No reduction	–
Wells Fargo Bank	10.0%	14.0%
Sears	21.0%	24.0%
American Express Optima	Reduced after DMP completion	21.7%

THE FRINGE SECTORS

(2) creditors can grant waivers or reduce fees, such as late-payment and over-the-credit-limit fees; and (3) creditors can reduce interest rates, although some CCIs, like Citibank, refuse to lower interest rates for those in credit counseling. Others, like Bank of America, lower interest rates to zero. In recent years, most CCIs have either raised their DMP interest rates or kept them above 9%.[18] In 1999 creditors offered the interest rate concessions shown in Table 10.2.

The failure rate (74%) of DMP enrollees is partly influenced by the concessions that creditors grant. If clients cannot significantly lower their monthly payments, they are more likely to drop out of a 60-month-long DMP. A 1999 Visa-funded survey of credit counseling agencies found that 34% of DMP dropouts believed they would have remained on the plan if creditors had waived or reduced additional interest or fees. Of the 42% of DMP dropouts who intended to file for bankruptcy, nearly half believed that it could have been avoided if their DMPs had contained more incentives.[19]

Some aggressive credit counseling agencies advertise that DMPs have no impact on a client's credit rating. One advertisement states: "The fact that we have creditor participation in our debt consolidation program indicates that our program will not negatively impact your credit. A debt consolidation plan enables you to reduce debt and have your payments recorded as prompt payments, both of which are excellent ways of improving your credit rating."[20] Despite this claim, a DMP is likely to have a negative impact on a consumer's credit rating. Specifically, participation in a DMP indicates financial difficulties, something that will influence the creditworthiness decisions made by potential lenders, landlords, or employers. Some creditors may also report that a consumer on a DMP is not paying as originally agreed, even though they accepted the reduced payment.[21]

THE IMPACT OF FAIR SHARE CUTS

Credit card issuers traditionally reimbursed CCAs at a rate of 15% for each DMP they initiated. However, by the late 1990s, CCIs began cutting their voluntary contributions, and by 2002, CCAs reported an average Fair

Table 10.3.
Fair Share creditor contributions.[22]

Credit card issuer	Fair Share contribution
Citibank	8%
Bank One Corp./First USA	0%–6.8%
MBNA	0%–10%
Chase Manhattan	6%–10%
Bank of America	0%–9%
Providian Financial Corp.	8%
Capital One Financial Corp.	9%
Fleet Boston Financial Corp.	6%–9%
Household Credit	3%–10%
Wells Fargo Bank	10%
Discover	7%
Sears	4%–10%
American Express	8%

Share contribution of only 8%, as shown in Table 10.3.[23] In addition, several CCIs pay no Fair Share contributions.

Cuts in Fair Share contributions are having a profound impact on CCAs. For one, some traditional agencies are eliminating services not directly funded by DMPs. Others charge for services that were formerly free. Still others are closing their doors, merging with other agencies, or operating at a deficit. To survive, some traditional CCAs have been forced to charge high service fees, to advertise aggressively, and to offer additional services, such as debt settlement. Other nonprofit CCAs are forced to operate like for-profit agencies by charging fees that cover their operating expenses and by denying services to those who can't afford to pay. Some traditional CCAs are turning to United Way and other charities to make up the shortfall.[24]

"Not-for-Profit" CCAs

Virtually every CCA has tax-exempt nonprofit status, making it eligible for benefits, such as sales tax, property tax, and income tax exemptions. An organization wanting to be classified as nonprofit must demonstrate that it

THE FRINGE SECTORS

engages primarily in activities involving charitable or educational purposes. Nonprofits must also operate in a "charitable manner" for the benefit of the public rather than the benefit of its officers. Many nonprofit CCAs don't meet this criterion.

The nonprofit designation is critical to CCAs for several reasons. First, the 1996 Credit Repair Organizations Act imposes strict regulations and disclosure requirements on credit counseling agencies while explicitly exempting nonprofits. Second, many state laws regulating debt-management services exempt nonprofit organizations. Other states restrict debt-management services to the nonprofit sector. Third, CCIs generally require agencies to have nonprofit status to receive Fair Share reimbursements. Finally, CCAs use their nonprofit status to convince debtors that they are charitable organizations, similar to the Boy Scouts, the Salvation Army, and other civic and social service agencies. Hijacking the nonprofit moniker to profit from vulnerable consumers is a cynical betrayal of public trust.

The Internal Revenue Service (IRS) states, "Federal and state regulators are concerned that some credit counseling organizations using questionable practices may seek tax-exempt status to avoid state and federal consumer protection laws."[25] This concern is a little too late, since the CCA industry is already inundated with "nonprofits" that are essentially for-profit businesses aggressively marketing DMPs and a wide range of "get-out-of-debt" services, such as debt-consolidation loans and debt-settlement services. Many of these agencies maintain close ties to for-profit corporations, deriving additional income from these relationships. Because of this, the nonprofit designation has become virtually meaningless.

Newer CCAs often pay their executives higher salaries than in the real nonprofit sector. In a *BusinessWeek* article, Christopher Schmitt, Heather Timmons, and John Cady wrote about the lavish salaries that are common among some newer CCAs. The former head of Genus, Bernard Dancel, drew a salary of $331,000 in 1996. In 2000 American Consumer Credit Counseling reported paying its president $462,000 plus $130,000 in benefits. Michael Hall, president of Credit Counselors of America, received more than $397,000 in 2002. In contrast, the average top salary nationwide for comparable nonprofits in 2002 was $134,000.[26] In short, many CCAs are clearly in violation of IRS rules governing nonprofit status, since they obviously exist to benefit company officers rather than to promote charitable or educational endeavors.

SCAM ARTISTS AND INDUSTRY ABUSES

Client funds lodged in a DMP make up a tempting pot of money for fringe economy operators. Some newer CCAs have been accused of failing to remit payments on time or of not remitting them at all. In other cases, CCAs have sent in payments on their own schedules (capturing as much of the float as possible), causing customers to be saddled with monthly late fees.

A *New York Times* article by Karen Alexander told the story of Robin Hardy, who owed $6,900 in credit card debt when she responded to an e-mail pitch about debt relief. Hardy signed a DMP contract in 2000 with Jubilee Financial Services, a California-based company that required her to pay 25% of her pre-tax salary for debt repayment. A year later, Hardy had paid Jubilee about $4,000, but none of her debt was reduced. Creditors were still hounding her, and Hardy's debt rose to $15,000. In the end, she was forced to file Chapter 7 bankruptcy.[27]

The challenge for shady CCAs is how to shift money from the nonprofit to the for-profit sector. Will Lund, director of the Maine Office of Consumer Credit Regulation, notes that it's common for a nonprofit CCA to be a shell for a for-profit company. Using their nonprofit status, these CCAs lease employees or farm out accounts to for-profit companies.[28]

AmeriDebt is a classic example of the inherent dangers in the loosely regulated CCA industry. In 2003 the Federal Trade Commission (FTC) filed a lawsuit in federal court charging that AmeriDebt—a nonprofit CCA—was engaging in deceptive practices. The FTC claimed that AmeriDebt fraudulently advertised that it charges no up-front fees, operates as a nonprofit, and educates consumers about managing their finances. After an investigation, the FTC found that AmeriDebt was a DMP mill that charged high up-front fees (the first month's DMP) without informing clients.[29] In 2003 AmeriDebt claimed it could better serve its

93,000 clients by suspending its television and radio advertising, downsizing, and refusing service to new clients. In early 2005 the FTC forced AmeriDebt to shut down entirely.

The AmeriDebt scandal points out the potential for abuse in the CCA industry. In September 1996 Andris Pukke pleaded guilty to a federal charge of defrauding consumers by falsely promising debt-consolidation loans. Pukke was sentenced to three years of probation and fined $5,000. In the same month, his wife, Pamela Shuster, started the nonprofit AmeriDebt (Pukke was the de facto co-founder) and served as its director until 1999. Across from AmeriDebt's headquarters was Pukke's new enterprise, DebtWorks (later called Ballenger Group), a for-profit corporation that processed DMPs for nine CCAs. DebtWorks charged CCAs $100 for each new client plus $25 a month to process their DMP accounts.[30]

Bernard Dancel started another "nonprofit" CCA, Genus Credit Management, in 1992. In 1996 Dancel launched Amerix, a for-profit corporation that processed accounts for CCAs, including Genus. The 1999 tax returns for Genus showed that $75 million of its $106 million in revenues went to Amerix.[31]

Massachusetts-based Cambridge Credit Counseling is one of the largest CCAs in the nation and another agency that has done substantial business with for-profit corporations in which its directors were involved. Until recently, Cambridge Credit's director was John Puccio, whose brother, Richard, was one of the other directors. In 1996 Richard Puccio was barred for five years by the Securities and Exchange Commission for scamming investors with hard-sell tactics. Even Puccio's lawyer conceded that his client's conduct was egregious.[32]

Cambridge Credit had done considerable business with other Puccio-owned or -controlled companies. For example, Cambridge Credit paid $940,000 in 2000 to a debt-referral company owned by John Puccio. In 1996 Cambridge Credit paid $1.3 million in principal and interest as part of a 50-year, 7% note to cover its $14.1 million purchase of two for-profit credit counseling firms started by the Puccios.[33] Besides Cambridge Credit, John Puccio was listed as president of Brighton Credit Management Corporation, Brighton Credit Corporation, and Debt Relief Clearinghouse. All are for-profit corporations.

In 2004 Massachusetts Attorney General Tom Reilly sued Cambridge Credit and its controlling directors and officers, John Puccio, Richard Puccio, Kurt Meyer, and Chris Viale, for funneling more than $60 million over two and one-half years to for-profit companies owned by insiders. According to Reilly, Cambridge Credit also misled thousands of consumers about the benefits of joining its credit counseling program.[34]

In 2000 the Puccio brothers received salaries of $312,000 each, well above the industry average for the nonprofit sector.[35] By 2003 their earnings had climbed to $624,000 each, and they also drew salaries and other benefits from affiliated for-profits totaling another $300,000 each.[36] The nonprofit CCA industry can be a lucrative venture for some "socially minded" entrepreneurs.

Debt Settlement

Rich Walsh, a forklift operator in Biloxi, Mississippi, had been struggling with $20,000 in high-interest credit card debt for almost five years. After paying the minimum all that time, Rich found that his balance was not dropping. In 2000 he got a solicitation call from a "nonprofit" CCA. Rich followed up, and after a 20-minute evaluation with a credit counselor he initiated a DMP with monthly payments of $520 for four years. Although Rich was told that the fees were voluntary, he soon found out that his contract required that he pay a full month's DMP as a setup fee. Since the CCA negotiated only with creditors who paid a Fair Share contribution, Rich was left with the responsibility for repaying two other unsecured loans.

Rich's take-home pay was $2,000 a month, which meant that the $520 was more than a quarter of his monthly post-tax income. The remaining $1,480 was supposed to cover his house payment, car loan, insurance, food, and other expenses. If Rich had received proper credit counseling, he would have been advised that paying this amount would be difficult, if not impossible. However, the credit counselor worked on commission, and DMPs were the source of his and the company's income. Rich dropped out after a year.

After he dropped out, his credit rating was worse than ever. He thought about bankruptcy but was afraid of the legal hassles and feared for his job if it became public. Rich eventually went to a debt-settlement agency, which promised to reduce his $20,000 debt to $10,000 for a 15% fee, or $3,000. His problem now was how to raise the $13,000, because the CCI demanded a cash settlement upfront. In the end, Rich was forced to refinance his home at an extremely high interest rate, and, in the process, he liquidated his home equity, increased his monthly costs, and destroyed his credit for at least seven years.

Some CCAs also offer debt-settlement (also known as debt-negotiation, debt-reduction, debt-workout, debt-relief, or third-party debt-negotiation) services. Debt settlement is designed to resolve a debt for less than the balance owed. Companies specializing in debt settlement claim they can reduce balances on unsecured loans from 20% to 80%, with the typical debt settled for less than 50 cents on the dollar.[37] Although debt-settlement agencies generally handle unsecured debt, some also claim to settle student loans, legal property claims, defaulted second mortgages, and home equity loans.[38]

Debt settlement works in the following manner: A debtor has cumulative credit card or other unsecured loans that he cannot repay. This debtor is often a poor candidate for a DMP, since he can't afford the high monthly payments. The debtor enlists the aid of a third-party debt specialist (an attorney or a debt-settlement agency), who negotiates with creditors to permanently settle the debt for a portion of the outstanding balance. In theory, lenders are agreeable to a settlement if they fear that a debtor may declare bankruptcy and they would receive little, if anything, through the bankruptcy courts. Creditors are also more likely to settle if the debtor has shown a repeated inability to pay, if he has no assets to protect, or when his income prohibits Chapter 13 reorganization. Table 10.4 shows an example of what a debt settlement might look like.[39]

Debt-settlement costs can vary, from hourly attorney fees to contingency-based agency fees. In particular, agency fees for debt settlement can range from a flat fee based on a percentage of the total settled debt to a percentage of the client's money saved through debt settlement. In the latter case, the more money an agency saves a client, the more it earns. Other agencies base their fees on the size and complexity of the debt, and costs can run from a few hundred dollars to more than $10,000. Settlement

Table 10.4.
A hypothetical debt settlement.

Credit card	Balance owed	Agreed-upon payment	Savings
Visa	$ 4,933.22	$ 2,158.00	$2,775.22 (56%)
First Card	$ 4,709.15	$ 2,060.00	$2,649.15 (56%)
Citibank	$ 5,791.54	$ 3,475.00	$2,316.54 (40%)
Universal Card	$10,724.49	$ 8,528.00	$2,196.49 (20%)
Total	$26,158.40	$16,221.00	$9,937.40 (38%)

agencies that base their fees on client savings normally appropriate 25%–33% of those savings. Fees are waived if an acceptable settlement cannot be reached, although some agencies require a fee for maintenance and setup. Debt-reduction fees can be paid up front, over time, or when a debt settlement is reached.[40]

Although some consumers might initially find debt reduction appealing, there are catches. Most creditors require that a debt settlement be paid in a lump sum. Even at 50 cents on the dollar, the settlement on a $15,000 debt costs $7,500 in cash plus agency fees. To compensate, some agencies allow debtors to build up their settlement funds through monthly deposits. Some creditors will also agree to a short payment plan (three to six months), especially when large amounts of credit card debt are involved. Other debt-reduction companies will stretch out the debt settlement for one to four years, although the interest on the balance builds during the negotiation and repayment period. The debtor can keep the settlement-fund account, or the debt-negotiation agency can hold it in escrow. Accounts are not negotiated all at once; instead, the settlement agency accumulates sufficient funds to pay off individual debts at the settlement discount. The process is repeated after each debt is paid off. The order of negotiation is generally based on the creditor closest to litigation.[41]

Debt settlements are reported almost as adversely as bankruptcy. While debt settlements are reported to credit bureaus as paid, they are noted on the credit report as a paid settlement rather than a paid-off balance. That notation stays on the credit report for 7–10 years.[42] On the other hand, by the time debtors opt for settlement, their credit is probably already ruined. Income taxes may also be owed on the debt settlement, because any write-off totaling $600 or more is considered income.

Debt Dispute and File Segregation

Numerous signs in low-income neighborhoods advertise: "Credit problems? No problem!" "We can erase your bad credit—100% guaranteed." Some of these advertisements are based on debt dispute. A consumer signs up for a debt-dispute service and orders a credit report from each of the three major credit reporting agencies (Experian, Equifax, and Trans-Union), costing about $12 each. The consumer then chooses the items she wants to dispute, and the debt-dispute service drafts letters on her behalf. In theory, the more items removed, the more the credit score will rise.

While debt-dispute companies make no guarantee that their letters will be successful, they do state that "statistically, participating clients have received, on average, 10.77 deletions by their third month, 15.15 deletions by the sixth month, and 25.8 deletions by the end of nine months."[43] What they fail to mention is that under federal law, credit reporting agencies can ignore disputes for a variety of reasons.

Debt dispute can be costly. One debt-dispute company charges $8 for each item a consumer wants expunged from his credit report. Other debt-dispute agencies charge an initial $75 fee plus $35 a month, or $420 a year.[44] Since some consumers with problematic credit have dozens of negative marks on their credit reports, trying to remove just 25 at $8 an item would cost $200.

Consumers filing for bankruptcy, or those who have exceptionally bad credit, may be targeted by companies offering file segregation. In this scheme, consumers are promised a chance to hide unfavorable credit information by establishing a new identity. For $60 to $70 the client is told to apply for an Employer Identification Number (EIN) from the IRS. EINs—which resemble Social Security numbers—are used by businesses to report financial information to the IRS and the Social Security Administration. After receiving the EIN, the customer is then instructed to use it instead of her Social Security number when applying for credit. File segregation is considered civil fraud in many states, and it is a federal crime to make false statements on a loan or credit application.[45]

Consumers now have some protection from being fleeced by credit-repair scams. The federal Credit Repair Organizations Act, originally passed in 1970 (and amended several times since then), states that it is a crime for credit-repair companies to make false claims about their services; charge customers before they complete the promised services; and perform any services until they have the customer's signature on a written contract and have completed a three-day waiting period.[46] To avoid prosecution, many scam artists have moved their operations offshore.

Reining In Runaway Consumer Credit Counseling Agencies

The credit counseling industry is a mixture of good intentions overshadowed by a growing number of unscrupulous entrepreneurs. Not surprisingly, the number of complaints lodged with the Better Business Bureau against credit counseling and debt-management companies jumped 78% in 2002.[47] According to the National Consumer Law Center, "The credit counseling industry has undergone an alarming transformation in the last decade. . . . Aggressive firms masquerading as 'non-profit organizations' are gouging consumers. Deceptive practices and outright scams are on the rise. More consumers are getting bad advice and access to fewer real counseling options. Meanwhile, most state and federal regulators appear to be asleep at the switch."[48]

Abuses by unethical consumer credit counseling agencies are in many ways the most reprehensible in the fringe economy. Drawn to the nonprofit status of CCAs, financially desperate consumers are led to believe they will find a safe harbor and an advocate who is sympathetic to their plight. Instead, they often encounter "credit counselors"—many of which are simply telemarketers who read from a prepared script—hungry for a commission and ready to sign them up for a DMP.[49]

Cynically, the "credit counselor" knows full well that most consumers will not be able to handle the high monthly DMP payments. For consumers with few resources and limited incomes, paying 9% instead of 17% on a $15,000 credit card debt will not make much difference. They simply can't afford to repay the debt, regardless of the interest rate. Since many of these clients are desperate to get their lives back on track, they are willing to undertake a sizeable DMP obligation, even though they're unsure how they will meet their other expenses. This explains why so many "non-

THE FRINGE SECTORS

profits" grab the money at the front end by requiring a "voluntary contribution" equal to a one-month DMP payment.

Credit counseling is a national rather than statewide industry, since CCAs routinely use telemarketing and the Internet to reach millions of consumers across the United States. Although some states license CCAs, it's essentially a futile task to regulate the thousand or more agencies that operate nationally. In many ways, the Internet has created a national economy for CCAs that supersedes state regulations.

Creditor funding through Fair Share reimbursements effectively makes CCAs "soft" debt collectors rather than charities. The Coalition for Responsible Credit Practices surmises that, based on two letters made public in 2004, the IRS may finally be willing to begin a crackdown of CCA "nonprofit," or charitable, tax-exempt status.[50] If that's the case, the long-term prospects for the less reputable elements of the CCA industry may be dicey.

As noted earlier, credit card companies reimburse CCAs only for a percentage of the debt recovered through DMPs, and that amount is declining. This trend is accelerating the demise of legitimate agencies and fostering the growth of DMP mills. Credit card issuers must reevaluate the policy of paying their Fair Share only through DMPs. In part, the CCI industry is responsible for the problem of credit card indebtedness by offering credit lines to financially marginal borrowers. Hence, CCIs should assume greater responsibility for solving this problem. Moreover, the current 8% Fair Share contribution is insufficient for reputable CCAs to offer much beyond DMPs. Either the Fair Share reimbursement should be raised, or additional monies should be allocated for supplemental services, such as credit counseling and consumer education.

CCIs should also be more cautious about which agencies receive Fair Share reimbursements. At this point, the credit counseling industry is incapable of policing itself, and CCIs must decide what constitutes a reputable CCA. One criterion should be whether the CCA offers a wide range of free or low-cost educational and counseling services.

Finding a reputable consumer credit counseling agency can be a daunting task. If you're looking for help, try calling your local United Way to see if it's funding any credit counseling agencies. You can also call the Better

Business Bureau and ask it for advice in locating an honest CCA in your area. If that doesn't work, you might try Jewish Family Services, Catholic Charities, or Lutheran Social Services. Getting a reference from a social worker who has worked with a particular CCA is also useful. It's hard to pick a good CCA from what's out there because the nonprofit designation doesn't always help.

The Impact of the New Bankruptcy Law

On April 20, 2005, at a time when many American families are financially overstretched and smarting from a shaky economy, President George W. Bush signed into law the harsh Bankruptcy Abuse Prevention and Consumer Protection Act of 2005. Among other things, this act—which intensifies the economic war on the poor and credit-challenged—will do the following:

- Impose a rigid means test by creating an inflexible formula to determine if a debtor can wipe away most of his debts in Chapter 7 bankruptcy. A debtor whose Chapter 7 case is challenged will have to litigate the issue, an expense that most won't be able to afford. Bankruptcy judges won't be able to waive the means test even if the debtor has experienced a circumstance such as a medical emergency. As many as 30,000–210,000 people—3.5%–20% of those who dissolve their debts in bankruptcy each year—will be disqualified from doing so under the legislation.

- Endanger child support by allowing more non-child-support debts to survive bankruptcy (for example, auto and credit card loans), thereby pitting custodial parents against creditors in a fight over the debtor's limited income.

- Allow the rich to continue to shelter their assets. The act will still permit some rich debtors in five states to declare bankruptcy and keep homes of unlimited value. The act also allows some rich debtors to continue to hide assets in complicated trust arrangements.

- Allow creditors to threaten debtors with costly litigation. Debtors who cannot afford to defend themselves in court will be coerced into giving up their legal rights.

- Make Chapter 13 plans to save homes and cars more difficult. Numerous provisions in the act (for example, requiring five-year instead of three-year repayment plans for many debtors) will increase the failure rate in Chapter 13. Two-thirds of those who enter Chapter 13 already fail to complete their plans.

- Make it easier for a residential landlord to evict a tenant who is in bankruptcy, even if the tenant has paid the back rent.

- Fail to deter reckless lending by credit card companies and other creditors. In fact, reckless and predatory lending could increase, since the act will make it harder for debtors to wipe away some debts, thereby lessening the financial risk for lenders and encouraging them to further lower their credit standards.[51]

The bankruptcy act will have a particularly destructive effect on African American and Latino homeowners, who are 500% more likely than white homeowners to find themselves in bankruptcy; laid-off workers, whose numbers are rising; and older Americans, who are now the fastest-growing age group in bankruptcy.[52]

The bankruptcy act will impact consumer credit counseling agencies. Among other things, it requires debtors in Chapter 7 and Chapter 13 bankruptcies to obtain pre- and post-bankruptcy credit counseling as a condition for eligibility and the discharge of debt. To satisfy bankruptcy courts, debtors will be required to file a certificate from an approved nonprofit credit counseling agency.[53] If the designation of an "approved nonprofit credit counseling agency" is based on the current CCA classification, debtors are likely to be subjected to deceptive practices and high costs.[54]

The act specifies that counseling services may be provided by telephone or over the Internet, the playground for deceptive practices. Although the bankruptcy act seeks to ensure that CCAs meet certain standards of quality,[55] no funds are authorized to investigate agencies, and their fees, practices, and success rates. The bankruptcy act may well lead to further growth in the discredited sector of the CCA industry. It could also foster the need for hundreds of new CCAs, many of them out to make a quick buck.

Although this chapter has investigated the scurrilous behavior of some CCAs, many, if not most, are aboveboard and look out for their clients' interests. Moreover, reputable CCAs have helped tens of thousands of debtors and are doing a remarkable job with few resources. It's unfortunate that the corrupt CCAs are besmirching the reputations of the many good ones.

PART

III

Looking Forward

Qui non improbat, aprobat.
(Who does not blame, approves.)

11

What Can Be Done to Control the Fringe Economy?

What was once a loose medley of family-owned pawnshops, used-car lots, neighborhood lenders, and small-time real estate speculators has evolved into an industry dominated by large corporations with revenues in the billions. Despite staking out different sectors of the fringe economy, all fringe businesses share a common goal: to extract the maximum amount of money possible from each customer.

Fringe businesses are connected to each other by their predatory relationship to consumers and communities. Specifically, in the fringe economy, customers make interest payments but receive no benefit from them. I know of no transaction in which consumers receive any interest compensation from a fringe economy corporation. Capital in the fringe economy flows in only one direction—from the pockets of consumers to industry coffers. Unlike mainstream financial institutions that allow customers to save money or invest, the fringe economy offers no investment services or financial products that lead to asset growth or increased household and community wealth. This feature alone marks the fringe economy as predatory. In the final analysis, the fringe economy preys upon society's most vulnerable members by charging them more for goods and financial services than it does the middle class, both in absolute dollars and relative to their income.[1]

Despite its often-deplorable business practices, the fringe sector addresses important financial needs not being met by government, traditional banks, or large retailers. Moreover, fringe economy businesses play an important role in the modern economy as some of the few lenders willing to serve poor and credit-challenged consumers who have been abandoned by mainstream financial institutions. In fact, given the dearth of economic alternatives, reliance on the fringe economy is unavoidable for many poor and credit-impaired consumers. Because of this, the fringe economy can't be simply outlawed without harming the very people who need it the most.

Consumer protection organizations, such as the U.S. Public Interest Research Group, Consumer Action, and the Consumer Federation of America, want the fringe economy more highly regulated, if not banned. But choking out this sector would only create an unfair advantage for mainstream financial institutions that would be likely to use this opportunity to

LOOKING FORWARD

institute their own brand of predatory economic activity.[2] Closing down the fringe economy would also lead to the resurgence of illegal loan-sharking, in much the same way as Prohibition led to bootlegging. Besides, the success rate of using legislation to curtail demand has been dismal at best. There's obviously no easy solution to the fringe economy.

Strategies for Reforming the Fringe Economy

Although reforming the fringe economy will be difficult, clearly its excesses must be curbed. Broad recommendations for reforming the fringe economy follow; they are based on an integrated four-pronged approach:

- Instituting more-robust federal and state regulation of the fringe economy

- Empowering consumers through advocacy and helping them achieve financial literacy

- Encouraging traditional banks and other mainstream financial institutions to serve low-income populations in a nonpredatory fashion

- Developing more and better-funded community-based financial institutions

Two caveats are necessary before we examine fringe economy reforms. First, space constraints dictate that the recommendations proposed here will be only skeletal. Readers wanting more detail about poverty and fringe economy reforms can find it in various books and in the research done by advocacy groups.[3]

Second, there are limits to reforming the fringe economy in the current economic context. For example, the growth of the alternative financial sector is a sign of serious structural economic and labor market problems, which include stagnant wages coupled with the rising prices of necessities (such as housing, health care, pharmaceuticals, and energy); a labor market increasingly marked by little employment security; a rising number of jobs that pay hourly wages without benefits; and the rapid creation of low-skilled and temporary jobs. The fringe economy is also tied to the increasing disparity of wealth in the United States. In 2004 the top 29,000 Americans had as much income as the bottom 96 million. In 1970 the bottom third of all Americans had more than ten times the income of the top 1/100 of 1%, or the top 29,000. By 2000 they were equal because the bottom third's income fell while the top group's income went through the roof.[4] In short, it's easy to blame the fringe economy for what is essentially an economic and labor market problem. Although labor market reforms are beyond the scope of this book, they must be part of any strategy to rein in the fringe economy. Lacking adequate wages, the poor will turn to easy sources of cash to make up the difference between their earnings and the real cost of living.

GOVERNMENTAL REGULATIONS AND THE FRINGE ECONOMY

The fringe economy is an untamed frontier with few rules other than the manic drive for profits. So far, both the states and the federal government have been unable to effectively control this runaway sector. According to Darrell McKigney, director of Consumers for Responsible Credit Solutions, "Across this country—and across the globe, for that matter— there have been countless news stories about the abuses of payday lending. While much attention has been raised, little appears to have been actually accomplished when it comes to enacting even the most basic regulation of this fast-growing industry. What attempts have been made have often been ineffective or even undermined by the very people assigned responsibility for watching out for vulnerable consumers."[5] What is true for payday lenders is also true for the fringe economy as a whole.

The fringe economy thrives in a milieu where government is increasingly abandoning its responsibility toward the poor through welfare reform and massive social welfare cuts, and where politically appointed federal and state regulators are more passionate about deregulation than about limiting the activities of rogue corporations. For the most part, financial misconduct toward the poor is either overlooked by regulators or justified by employing calculated euphemisms such as "subprime lending."[6] Apart from warnings and occasional high-profile sting operations, federal regulatory agencies have done little to promulgate new legislation that protects consumers from the rapaciousness of the fringe economy. Indeed, the

LOOKING FORWARD

unfettered growth of the fringe economy partly results from the relaxed attitudes of federal and state watchdog agencies.

This growth illustrates the chasm between government regulatory policies and modern economic realities. For example, despite its national reach, the fringe economy is often viewed as a state rather than federal problem. However, this approach disregards its national scope and the impact of technology.

Several factors help explain why states have been largely unsuccessful in regulating the fringe economy. For one, large, well-funded corporations are increasingly dominating the alternative financial sector. With billions in revenues, these publicly traded corporations—backed by large mainstream banks and financial houses—serve clients in almost all states. Second, Internet technology has created a virtual marketplace where consumers can get their financial needs met regardless of their location or the locations of financial vendors. Consequently, it is hard to enforce usury statutes in states where these laws are porous. Clearly, it's easier to regulate brick-and-mortar lenders than cables and fiber-optic phone lines. Third, while interest rates are theoretically regulated by state usury laws, fewer than half of all states cap credit card interest rates. Not surprisingly, most CCIs base their headquarters in states without usury laws or with few interest-rate restrictions, such as South Dakota, Delaware, Georgia, Illinois, Nebraska, Nevada, Rhode Island, and Utah.[7] Fourth, the fringe economy got a boost from the 1978 Supreme Court decision in *Marquette v. First Omaha Service Corp.*, which allowed national banks to charge the highest interest rate permitted in their home state to customers living anywhere in the United States. This ruling made it possible for fringe corporations to bypass state usury laws by partnering with out-of-state banks. When the Office of the Comptroller of the Currency (OCC) curtailed this rent-a-bank arrangement, fringe businesses partnered with in-state banks.

Even modest amounts of financial and legal manipulation can circumvent most state usury laws. In fact, fringe economy corporations employ an army of high-priced legal talent in their ongoing search to find and exploit federal and state banking loopholes. Besieged by industry pressure, state usury laws are becoming anachronistic as individual states try to compete against the juggernaut of the fringe sector. When states do enforce usury laws, it is often against indigenous fringe businesses rather than large nationally based corporations. This "feel-good" enforcement succeeds in driving out local fringe businesses while giving national corporations a larger share of the market.

Federal regulation of the fringe economy poses a knotty question: Which agency should be responsible for overseeing the fringe economy? Since the fringe sector involves credit and banking, it might logically fall within the purview of the OCC, "which charters, regulates, and supervises national banks to ensure a safe, sound, and competitive banking system that supports the citizens, communities, and economy of the United States." Alternatively, this charge could be lodged with the Federal Reserve Board, whose job is "supervising and regulating banking institutions to ensure the safety and soundness of the nation's banking and financial system and to protect the credit rights of consumers."[8] This responsibility could also go to the Federal Trade Commission (FTC), which has a long-standing interest in fringe economy activities. Or it could be assigned to the FDIC (Federal Deposit Insurance Corporation), which regulates state-chartered banks.

While the OCC, the Federal Reserve, the FDIC, and the FTC have expressed concerns about the fringe economy, their actions are neither coordinated nor consistent, thus allowing fringe economic activities to fall between the cracks. Instead of promulgating strict laws against predatory lending, government has relied on mountains of disclosure documents that virtually no one reads, least of all those in the heat of a major purchase. What is needed is one federal agency explicitly charged with overseeing and regulating the fringe economy. Operating under a federal mandate, this agency would coordinate the efforts of the various governmental agencies whose direct or indirect missions involve alternative financial services.

CONSUMER EDUCATION

Many government officials and consumer advocates believe that the poor need financial literacy training to ward off the siren call of the fringe economy. The assumption is that the economic behavior of the poor will change once they understand the real costs of their decisions. This may be true, since comprehensive consumer education is clearly necessary due to the low level of financial literacy in many sectors of the population. For example, when a group of adults were given a 14-question test of financial literacy, the average score was 42%. Eighty-two percent of high school seniors failed a 13-question quiz examining their knowledge of issues like interest rates, savings, loans, credit cards, and calculating net worth.[9]

One reason why millions of Americans don't use checking or savings accounts is that they lack knowledge about how banks and other financial institutions work. Many lower-income households with limited financial savvy struggle with even the most basic aspects of household budgeting. Consumers must be better educated about the types of institutions, products, and financial services that are available in order to more effectively manage their finances.

Economic transactions have become increasingly more complex as disclosure documents and loan terms have grown long, complicated, and tricky. For example, the initial terms brochure for Chase's Visa card is nine pages long. The paperwork for a home mortgage can fill up a small briefcase. The devil lies in the details of these transactions. Yet, despite the complexities of modern finance, financial literacy is not taught in most high schools or colleges. Nor are courses offered through most social service agencies. Consumers are simply left to their own devices.

Finance is full of minefields, and even good consumer education isn't enough to navigate them. If these minefields exist for creditworthy middle-class consumers, they are even more treacherous for the poor who rely on tricky subprime lending. To protect the poor and credit-challenged, free legal assistance should available to help borrowers understand contracts before they sign them. The poor should also have access to the services of an attorney, paralegal, or ombudsman on request in high-dollar contractual proceedings, such as mortgages and refinancing.

Consumer education can occur in many places. For instance, banks can use their branches in low-income neighborhoods as classrooms for financial education. The banks need not conduct financial education themselves—especially since they may not be the most objective institutions to deliver the information—but they can open their offices to community-based organizations and even to legitimate consumer credit counseling agencies. Public schools, community centers, supermarkets, churches, and other public settings would also make excellent classrooms for teaching financial literacy.

Government funding should be available for mass-based consumer education. This would be a sound investment, because victims of predatory lending can end up on the public dole, draining much more of the public's resources than would be spent in relatively inexpensive consumer education programs. Additionally, if legitimate consumer credit counseling agencies received government funding for consumer education, it would help wean them from their dependence on the Fair Share contributions of the credit card industry.

THE NEED FOR MAINSTREAM BANKS TO SERVE THE POOR

Mainstream financial institutions have several important reasons for reaching underbanked and unbanked populations. For instance, banks that develop relationships with low-income consumers by providing even rudimentary services could soon foster new full-service customers. Maintaining bank branches in poor areas, even if they weren't as profitable as those in higher-income ones, would facilitate better community relations and improve the banks' ratings under the Community Reinvestment Act (CRA).[10]

Transitioning into the financial mainstream would help low-income and credit-challenged consumers avoid carrying large amounts of cash (check-cashing outlets are notorious magnets for muggers and street predators) and would be likely to reduce their overall costs for financial transactions. Joining the economic mainstream would also help low-income households build savings and improve their credit scores, thereby lowering their costs for financial services and gaining them access to lower-cost sources of credit.

To help underbanked and unbanked households to make this transition, banks must develop low-cost and innovative financial products and services. For example, in low-income neighborhoods banks can open small branches that have flexible hours, including nights and weekends. (One of the attractions of the fringe economy is convenience: most check cashers and payday lenders are open on weekends and often late into the night. Some are even open 24 hours a day.) These banks can be freestanding or occupy a small space in a supermarket or other retail operation. In addition to normal banking products the branches should offer nontraditional services, including the following:

- Free check-cashing services for relatively secure payroll and government checks.

- The use of currently available ATM machines capable of check cashing. In addition, these machines could be used to dispense money orders (thereby freeing up tellers) and stamped envelopes.

- A basic savings account—that also provides money orders—designed to help customers accumulate savings. This savings account could be a modest financial buffer to provide "crisis cash" for an emergency. Even a small savings account would help discourage consumers from turning to expensive payday lenders.

- Secured deposit loans to customers whose credit histories make them ineligible for mainstream credit. These loans could be tied to a savings account, whereby the balance would be frozen until the loan was paid off. Interest would be moderate, since the loan would be secured by the funds lodged in the account. If these types of loans were offered, customers might have an increased incentive to regularly deposit money into a savings account. Plus, banks could charge considerably lower fees than payday lenders, yet still make a profit with relatively low risk.

- Debit cards, which are essentially stored-value cards in that they can't be overdrawn. These debit cards would be tied to a customer's checking or savings account and would serve multiple functions. For one, checks are quickly becoming an anachronism, because most bills can now be paid online using a debit or credit card. Second, many lower-income individuals have a history of writing bad checks or fear that they'll write them in the future. Because non-sufficient fund checks are costly for consumers in bounced-check fees, many low-income individuals steer away from checking accounts. These consumers need deposit accounts that can't be overdrawn but that offer an affordable and convenient way to pay bills, buy groceries, and so forth. Debit cards could also be tied to electronic bill-paying services through the use of Internet-access computers in local bank branches. Banks could either offer this service for free or charge a minimal user fee. There's little reason why consumers should pay extortionate bill-paying fees at check cashers, sometimes as much as $6.50 for a bill, for something they can do themselves with only a few keystrokes.

The creation of innovative products and financial services for low-income and credit-impaired populations can be a winning situation for both sides. It can also help discourage economically at-risk groups from relying on the fringe economy to meet their financial needs.

ALTERNATIVE CREDIT AND LENDING INSTITUTIONS

In 1976 the Grameen Bank Project, under the leadership of economist Muhammad Yunus, lent a total of $25 to 10 landless people in Jobra, Bangladesh. The Grameen project formally became a bank in 1983; by 2004 it was disbursing more than $37 million in loans each month to 4 million borrowers, 96% of them poor women. Since 1976 the Grameen Bank has loaned more than $4.57 billion. In fact, the growth of the bank was so stunning that in only 28 years it grew to 1,326 branches, had 12,903 staff members, and operated in 48,000 of Bangladesh's 68,000 villages. Using the concept of microcredit, the Grameen Bank offers collateral-free loans sometimes worth just a few U.S. dollars and rarely more than $200. The bank doesn't provide charity—it charges an annual interest rate of 20% and is strict about the terms. Ninety-eight percent of the loans are repaid.[11]

In 1987 former president Bill Clinton, then the governor of Arkansas, approached the Grameen Bank to ask for help in replicating the model in the United States. Although at one point there were 20 Grameen-style programs in the United States, the microcredit concept never really took hold on a large scale. Nevertheless, through one form or another, several groups continue to work toward developing the concept of microcredit in the United States, and it continues to represent a viable model for local community development.

The federal government is involved in helping the unbanked get banked. For example, the Federal Deposit Insurance Corporation (FDIC) created the Money Smart program, an educational outreach initiative aimed at increasing financial literacy. The U.S. Treasury's First Accounts program is designed to make basic financial institution accounts available to low- and moderate-income consumers. Under this program, the Treasury provides grants to eligible entities, such as credit unions, to offer low-cost savings and share-based draft/checking accounts to low- and moderate-income consumers. The program also stresses financial education. As a result of First Accounts, more than 50 credit unions in Texas, New York, California, Washington, Oregon, Idaho, Montana, and South Dakota have moved thousands of unbanked people into their first credit union accounts.

One example of the success of the First Accounts program is Chicago's ShoreBank, which has opened 912 new bank accounts, representing more than one quarter of all the program's accounts started in the country. ShoreBank is one of the nation's foremost community-development banks and focuses on improving the economic conditions in the neighborhoods it serves.

The idea of ShoreBank began in the late 1960s when four friends— Milton Davis, James Fletcher, Ronald Grzywinski, and Mary Houghton— began meeting at a neighborhood hangout near the University of Chicago to exchange ideas. ShoreBank grew out of those discussions and was started in 1973. The bank was so successful that by 1993 it had lent over $600 million to more than 13,000 businesses and individuals. ShoreBank grew so rapidly that by 2004 it had locations in Chicago, Detroit, Cleveland, Michigan, Oregon, Washington, and the District of Columbia. The bank has been profitable every year since 1975.[12]

Although credit unions are not community-development banks per se, they are member-owned alternatives to commercial banks and generally charge lower fees. For example, ATM users at commercial banks paid about $1.45 a transaction in 2000 compared with $1.21 for credit union members. The interest rate on credit cards averages three percentage points less than the rate charged by banks. Credit unions also typically charge only half of the credit card late fees and bounced-check charges assessed by mainstream banks. In 2001 the average bounced-check fee at commercial banks was $25; credit unions charged $3–$8 less. On average, credit unions pay customers nearly one percentage point more than other financial institutions in dividends on interest-bearing checking accounts, money market deposit accounts, and share certificates of deposit. A 2001 report by the U.S. Public Interest Research Group found that credit union customers using regular checking accounts could save $90 a year compared with what they'd pay at small community banks and $165 a year compared with what they'd pay at the 300 largest U.S. banks.[13]

Alternative financial institutions like credit unions can help millions of unbanked households that lack ties to mainstream banks. For example, the National Community Investment Fund (NCIF) launched a three-year project in 2002 to expand access to financial services for the unbanked. NCIF is a nonprofit organization that invests in community-based financial institutions targeted at underserved markets. With $750,000 from the Ford Foundation, the project, known as the Retail Financial Services Initiative, has provided seed capital to 12 credit unions and community banks that have a mission to build wealth and create economic opportunity for underserved communities. The hope is that the participating banks and credit unions can develop consumer lending models that will be adopted by the commercial banking sector.

Some credit unions have also developed affordable alternatives to high-cost payday loans. For example, they offer their members up to $300 at an 18% interest rate for up to six months, as long as the members have direct deposit. Other credit unions offer emergency loans with no fees or interest attached. Some credit unions have opened facilities in underserved neighborhoods and offer not only small unsecured loans, but also low-cost check cashing, affordable money orders, bill-paying services, bus tokens, and free credit counseling.

Credit unions have developed a variety of subprime lending programs to help consumers build credit and get into homes with as little as 1% down. For example, one credit union program offers subprime loans at 2%–4% above normal rates, depending on collateral. This subprime rate drops to the prime rate when the borrower makes 12 on-time payments. Another credit union offers its subprime borrowers several ways to reduce their interest rates. For example, attending one consumer credit counseling class reduces the rate by .5%; attending more than one class reduces

LOOKING FORWARD

the rate by 1%; depositing $15 a month into a savings account for a year reduces the rate by 0.5%; and for each year the debt does not increase, the rate drops 1%.

Alternatives Federal Credit Union, in Ithaca, New York, helped local residents eligible for the Earned Income Tax Credit to secure their tax refunds. In the process, it used the opportunity to build its membership. In 2003 low- and moderate-income families in the area were forgoing about $1 million in unclaimed benefits. The credit union allowed members to take out a tax anticipation note as a low-cost alternative to a fringe economy "rapid-refund" loan. For a $20 fee, customers are given a line of credit in the amount of their anticipated refund, at an annual interest rate of 11.5%. Once the IRS distributes the refund, a loan officer evaluates the member's credit history and decides if a line of credit should be extended.

Legacy Bank, in Milwaukee, Wisconsin, is another success story. In 1999 the bank started with $7.5 million in seed capital. By 2003 that had increased to $92 million. Most of Legacy's short-term growth has come from small-business loans, mortgages, and financing for housing preservation and development. However, Legacy also offers low- and moderate-income people with credit problems a second chance to join the financial mainstream through its Financial Liberty Accounts, which combine consumer education, outreach, and financial monitoring to make sure that customers stay solvent. Customers can open a Financial Liberty checking or savings account with as little as $10. There are no minimum balance requirements and no monthly service charges, and checking accounts come with free unlimited check writing and ATM transactions. In just two years, the bank has opened more than 700 new low-income accounts that it regards as sound long-term investments.

The Baltimore Social Security Administration (SSA) Federal Credit Union saw an opportunity to rebuild its dwindling membership. In 2002 it joined forces with Operation ReachOut Southwest, a coalition of churches and neighborhood organizations, and A&B Check Cashing, Maryland's leading fringe check-cashing company. Together they opened Our Money Place, a one-stop shop for financial services. At Our Money Place, A&B offers quick check cashing, money orders, and photocopies; an SSA Baltimore employee handles all non-cash bank transactions, including new accounts, deposits, transfers, and auto and small-business loans; and an Operation ReachOut staff member signs up customers for weekly financial-literacy classes. A&B Check Cashing accounted for 90% of the traffic at Our Money Place in the first few weeks. But as people enrolled in Operation ReachOut's financial-education classes, customers began to move into the banking mainstream and quit using Our Money Place.

Chicago's North Side Community Federal Credit Union managed to create a product to compete directly with expensive commercial payday lenders. In 2002 the credit union introduced the Payday Alternative Loan (PAL), which allows credit union members and nonmembers alike to borrow up to $500 for six months at an annual interest rate of 16.5%, considerably lower than the 400% charged by commercial payday lenders. With a $20,000 loan loss reserve fund from one of Chicago's largest banks, North Side can automatically approve loans for any community resident with an income of at least $1,000 per month, regardless of his or her credit history. PAL has proved almost too popular. More than half of the outstanding loans are to repeat borrowers, many of whom have taken out second loans before paying off their first. Because of this repeat business, North Side has decided to advance only two loans a year, worth a maximum of $500, per customer.[14]

One of the most striking examples of a successful alternative financial services institution is North Carolina's Self-Help credit union, which from 1980 to 2003 provided $3.5 billion in mortgage financing to 40,000 home buyers. Self-Help's mortgages are made possible by deposits from individuals, religious groups, businesses, and other institutions that have accounts with the credit union. It provides mortgages to home buyers unable to qualify for conventional financing by requiring down payments as low as 3%; the loans have low closing costs and no discount points. About 60% of Self-Help's mortgages go to minorities; almost 50% go to female-headed households; 72% go to low-income families; and 42% go to rural families. Besides mortgages, Self-Help also provides small-business, micro, and fixed-asset loans. Despite serving a high-risk population, Self-Help reports losses of less than 1%.[15]

Self-Help has been so successful that the Ford Foundation gave it $50 million (its largest grant ever) in 1998 to purchase secondary-market mort-

LOOKING FORWARD

gages. In 2003 Self-Help, Fannie Mae, the Ford Foundation, Bank of America, and Chevy Chase Bank gathered in Washington, DC, to announce the success of Self-Help's $2 billion Community Advantage home-loan secondary-market program. Fannie Mae's CEO also announced the corporation's commitment to continue the program through 2008 by purchasing another $2.5 billion in home loans from Self-Help.[16]

One of the more innovative concepts to emerge in the last few decades has been Individual Development Accounts (IDAs). Pioneered by Michael Sherraden, IDAs are based on the idea that the accumulation of assets plays a major role in allowing people to escape poverty. IDAs are leveraged, restricted investment accounts that help low- and moderate-income individuals build savings that can be used for education and training, for home ownership, and for developing home-based and micro-enterprise businesses. A typical IDA program matches the savings of the working poor at rates of 1:4 to 4:1 using external sources such as government, foundations, corporations, and religious institutions. IDA participants are also required to attend personal finance training. As of this writing, more than 400 communities, 300 banks and financial institutions, 47 states, and the federal government have begun to invest in IDAs for low-income people.[17]

The Future of the Fringe Economy

The fringe economy is undergoing a dramatic transformation: it is turning many fringe businesses into full-service centers that offer a wide range of financial products once available only from mainstream economic institutions. At the same time, the industry is being assaulted on multiple fronts, including consumer groups demanding more regulation, federal and state regulators concerned about industry practices, a public that stigmatizes it, and increased market saturation that is carving up the customer base. Perhaps most important, fringe businesses are under attack by some large mainstream financial institutions that want to claim their economic territory.

The profitability of the fringe sector is alluring in a marketplace where many retailers and financial institutions are desperately trying to increase their slim profit margins. As a result, mainstream banks, supermarkets, and convenience stores are entering the check-cashing business in droves, and some are charging less than fringe check cashers. Large auto dealers are competing with fringe used-car lots by advertising second- and third-chance financing. Mainstream banks are offering secured high-interest credit cards to consumers with checkered credit histories and providing payday loans disguised as bounced-check protection or cash advances. Traditional mortgage companies are writing subprime and even predatory loans directly or through their affiliates. Growing numbers of furniture and appliance stores are offering deferred-interest plans that resemble rent-to-own transactions. The success of the fringe economy has awakened corporate giants, and the industry is experiencing pressure from all sides.

While many of the business practices of fringe enterprises are reprehensible, traditional institutions may prove to be equally as ruthless in exploiting impoverished consumers. For one, mainstream economic institutions and well-known retailers are not sullied by the stigma associated with check cashers, payday lenders, and the like. They also have institutional credibility resulting from their size and reputation. In short, these businesses don't have to prove that their intentions are aboveboard. Second, as large institutions adopt more fringe economy practices, these are likely to be hidden within larger and more complex banking and retail policies. As fringe financial services become less visible, they will undergo less scrutiny by regulators.

Large financial and retail institutions also have enough political and economic clout that regulators and legislatures are hesitant to confront them. Despite the fringe economy trade groups' lobbying efforts, they obviously lack the political power of Bank of America, Citigroup, Wells Fargo, Sears, or Wal-Mart. Moreover, even when large, well-known corporations falter in their conduct, the public seems more concerned with their prices than with their behavior. For example, sales at Wal-Mart didn't decline in the wake of headlines accusing the company of paying low wages, having overnight lock-ins of workers, failing to promote significant numbers of women into management, using low-paid undocumented workers to clean stores, and making employees work off the clock (working hours they're not paid for).

America's fringe sector may well be the precursor to a larger and more aggressive international fringe economy. For instance, Cash America entered the European market in 1992 when it bought Harvey and Thompson, the London-based pawnbroker and market leader in the United Kingdom. Today, Harvey and Thompson offers pawn loans, check cashing, and cash advances. Cash America acquired Svensk Pantbelåning (like Harvey and Thompson, founded at the turn of the twentieth century) in the same year. Cash America sold its European holdings to the Rutland Fund in 2004.

Another example of the export of the fringe economy is EZCORP, the owner of EZ Pawn, which owns 29% of Albemarle & Bond Holdings, a leading pawn and financial-services company in the United Kingdom. First Cash, the third-largest U.S. pawnshop operator, is aggressively opening more storefronts in Mexico (it already owns 90), where demand is especially robust.

In 2004 a federal court judge in Chicago upheld a class-action racketeering lawsuit against H&R Block and Household International. The suit accuses the companies of conspiring to trick poor customers into taking out high-interest tax refund anticipation loans.[18] H&R Block operates in 11 countries.

Perhaps the most dramatic example of the export of America's fringe economy is the HSBC Group's $14 billion purchase of Household International (and its subsidiary Beneficial Finance) in 2003. Headquartered in London, HSBC is the world's second-largest bank (the 10th-largest U.S. commercial bank in terms of assets) and serves more than 90 million customers through an international network of 9,500 offices in 80 countries. Household International is a U.S.-based consumer finance company with 53 million customers and more than 1,300 branches in 45 states. It's also a predatory lender. In 2002 a $484 million settlement was reached between all 50 states and the District of Columbia with Household, which was accused of duping tens of thousands of low-income home buyers into loans that included unnecessary hidden costs. In 2003 another $100 million settlement was reached regarding Household's abusive mortgage lending practices. Officials alleged that Household violated state laws by misrepresenting loan terms and failing to disclose material information to borrowers.[19]

Ominously, HSBC plans to export Household's operations to Poland, China, Mexico, the United Kingdom, France, India, and Brazil, for starters.[20] Presumably, HSBC believes that predatory lending will not tarnish the reputations of the seven British lords and one baroness who sit on its 20-member board of directors. One can only imagine how the exploitative qualities of the fringe economy will develop in nations with even fewer regulatory safeguards than the United States.

■ ■ ■

For many of us, the economic injustices in the fringe economy are morally offensive. It's simply wrong and immoral to exploit vulnerable populations through seedy financial transactions. Nevertheless, the fringe economy is emblematic of the separation of morality from economics, and its very existence is evidence that free-market ideology supersedes morality. To effectively address the injustices of the fringe economy, reformers must reclaim the concept of morality and apply it to market economics. Legislative regulation alone will not eliminate the fringe economy. Nor will regulation reform a marketplace that has lost its moral center. Instead, the interests of economically powerless consumers can be protected only when American society applies basic moral principles to the marketplace.

Glossary

APR (annual percentage rate): Loan interest calculated on a yearly basis.

assisted refund transfer: A tax filer pays a tax preparer to act as an intermediary in processing a tax refund into his or her bank account.

balloon loan: A loan that includes a high payment (often the size of the original loan) at the end of the loan term.

buy here, pay here lots: Used-car lots providing in-house financing.

cash leasing: Loans based on transferring collateral to a lender and then leasing it back to the borrower. These loans are often used to bypass state usury laws.

charge-off: The designation by a creditor—usually a credit card issuer—that an account is severely in default and uncollectible.

check-cashing outlet (CCO): A business that charges a fee for cashing checks.

Child Tax Credit: A federal tax credit worth up to $1,000 per child. This credit can be deducted from taxes owed or received as a refund.

conforming loan: A mortgage loan that qualifies for sale to Fannie Mae or Freddie Mac. These mortgages have a maximum loan value and conform to other terms, such as a 20% down payment. Jumbo loans are mortgages that exceed the maximum loan limit or otherwise bypass conventional loan conditions.

consumer credit counseling agency (CCA): A nonprofit agency that specializes in consolidating consumer debt through debt-management plans.

consumer financial lender (CFL): A lender that serves consumers who have trouble securing conventional bank loans.

convenience checks: Blank checks, sent to cardholders, that function as cash advances.

collateral-based loan: A loan guaranteed by collateral such as a home or vehicle.

credit card issuer (CCI): A bank or other financial institution that offers consumer credit cards.

debt-management plan (DMP): A repayment plan offered by CCAs that involves consolidating unsecured debts by negotiating with creditors to lower interest rates and fees.

debt-to-asset ratio: A numerical rating measuring the percentage of assets financed by debt. This rating helps lenders determine the security of a loan.

default rate category: The highest interest-rate category used by a credit card issuer.

discount points: A percentage of the loan amount that lenders charge to reduce interest rates. In subprime lending, they are simply fees paid that do not lower interest costs.

Earned Income Tax Credit (EITC or EIC): A federal program that refunds income taxes to low-income wage earners. Low- and moderate-income tax filers receive a tax refund greater than what they paid in taxes.

e-file: The electronic filing of federal income taxes.

Electronic Return Originator: A tax preparer or tax preparation service authorized by the Internal Revenue Service (IRS) to transmit federal income tax returns electronically.

equity: The difference between what is owed on a mortgage and the current market value of the property.

Fair Share Plan: Credit card companies make a voluntary contribution to a CCA when they accept a debt-management plan.

Fannie Mae (Federal National Mortgage Association) and **Freddie Mac (Federal Home Loan Mortgage Corporation):** Privately held corporations operating under a federal charter in a similar manner. Lenders package a portfolio of mortgages and sell them to Fannie Mae or Freddie Mac, which then backs the notes with mortgage guarantees and resells them to investors.

Federal Deposit Insurance Corporation (FDIC): An independent agency created by Congress that supervises banks, insures deposits up to $100,000, and helps maintain the banking system.

float: The lag time between when a customer requests money and when the financial institution releases it.

Free File: A public-private partnership between the IRS and tax-software companies to provide free tax preparation and electronic filing services.

grace period: The time allowed a customer before interest is added to a credit card purchase.

Home Investment Partnerships Program (HOME): Part of the 1990 Cranston-Gonzalez National Affordable Housing Act, HOME is a federal block grant to state and local governments designed to create affordable housing for low-income households.

Home Mortgage Disclosure Act (HMDA): Provides loan data used to investigate whether a financial institution is serving the community or if discriminatory lending patterns exist.

insurance scoring: The use of credit scores to determine a consumer's insurability.

LMI: Low and moderate income.

loan flipping: Successive initiation of mortgage or refinancing loans that systematically depletes home equity.

loan packing: The inclusion of hidden charges, overcharges, and unnecessary items like credit life, disability, and unemployment insurance in a loan.

loan-to-value ratio (LTV): The relationship between the amount of a mortgage and the value of a property. In a common 80% LTV, the mortgage equals 80% of the home's value.

nonprofit: A state and federal designation for organizations engaged in charitable or educational endeavors.

Office of the Comptroller of the Currency (OCC): A federal agency that charters, regulates, and supervises national banks.

overdraft protection: A bank line of credit that allows customers to overdraw their checking accounts.

over-the-limit fee: A penalty fee paid by credit card holders when they exceed their credit limit.

payday loan: A high-interest loan (usually for 14–18 days) secured by a postdated check or an electronic debit authorization.

prime-rate loan: The interest rate that a bank charges its best, or "prime," customers.

private mortgage insurance (PMI): Protects the lender if a borrower defaults on a home mortgage. Borrowers must pay for this insurance if a mortgage is greater than 80% of the purchase price of a home.

redlining: The refusal of financial institutions to make loans in LMI or minority communities. Also refers to the refusal of insurance companies to write home or auto policies in these neighborhoods.

refund anticipation loan (RAL): A loan facilitated by a tax preparer based on the anticipated refund that a tax filer will receive.

rent-a-bank: The partnership between a fringe lender and an FDIC-insured bank for the purpose of funding high-interest consumer loans.

second- and third-chance financing: Loans, usually for autos, made to customers who don't qualify for standard financing. The interest on these loans is high and based on the severity of the borrower's credit problems.

secured credit card: A credit card using a credit line secured by cash collateral deposited into an interest-bearing account controlled by the credit card issuer.

stored-value credit card: A debit card (similar to a phone card) preloaded with funds.

subprime loan: A loan targeted at consumers with blemished or limited credit histories. Subprime loans carry a higher interest rate (and often more stringent terms) than prime loans.

teaser rate: The rate on a time-limited low- or no-interest credit card offer. Teaser rates often apply only to balance transfers rather than to new purchases.

unsecured loan: A loan based on the promise of the borrower to repay it. These loans are not secured by collateral.

usury laws: State laws that limit the amount of interest that can be charged on a loan.

variable interest rate: A rate that fluctuates based on economic indexes such as the prime rate.

Volunteer Income Tax Assistance Program (VITA): An IRS service that provides free federal tax return preparation for low- and moderate-income taxpayers.

Notes

PREFACE

1   Chi Chi Wu and Jean Ann Fox, *The High Cost of Quick Tax Money: Tax Preparation, "Instant Refund" Loans, and Check Cashing Fees Target the Working Poor* (Washington, DC: National Consumer Law Center and the Consumer Federation of America, January 2003).

2   Michael Hudson, ed., *Merchants of Misery* (Monroe, ME: Common Courage, 1996).

3   U.S. Department of Justice, "Captain, Soldier and Four Associates of the Colombo Organized Crime Family Charged with Racketeering, Loansharking, Illegal Gambling and Witness Tampering," press release, June 17, 2003.

4   Robert W. Snarr, *No Cash 'Til Payday: The Payday Lending Industry*, CCRA Compliance Center, Federal Reserve Bank of Philadelphia, First Quarter 2002.

CHAPTER 1: AMERICA'S CHANGING FRINGE ECONOMY

1   Fannie Mae Foundation, "Low-Income and Minority Families Rely Increasingly on High-Cost Financial Services," August 2, 2001, www.fanniemaefoundation.org.

2   General Electric Mortgage Insurance, "Homebuyer Resources," 2000, www.gehomebuyerprivileges.com/Homebuyer/glossary.asp.

3   Board of Governors of the Federal Reserve System, *Interagency Guidance on Subprime Lending*, March 1, 1999.

4   Federal Deposit Insurance Corporation, *FDIC Federal Register Citations*, 2002.

5   Fannie Mae Foundation, *Low-Income and Minority Families Rely Increasingly on High-Cost Financial Services*, August 2, 2001.

6   Subprime loans are targeted toward borrowers with blemished or limited credit histories. Compared with prime-rate loans—given to the most creditworthy—subprime loans carry a higher interest rate and often include more stringent loan terms.

7   Community Financial Services Association of America, "The Payday Advance Service," 2003, www.cfsa.net/genfo/ageninf.html.

8   Sougata Mukherjee, "Consumer Group Pushes for Regulation of Check Cashing Industry," *Houston Business Journal*, August 29, 1997: 18; and Financial Service Centers of America, *Quick Facts about FiSCA*.

9   ACE Cash Express, 2004 Annual Report. Although this number may be inflated, since many check cashers also offer payday loans, it doesn't include rent-to-own stores, fringe economy used-car lots, tax refund lenders, auto title pawns, and pawnshops. Adding those sectors would likely double that number to at least 50,000.

10 ACE Cash Express, Inc., 2004 Annual Report.

11 Hoover's Online, Advance America, Cash Advance Centers, Inc., www.hoovers.com.

12 Advance America, Cash Advance Centers, 2004, http://aea.client.shareholder.com/ReleaseDetail.cfm?ReleaseID=147042.

13 NASDAQ Stock Report for Cash America, EZ Pawn, and First Cash, November 28, 2003.

14 APRO (Association of Progressive Rental Organizations), RTO Industry Statistics, 2003.

15 Hoover's Online, 2004, www.hoovers.com.

16 Alan Berube, Anne Kim, Benjamin Forman, and Megan Burns, *The Price of Paying Taxes: How Tax Preparation and Refund Loan Fees Erode the Benefits of the EITC* (Washington, DC: Brookings Institution, May 2002).

17 See Consumer Federation of America, *Predatory Lending*, 2002; and H&R Block, "Company Fast Facts," *H&R Block By-The-Numbers*, 2003.

18 Governor Edward M. Gramlich, remarks made at the Federal Reserve Bank of Philadelphia, December 6, 2000.

19 David Tice, "The New Telecom: The Mortgage Industry Will Be the Next to See a Bust, and the Impact Will Be Dramatic," *On Wall Street*, January 1, 2005.

20 ACE Cash Express, 2004 Annual Report.

21 Ace Cash Express, Retail Financial Services, *The Evolving Needs of U.S. Consumers: A Status Report from ACE Cash Express*, December 2004.

22 Forbes.com, "People Tracker, 2004," www.forbes.com/peopletracker.

23 This was calculated at a share price of $21.80, the average stock price in late 2004.

24 See South Carolina Business Hall of Fame, 1999; Advance America, Cash Advance, Securities and Exchange Form, 13D; and Forbes.com "People-Tracker."

25 See ACE Cash Express, Inc., Annual Report on Form 10-K for the Fiscal Year Ended June 30, 2000 (filed with the U.S. Securities and Exchange Commission).

26 Mary Kane, "Fringe Banks Profit from Customers without Banks," in Michael Hudson, ed., *The Merchants of Misery* (Monroe, ME: Common Courage Press, 1996).

27 John P. Caskey, "Bringing Unbanked Households into the Banking System," *Capitol Xchange* (Washington, DC: Brookings Institution, January 2002).

28 Ibid.

29 Rob Schneider, "Big Banks' Check-Cashing Fees Target Low-Income Consumers," *Times Guardian*, January 23, 2002.

30 ACE Cash Express, 2004 Annual Report.

31 Michael Hudson, "Citigroup, Wall Street, and the Fleecing of the South," *Southern Exposure* 31, no. 2 (Summer 2003): 3-4.

32 Helen Stock, Susan Decker, Michael Nol, George Stein, Scott Silvestri, "Citigroup to Pay $240 Million to Settle Lending Charges," *Bloomberg News*, September 19, 2002: 3.

33 Jonathan Stempel, "Citigroup 4th-Quarter Profit Nearly Doubles," *Forbes*, January 20, 2004.

34 Ibid.

35 "State Sues Wells Fargo Financial," *Silicon Valley/San Jose Business Journal*, January 10, 2003.

36 John DiStefano, "Bank to Refund Fees in 'Predatory-lending' Cases," *Philadelphia Inquirer*, April 26, 2002: 19.

37 Joseph Coleman, testimony before the Federal Reserve Bank of Boston opposing the acquisition of Fleet Boston by Bank of America, FiSCA.

CHAPTER 2: WHY THE FRINGE ECONOMY IS GROWING

1 Dick Mendel, "Double Jeopardy," *Advocasey* (Annie E. Casey Foundation, Baltimore, MD) 7, no. 1 (Winter 2005): 10.

2 Federal Reserve Board, "The Unbanked: Who Are They?" *Capital Connections*, 2001.

3 Arthur Kennickell, Martha Starr-McCluer, and Brian J. Surette, "Recent Changes in U.S. Family Finances," *Federal Reserve Bulletin*, January 2000: 1-29.

4 Io Data Corporation, 2002.

5 Representative George Miller, *Everyday Low Wages: The Hidden Price We Pay for Wal-Mart*, Committee on Education and the Workforce, U.S. House of Representatives, February 16, 2004.

6 Ibid.

7 Ibid.

8 David Shipler, *The Working Poor: Invisible in America* (New York: Knopf, 2004), 1.

9 Beth Shulman, *The Betrayal of Work* (New York: The New Press, 2003).

10 Lawrence Mishel, Jared Bernstein, and John Schmitt, *The State of Working America 2000 /2001* (Ithaca, NY: Cornell University Press, 2001).

11 Jared Bernstein, *Economic Growth Not Reaching Middle- and Lower-Wage Earners*, Economic Policy Institute, Washington, DC, January 28, 2004.

12 "House Passes Minimum Wage Increase of 90 Cents," *Houston Chronicle*, March 30, 1996.

13 The Bureau of Labor Statistics, Table 44, "Household Data and Averages, Wage and Salary Workers Paid Hourly Rates with Earnings at or Below Prevailing Minimum Wage by Selected Characteristics," 2001.

14 U.S. Census Bureau, *Poverty Thresholds*, January 30, 2004.

15 Barbara Ehrenreich, *Nickel and Dimed* (New York: Owl Books, 2001), 213.

16 See American Friends Service Committee, *Five Years and Counting*, Philadelphia, June 5, 2001; and Wendell Primus, Lynette Rawlings, Kathy Larin, and Kathryn Porter, *The Initial Impacts of Welfare Reform on the Incomes of Single-Mother Families*, Center on Budget and Policy Priorities, Washington, DC, 1999.

17 Jack Tweedie, Dana Reichert, and Matthew O'Connor, *Tracking Recipients After They Leave Welfare*, National Conference of State Legislatures, August 1999.

18 Howard Jacob Karger and David Stoesz, *American Social Welfare Policy*, 4th ed. (Boston: Allyn & Bacon, 2002).

19 Io Data Corporation, Salt Lake City, September 2002.

20 Nancy Rytina, *Estimates of the Legal Permanent Resident Population and Population Eligible to Naturalize in 2002*, U.S. Department of Homeland Security, Washington, DC, May 2004.

21 Pia Orrenius, "U.S. Immigration and Economic Growth: Putting Policy on Hold," Federal Reserve Bank of Dallas, *Southwest Economy* 6, November/December 2003: 3.

22 Ibid.

23 Ibid.

24 Jeffrey Passel, Randy Capps, and Michael Fix, *Undocumented Immigrants: Facts and Figures*, Urban Institute Immigration Studies Program, Washington, DC, January 12, 2004.

25 Patty Reinert, "Federal Welfare Plan Hits Legal Immigrants," *Houston Chronicle*, August 2, 1996.

26 National Telecommunications and Information Agency, "A Nation Online: How Americans Are Expanding Their Use of the Internet," U.S. Department of Commerce, February 2002, www.ntia.doc.gov/ntiahome/dn/index.html.

27 Forrester Research, 2004.

28 Kenneth Cline, *The Friction Factor*, Banking Strategies, 2003.

CHAPTER 3: DEBT AND THE FUNCTIONALLY POOR MIDDLE CLASS

1 Mary Pattillo-McCoy, *Black Picket Fences: Privilege and Peril Among the Black Middle Class* (Chicago, IL: University of Chicago Press, 1999).

2 Andrew Cassel, "Black Middle Class Continues to Grow, but Gaps Remain," *Philadelphia Inquirer*, July 12, 2004; Frank D. Bean, Stephen J. Trejo, Randy Crapps, and Michael Tyler, *The Latino Middle Class: Myth, Reality and Potential*, the Tomás Rivera Policy Institute, University of Southern California, April 2001.

3 Carmen DeNavas-Walt, Bernadette Proctor, and Robert Mills, U.S. Census Bureau, *Current Population Reports, Income, Poverty, and Health Insurance Coverage in the United States: 2003*, Washington, DC, August 26, 2004.

4 There is occasional confusion between the terms "deficit" and "debt." Government refers to the deficit as the yearly shortfall, while debt is the cumulative amount of money owed.

5 Nicholas von Hoffman, "America's Debt Crisis Starts in Corporate Suites," *The New York Observer*, December 17, 2001.

6 Louis Uchitelle, "Families, Deep in Debt, Facing Pain of Growing Interest Rates," *The New York Times*, June 28, 2004.

7 Steve Lohr, "Maybe It's Not All Your Fault," *The New York Times*, December 5, 2004.

8 Ibid.

9 Teresa Murray, "Experts Warn Against Milking Home Equity to Extend Debt," *Star Tribune*, November 4, 2000.

10 Noel Paul, "Culture of Consumption," *The Christian Science Monitor*, June 12, 2003.

11 Joint Center for Housing Studies of Harvard University, *The State of the Nation's Housing*, Graduate School of Design, John F. Kennedy School of Government, Harvard University, Cambridge, MA, 2003.

12 Source: U.S. Census Bureau, Population Reports, 1990-2002.

13 Coalition for Responsible Credit Practices, "The Crisis of Growing Consumer Debt," 2004, www.responsiblecreditpractices.com/issues/growing.php.

14 Joint Center for Housing Studies of Harvard University, 2003.

15 Coalition for Responsible Credit Practices, "The Crisis of Growing Consumer Debt."

16 Elizabeth Warren and Amelia Warren Tyagi, *The Two-Income Trap* (New York: Basic Books, 2003).

17 Tom Feran, "Two Incomes Don't Add Up," *Houston Chronicle*, September 22, 2003.

18 Runzheimer International, "Runzheimer Analyzes Daycare Costs Nationwide," January 20, 2004, www.runzheimer.com /corpc/news/scripts/012004.asp.

19 Steven Harris, "Taking Aim at Male/Female Wage Gap," *The Christian Science Monitor*, January 31, 2000.

20 Eileen Applebaum, Annette Bernhardt, and Richard Murnane, eds., *Low-Wage America* (New York: Russell Sage Foundation, 2003).

21 Juliet B. Schor, *The Overspent American* (New York: Perennial, 1999).

22 John de Graaf, David Wann, and Thomas Naylor, *Affluenza* (San Francisco: Berrett-Koehler, 2002).

23 Warren and Tyagi, *The Two-Income Trap*.

24 Stephanie Armour and Julie Appleby, "As Health Care Costs Rise, Workers Shoulder Burden," *USA Today*, October 21, 2003; College Board, *College Costs: Keep Rising Prices in Perspective, 2003-2004*; and Robert Hartwig, *What's Behind the Rising Cost of Auto and Homeowners Insurance?* Insurance Information Institute, 2003.

25 American Bankruptcy Institute, www.abiworld.org.

26 Teresa Sullivan, Elizabeth Warren, and Jay Lawrence Westbrook, *The Fragile Middle Class* (New Haven, CT: Yale University Press, 2001).

27 Teresa Sullivan, Elizabeth Warren, and Jay Lawrence Westbrook, *As We Forgive Our Debtors* (New York: Oxford University Press, 1989).

28 Warren and Tyagi, *The Two-Income Trap*.

29 Juliet Schor, *Born to Buy* (New York: Charles Scribner's Sons, 2004).

CHAPTER 4: THE CREDIT CARD INDUSTRY

1 Robert Manning, *Credit Card Nation* (New York: Basic Books, 2000).

2 Randy Martin, *The Financialization of Daily Life* (Philadelphia: Temple University Press, 2002).

3 Lloyd Klein, *It's in the Cards* (Westport, CT: Praeger Publishers, 1999).

4   CNN, "Late Payments at 5-Year High, Past-Due Credit Card Debt Highest Since '97," April 29, 2002.

5   Manning, *Credit Card Nation;* the Motley Fool, "Industry Secrets, Scary Debt Stats," 2003, www.motleyfool.com; CNN Money, "Credit Card Noose Still Tight," March 14, 2003, http://money.cnn.com/2003/03/13/pf/banking/creditcard_survey/; NFO WorldGroup, "Younger Consumers Paying the Piper for Excessive Credit Card Spending," November 21, 2002; and Cardweb.com, "Foggy 2003," www.cardweb.com/cardtrak/pastissues/jan03.html.

6   Coalition for Responsible Credit Practices, *The Crisis of Growing Consumer Debt.*

7   Source: Fair Isaac Corporation, 2004.

8   Source: Fair Isaac Corporation, 2004.

9   Consumerinfo.com, "Credit Scoring Made Simple," 2003, www.consumerinfo.com/credit-scoring-simple.asp.

10 Merchant Bankcard Network, 2003.

11 U.S. Court of Appeals, Second Circuit, United States v. Visa U.S.A., Inc., Visa International Corp., and MasterCard International, Inc., Washington, DC, September 17, 2003.

12 Manning, *Credit Card Nation.*

13 The London Interbank Offered Rate Index (LIBOR) is an average of the interest rates that major international banks charge each other to borrow U.S. dollars in the London money market.

14 Patrick McGeehan, "The Plastic Trap: Soaring Interest Compounds Credit Card Pain for Millions," *The New York Times,* November 21, 2004.

15 Consumer Action, *Annual Credit Card Survey,* San Francisco, CA, March 2003.

16 Ibid.

17 Ibid.

18 Consumers for Responsible Credit Solutions, "A New Report Issued by Consumers for Responsible Credit Solutions Carries Strong Warnings for Consumers Seeking Credit Counseling Services," July 12, 2004, www.responsiblecredit.com/releases/071204.php.

19 McGeehan, "The Plastic Trap."

20 Consumer Action, *Annual Credit Card Survey,* 2003.

21 Kathleen Day and Caroline Mayer, "Credit Card Penalties, Fees Bury Debtors," *The Washington Post,* March 6, 2005.

22 Quoted in ibid.

23 Ibid.

24 Candace Heckman, "Lawmakers Mull Ban on Credit Card 'Convenience Checks,'" *Seattle Post-Intelligencer Reporter,* February 12, 2003.

25 Quoted in Bonnie Rubin, "College Students Charge Right into Valley of Debt," *Chicago Tribune,* August 16, 1998.

26 U.S. Public Interest Research Group, *The Campus Credit Card Trap,* Washington, DC, September 17, 1998.

27 Coalition for Responsible Credit Practices, "The Crisis of Growing Consumer Debt," 2004, www.responsiblecreditpractices.com/issues/growing.php.

28 RAM Research Group, "October Top News," October 2003, www.ramresearch .com/press.amp (accessed January 4, 2003).

29 Joanna Stavins, "Credit Card Borrowing, Delinquency and Personal Bankruptcy," *Questia*, September 2000.

30 First Premier Bank of South Dakota, "Rates, Fees, Costs and Limitations," 2003.

31 Cardweb, www.cardweb.com (accessed 2003).

32 Wired Plastic, www.wiredplastic.com (accessed 2003).

33 Center for Financial Services Innovation, *Stored Value Cards: A Scan of Current Trends and Future Opportunities*, Research Series, Chicago, IL, July 2004.

34 FSV Payment System, Houston, TX, 2004.

35 Neil Carlson, "Five New Ways to Serve America's Unbanked," *Ford Foundation Report*, New York, Fall 2004.

36 Center for Financial Services Innovation.

37 Ibid.

38 Four Oaks Bank & Trust Company, Elite Plus Cash Card, 2003.

39 CJAD (Canadian Radio), "American Consumer Debt More Than Doubles in 10 Years as Savings Slide," January 5, 2004.

40 Ibid.

41 Lucy Lazarony, "Credit Card Companies Sidestep Usury Laws," *Bankrate*, March 20, 2002.

42 Consumer Action, *Annual Credit Card Survey*, 2003.

CHAPTER 5: STOREFRONT LOANS: PAWNSHOPS, PAYDAY LOANS, AND TAX REFUND LENDERS

1 John Caskey, *Fringe Banking* (New York: Russell Sage Foundation, 1994), 5-9.

2 Ibid.

3 Fannie Mae Foundation, *Low-Income and Minority Families Rely Increasingly on High-Cost Financial Services*, August 2, 2001; and Michael Hudson, ed., *Merchants of Misery* (Monroe, ME: Common Courage Press); Caskey, *Fringe Banking*, 36; and CompuPawn Industry Information, 1998.

4 Empire Loan, "About Pawnbroking," www.empireloan.com.

5 John Caskey, *Lower Income American, Higher Cost Financial Services* (Madison, WI: Filene Research Institute, 1997).

6 American Financial Services Association, *Pawnshops Struggle*, 2002.

7 The claim that 70% of borrowers retrieve their pawns is based on industry statistics. From interviews and other anecdotal data I suspect that number is much lower.

8 NASDAQ, *Report for Cash America, EZ Pawn, and First Cash*, November 28, 2003.

9 Gregory Elliehausen and Edward Lawrence, *Payday Advance Credit in America*, Georgetown University Credit Research Center, Washington, DC, April 2001.

10 Center for Responsible Lending and Charles Gerena, *Need Quick Cash?* Issue Archives, Federal Reserve Bank of Richmond, Summer 2002.

11 Neil F. Carlson, "Five New Ways to Serve America's Unbanked," *Ford Foundation Report*, Fall 2004.

12 Robert W. Snarr, *No Cash 'til Payday: The Payday Lending Industry*, CCRA Compliance Center, Federal Reserve Bank of Philadelphia, 1st Quarter 2002.

13 Keith Ernst, John Farris, and Uriah King, *Quantifying the Economic Cost of Predatory Payday Lending*, Center for Responsible Lending, Wilmington, NC, February 24, 2004.

14 Jean Ann Fox and Edmund Mierzwinski, *Rent-a-Bank Payday Lending*, Consumer Federation of America, Washington, DC, November 2001.

15 Michael Bush, "3 'Fringe Financiers' Turn a Profit on Poverty," *Moneycentral*, 2003.

16 Ernst, Farris, and King, *Quantifying the Economic Cost of Predatory Payday Lending*.

17 Center for Responsible Lending, *Payday Lending Basics*, 2004.

18 Trihouse Enterprises, Las Vegas, Nevada.

19 Fox and Mierzwinski, *Rent-a-Bank Payday Lending*.

20 Ibid.

21 Nolo Press, the 'Lectric Law Library, 1995, www.lectlaw.com.

22 Quik Payday, APR disclosure, 2002, www.quikpayday.com.

23 Center for Responsible Lending, *Payday Lending Basics*.

24 Cited in Ernst, Farris, and King, *Quantifying the Economic Cost of Predatory Payday Lending*.

25 Check 'n Go, www.checkngo.com/questions.asp.

26 Amanda Sapir and Karen Uhlich, *Pay Day Lending in Pima County, Arizona*, Southwest Center for Economic Integrity, Tucson, AZ, December 2003.

27 Ernst, Farris, and King, *Quantifying the Economic Cost of Predatory Payday Lending*.

28 Sapir and Uhlich, *Pay Day Lending in Pima County, Arizona*.

29 Center for Responsible Lending, *Payday Lending Basics*.

30 Elliehausen and Lawrence, *Payday Advance Credit in America*.

31 Community Financial Services Association of America (CFSAA).

32 Tim Schooley, "Neighborhood Groups Oppose Cash Advance Stores," *Pittsburgh Business Times*, May 7, 2004.

33 Madis Senner, "Financial Deregulation-Promoting Discrimination and the Rise of Fringe Banking," Jubilee Initiative, www.jubileeinitiative.org/RiggedDeregulation.htm, July 2001.

34 James Carr, Lopa Kolluri, and Jennie Schuetz, *Financial Services in Distressed Communities*, Washington, DC, Fannie Mae Foundation, 2001.

35 Fast Cash Leasing, 2003, www.fastcashleasing.com.

36 Fox and Mierzwinski, *Rent-a-Bank Payday Lending*.

37 Alex Berenson, "Banks Are Reaping Billions from Stealth Overdraft Charges," *The New York Times*, January 23, 2003.

38 Lucy Lazarony, "States Act Against Bank Policies That Create Extra Bounced Checks," *Bankrate*, January 31, 2002.

39 Chi Chi Wu and Jean Ann Fox, *Consumer Groups Urge Federal Reserve Board to Stop Abusive Bank Overdraft Charges*, National Consumer Law Center, January 28, 2003.

40 David Shipler, *The Working Poor* (New York: Alfred A. Knopf, 2004), 8-9.

41 Internal Revenue Service, *Earned Income Tax Credit*, 2003.

42 Alan Berube, Anne Kim, Benjamin Forman, and Megan Burns, *The Price of Paying Taxes*, Center on Urban and Metropolitan Policy, Brookings Institution, Washington, DC, 2002.

43 Ibid.

44 Ibid.

45 Chi Chi Wu and Jean Ann Fox, *The High Cost of Quick Tax Money*, National Consumer Law Center, Washington, DC, January 2003.

46 Quoted in Berube, et al., *The Price of Paying Taxes*.

47 Wu and Fox, *The High Cost of Quick Tax Money*.

48 New York City Department of Consumer Affairs, *More Than $4 Million in Restitution, Fines and EITC Outreach Funds from H&R Block in Largest Settlement in Agency's History*, December 12, 2002; "Block Faces Another Shareholder Class Action," *The Business Journal*, December 16, 2002.

49 Wu and Fox, *The High Cost of Quick Tax Money*.

50 Berube, et al., *The Price of Paying Taxes*.

51 Source: Wu and Fox, *The High Cost of Quick Tax Money*.

52 This was based on 40% of low-income tax filers using a check-cashing service.

53 H&R Block, *Company Fast Facts: H&R Block By-The-Numbers*, 2003.

54 Jackson Hewitt, *About Us*, 2003.

55 Some of these suggestions are taken from the Center for Responsible Lending, www.responsiblelending.org/pdfs/2b002-payday.pdf.

56 Internal Revenue Service, "Free File, 2003," www.irs.gov/efile/article/0,,id=118986 ,00.html.

57 SmartPros Editorial Staff, "H&R Block Under Fire-Again," March 31, 2003, SmartPros, http://finance.pro2net.com/x37631.xml; Consumer Federation of America, Consumers Union, Electronic Privacy Information Center, National Consumer Law Center, and U.S. PIRG, letter to Pamela Olson, U.S. Treasury, "Re: Subprime Mortgage Marketing through IRS Free File," March 24, 2003.

Chapter 6: Alternative Services: Check Cashers, the Rent-to-Own Industry, and Telecommunications

1 While most large check cashers also offer payday loans, the two have been separated here because of their different functions—check cashing is not a loan service.

2 Anne Kim, "The Unbanked and the Alternative Financial Sector" (presented at the Changing Financial Markets and Community Development Conference, Federal

Reserve Bank of Chicago, April 5, 2001); and Financial Service Centers of America (FiSCA), *Quick Facts About FiSCA*, 2000.

3 Financial Service Centers of America (FiSCA), 2000.

4 Sougata Mukherjee, "Consumer Group Pushes for Regulation of Check Cashing Industry," *Houston Business Journal*, August 29, 1997.

5 Kim, "The Unbanked and the Alternative Financial Sector."

6 ACE Cash Express Inc., SEC Annual Report on Form 10-K for FY 2000; and Dollar Financial Group, SEC Annual Report on Form 10-K for FY 2000.

7 ACE Cash Express, "ACE Cash Express Extends Money Order Relationship with Travelers Express, ACE to Receive $3.4 Million in Signing and Annual Bonuses," October 20, 2003.

8 Ibid.

9 Kim, "The Unbanked and the Alternative Financial Sector."

10 Cash America International, 2003, www.cashamerica.com.

11 "A New Twist on Bank Fees," *Consumer Reports* 2, February 2002: 35.

12 Michael Brush, "3 Fringe Financiers Turn a Profit on Poverty, 2003," MSN Money, 2003, http://moneycentral.msn.com/content/P57042.asp.

13 Liz Pulliam Weston, "Ditch All Fees for Online Banking Services," MSN Money, 2003, http://moneycentral.msn.com/content/Banking/Betterbanking/P38219.asp.

14 Rent-A-Center, 2004, www.rentacenter.com; Aaron Rents, 2004, www.aaronrents .com; RentWay, 2004, www.rentway.com.

15 Ibid.

16 U.S. Public Interest Research Group (U.S. PIRG), *Don't Rent to Own: The 1997 PIRG Rent-to-Own Survey*, U.S. Public Interest Research Group, Washington, DC, June 11, 1997.

17 Ibid.

18 Alix Freedman, "Peddling Dreams: A Market Giant Uses Its Sales Prowess to Profit on Poverty," *Wall Street Journal*, September 22, 1993.

19 Association of Progressive Rental Organizations, 2003.

20 Quoted in Freedman, "Peddling Dreams."

21 DPI Teleconnect, "Our Market," 2004, www.dpiteleconnect.com.

22 Direct Telephone Company, Houston, TX; 1-800-Reconex, Hubbard, OR, www .reconex.com.

23 The costs of the alternative phone services were based on 2004 and 2005 charges, but competition in the fringe economy make these rates and terms subject to change.

24 DPI Teleconnect, "Our Market," 2004.

25 Sprint PCS, 2005, www1.sprintpcs.com; Cingular Wireless, 2005, www.cingular .com. These rates were in effect in 2005, but the cell phone market is rapidly changing, and new terms and rates are always being developed.

26 Dana Dratch, "Getting the Best Deal on Prepaid Cellular Service, 2004, Bankrate.com.

27 Ibid.

28 APRO, *RTO Industry Stats*, 2003.

29 James M. Lacko, Signe-Mary McKernan, and Manoj Hastak, *Survey of Rent-to-Own Customers*, Federal Trade Commission, Washington, DC, 1999.

30 Financial Services of America, *About FiSCA*, 2000.

31 Household International, *Community Commitment*, 2003.

32 APRO, 2003.

33 Lacko, McKernan, and Hastak, *Survey of Rent-to-Own Customers*.

34 John Caskey, *Lower Income American, Higher Cost Financial Services* (Madison, WI: Filene Research Institute, 1997).

Chapter 7: Fringe Housing

1 Joint Center for Housing Studies of Harvard University, *The State of the Nation's Housing* (Cambridge, MA: Harvard University, 2003), 22.

2 Eric Stein, *Quantifying the Economic Cost of Predatory Lending*, Coalition for Responsible Lending and the Reinvestment Fund, Durham, NC, 2001.

3 Prime-rate mortgages are low-interest loans given to a bank's most creditworthy customers.

4 Thomas Feran, "Two Incomes Still Don't Add Up," *Houston Chronicle*, September 22, 2003.

5 Joint Center for Housing Studies of Harvard University, *The State of the Nation's Housing*.

6 Edward Gramlich, remarks, Federal Reserve Bank of Philadelphia, Community and Consumer Affairs, Washington, DC, December 6, 2000.

7 Ibid.

8 Ibid.

9 Securitization is the process of aggregating similar instruments, such as loans or mortgages, into a negotiable security.

10 National Low Income Housing Coalition, *2003 Advocates' Guide to Housing and Community Development Policy*, Washington, DC, 2003; Jonathan Epstein, "Subprime Loan Growth: Minorities in Wilmington Pay Higher Fees," *The News Journal*, November 27, 2002.

11 Center for Responsible Lending, "Newsbrief: Predatory Loan Terms and Subprime Foreclosures," January 26, 2005, www.responsiblelending.org/news_headlines/nb012605.cfm.

12 Thomas Goetz, "Loan Sharks, Inc.," *The Village Voice* , July 15, 1997.

13 Edward M. Gramlich, "Subprime Mortgage Lending" (presentation to Roundtable Annual Housing Policy Meeting, Chicago, Illinois, May 21, 2004.

14 Roberto G. Quercia, Michael A. Stegman, and Walter R. Davis, *The Impact of Predatory Loan Terms on Subprime Foreclosures: The Special Case of Prepayment Penalties and Balloon Payments*, Center for Community Capitalism, Keenan Institute for Private Enterprise, University of North Carolina at Chapel Hill, January 25, 2005.

15 Goetz, "Loan Sharks, Inc."

16 U.S. Department of Housing and Urban Development, Office of Policy Development and Research, *First-Time Homebuyers*, Washington, DC, Fall 2001.

17 Association of Community Organizations for Reform Now, *Predatory Lending in Arizona*, Phoenix, AZ, February 2003.

18 For an excellent discussion of discrimination in the mortgage market, see Stephen L. Ross and John Yinger, *The Color of Credit: Mortgage Discrimination, Research Methodology and Fair Lending Enforcement* (Cambridge, MA: MIT Press, 2003).

19 Federal Financial Institutions Examination Council (FFIEC), *Nationwide Summary Statistics for 2002 HMDA Data*, Washington, DC, August 2003.

20 Quercia, Stegman, and Davis, *The Impact of Predatory Loan Terms on Subprime Foreclosures*.

21 ACORN, *Predatory Lending Practices*, Washington, DC, 2004.

22 Quercia, Stegman, and Davis, *The Impact of Predatory Loan Terms on Subprime Foreclosures*.

23 Ibid.

24 *CBS Evening News*, "Unaffordable Housing," aired February 14, 2003.

25 HSH Associates, Financial Publishers, *Shared Appreciation Mortgages Re-Debut*, 2003.

26 Office of the Comptroller, *Comptroller Charts Increase in Mortgage Complaints*, Florida Department of Banking and Finance, Tallahassee, FL, May 13, 1997.

27 Quercia, Stegman, and Davis, *The Impact of Predatory Loan Terms on Subprime Foreclosures*, 2005.

28 Bill Brennan, *History of Predatory Lending*, Atlanta Legal Aid Society, March 6, 1998; *CBS News*, "What's Hiding in Some Home Contracts," aired February 14, 2003.

29 Bill Brennan, "History of Predatory Lending," March 6, 1998, Atlanta Legal Aid Society, http://legalaid-ga.org (Housing > Home Loans, Foreclosure, Home Loan Scams). See also *CBS News*, "What's Hiding in Some Home Contracts," aired February 14, 2003.

30 Consumer Federation of America, *While Home Ownership Rises, Home Equity Stagnates*, Washington, DC, 2000.

31 Ibid.

32 Joint Center for Housing Studies of Harvard University, *The State of the Nation's Housing*; and Teresa Murray, "Experts Warn Against Milking Home Equity to Extend Debt," *Star Tribune*, November 4, 2000.

33 Brennan, *History of Predatory Lending*.

34 Ibid.

35 Scott Reckard, "Consumer Group Joins Opposition to Wells Mergers," *Los Angeles Times*, July 30, 2003.

36 Jeff Bailey, "A Man and His Loan: Why Bennie Roberts Refinanced Ten Times," *The Wall Street Journal*, April 23, 1997.

37 Brennan, *History of Predatory Lending*.

Chapter 8: Real Estate Speculation and Foreclosure

1 EZ-2-Own Homes, Kansas City, KS, 2003, www.startowningtoday.com.

2 Ibid.

3 John Reed, "Real Estate Investment Information," 2003, www.johntreed.com/rateseminars.html.

4 Quick House Buyer, "Basics of Owner Financing," 2003, www.quickhousebuyer.com.

5 John T. Reed's Home Page, 2003, www.johntreed.com.

6 HomeVestors of America, *About the "We Buy Ugly Houses" People*, Dallas, 2005.

7 Heather Vogel, "A Franchise for Fixers: Pretty Good Profit from 'Ugly' Houses," *The Charlotte Observer*, July 20, 2003.

8 Vogel, "A Franchise for Fixers."

9 Kathy Hoke, "Call for Ugly Houses: Firm Says Area's Aging Housing Stock Can Be Hot Property," *Business First of Columbus*, January 7, 2002.

10 Laura Armstrong and Matthew Royce, *Second-Quarter 2003 National Delinquency Survey Results*, Mortgage Bankers Association of America, September 10, 2003.

11 Joseph Haas, "Companies to Watch: HomeVestors of America," 2004, Realtor Online, www.realtor.org/rmomag.NSF/pages/companieswatchjan04.

12 John T. Reed's Home Page, 2002, www.johntreed.com.

13 Vena Jones-Cox, "Real Estate 101: A Comprehensive Basic Education for New Investors," 2003, www.regoddess.com/seminars/RealEstate101.asp.

14 Carleton Sheets, "The Home of No Down Payment Real Estate Investing," 2003, www.carletonsheets.com/webapp/wcs/stores/cs/index.jsp.

15 Sandra Fleishman, "2nd Quarter Foreclosure Rates Highest in 30 Years," *The Washington Post*, September 14, 2002.

16 Peter Kilborn, "Easy Credit and Hard Times Bring Mortgage Foreclosures," *The New York Times*, November 24, 2002.

17 Roberto G. Quercia, Michael A. Stegman, and Walter R. Davis, *The Impact of Predatory Loan Terms on Subprime Foreclosures: The Special Case of Prepayment Penalties and Balloon Payments*, Center for Community Capitalism, Keenan Institute for Private Enterprise, University of North Carolina at Chapel Hill, January 25, 2005.

18 HousingBubble.com, "Foreclosures.com Reports Foreclosure Activity in Chicagoland Still High," July 1, 2003.

19 National Training and Information Center, *Subprime Mortgage Lending and Chicagoland Foreclosures*, Chicago, IL, September 21, 1999.

20 Sandra Fleishman, "From Foreclosure to the Cleaners," *The Washington Post*, December 24, 2004.

21 Ibid.

22 Robert K. Heady, "Banking: Foreclosure Scams Are Prevalent," *St. Paul Pioneer Press*, September 28, 2003.

23 U.S. Department of Housing and Urban Development, *First-Time Homebuyers*.

24 John T. Reed, "Real Estate Investment Information," 2003, www.johntreed.com/rateseminars.html.

CHAPTER 9: THE FRINGE AUTO INDUSTRY

1 Consumers Union, "The Certified Option," 2005, *Consumer Reports*, http://used-cars.autos.yahoo.com/consumerreports/article/certified_option.html.
2 "Manheim Auction Report," 2002, Manheim Auctions, www.manheimauctions.com.
3 Ibid.
4 Carfax is a fee-based company that accesses records of used cars based on their VIN. See www.carfax.com.
5 "2001 Used Car Market Report," Manheim Auctions, www.manheimauctions.com/HTML/ucmr/dealership2.html#.
6 Ron Feldman, *An Introduction to Subprime Auto Lending for Examiners*, Banking Supervision Department, Federal Reserve Bank of Minneapolis, April 1998.
7 James Bragg, "And They Call This Consumer Friendly?" 2002, www.carinfo.com.
8 Richard Tortoriello, "Advice from Standard & Poor's: Focus Stock of the Week," *Business Week*, January 19, 2001.
9 Feldman, *An Introduction to Subprime Auto Lending for Examiners*.
10 Carinfo.com, "Car Buying Secrets," 2002, www.CarInfo.com.
11 Holden Lewis, "Fed Tightens Rules on Subprime Lending," *Bankrate*, December 20, 2001.
12 Terry Box, "Used Car Lots Thrive When Going Gets Tough: High-Interest Dealers among Fastest-Growing Segments in Industry," *The Dallas Morning News*, June 28, 2004.
13 Ashley Herndon, "R.O.I.," *World of Special Finance,* 2004, www.wosfmagazine.com/aherndon.cfm.
14 National Association of Automobile Dealers, *NADA Data: Dealership Financial Trends*, 2000.
15 Sources: IndependentDealer.com, 2002; *Auto Auction Shopper-Used Car News,* 2002, www.eusedcarnews.com.
16 *Automotive Digest,* "Average Retail vs. Buy-Here-Pay-Here Dealer Sales Data—2002."
17 Chris Leedom, "Some Buy-Here, Pay-Here Predictions," *World of Special Finance,* 2002, www.wosfmagazine.com.
18 Source: Auto Auction Shopper-Used Car News, 2000, September 2002, www.eusedcarnews.com.
19 *Hoover's,* 2004, www.hoovers.com.
20 America's Car-Mart, "Investor Relations," www.car-mart.com/investor.htm.
21 J.D. Byrider, 2002, www.jdbyrider.com.
22 ConsumerAffairs.com, "Kentucky Sues J.D. Byrider," December 17, 2004, www.consumeraffairs.com/news04/ky_jdbyrider.html.
23 Quoted in Terry Box, "Used Car Lots Thrive When Going Gets Tough."
24 Quoted in Herndon, "R.O.I."

25 Chuck Bonanno, "The Best of 2004: The Best Buy-Here, Pay-Here Practices," *World of Special Finance,* 2004, www.wosfmagazine.com.

26 Bonanno, "The Best of 2004: The Best Buy-Here, Pay-Here Practices."

27 *Insurance Journal,* "Conning & Co. Study Says Auto Insurers are Paying Closer Attention to Credit Scores," August 2, 2001.

28 National Association of Independent Insurers, *Industry Issues: Credit-Based Insurance Scoring,* 2002; A.M. Best Company, "Insurers Expect Battle on Use of Credit Scores in about Half the United States," *BestWire,* January 30, 2002.

29 Center for Economic Justice, "Redlining," www.cej-online.org; and Consumers Union, "Reducing the Number of Uninsured Motorists," Consumers Union SWRO Issue Pages for the 77th Texas Legislature, Austin, TX, January 2001.

30 A.M. Best Company, "Insurers Expect Battle on Use of Credit Scores in about Half the United States," *BestWire,* January 30, 2002.

31 AAA Auto Club South, "Insurance Tips: Is Your Insurer Healthy?" 2002, www.aaasouth.com.

32 John Jonik, "Who Are the Scofflaws?" *Counter Punch,* March 7, 2002; Southwestern Insurance Information Service, *Texas Ranks Ninth in Uninsured Driver Study,* August 12, 1999.

33 Missouri Department of Insurance, *Missouri Uninsured Vehicle Rate,* Jefferson City, Missouri, February 7, 2002.

34 Car Title Loans of America, Inc., Laurel, MS, 2002.

35 *Today's Pawnbroker,* "Title Loans Come to Florida," Fall 1995: 37.

36 Susan Brenna, "Deals on Wheels," *Advocasey* (Annie E. Casey Foundation, Baltimore, MD) 7, no. 1 (Winter 2005): 35.

37 Ibid.

CHAPTER 10: THE GETTING-OUT-OF-DEBT INDUSTRY

1 Quoted in *CJAD* (Canadian Radio), "American Consumer Debt More Than Doubles in 10 Years as Savings Slide," January 5, 2004.

2 Robert Samuelson, "A 60-Year Credit Binge," *Washington Post,* August 27, 2003.

3 U.S. Department of Commerce, Bureau of Economic Analysis, *National Income and Product Accounts, Release G.19, Consumer Credit,* Washington, DC, 2004.

4 Deanna Loonin and Travis Plunkett, *Credit Counseling in Crisis: The Impact on Consumers of Funding Cuts, Higher Fees and Aggressive New Market Entrants,* Consumer Federation of America, Washington, DC, and National Consumer Law Center, Boston, April 2003.

5 Ibid.

6 National Foundation for Credit Counseling, "Credit 101," 2003, www.debtadvice.org.

7 Consumers for Responsible Credit Solutions, "A New Report Issued by Consumers for Responsible Credit Solutions Carries Strong Warnings for Consumers Seeking Credit Counseling Services," July 12, 2004, www.responsiblecredit.com/releases/071204.php.

8 Ibid.

9 Alan Joch, "Professional 'Negotiators' May Promise Quick Fixes, But the Best Counselors Aim at Roots of Debt," *The Christian Science Monitor*, December 10, 2001.

10 Consolidated Credit Counseling Services, "How It Works," 2004, www.debtfree.org.

11 This table leaves out the monthly payment. The only way the debt could be paid so quickly with consolidation would be if the monthly payments were much higher than without consolidation, which might be impossible for the borrower to manage.

12 Loonin and Plunkett, *Credit Counseling in Crisis*.

13 Quoted in Christine Dugas, "All Debt Counselors Are Not the Same," *USA Today*, May 27, 2002.

14 Ibid.

15 Consumers for Responsible Credit Solutions, "Nonprofits in Service to One of America's Most Profitable Industries," July 2004, www.responsiblecredit.com.

16 Ibid., and CardWeb, 2004, www.cardweb.com.

17 Source: Loonin and Plunkett, *Credit Counseling in Crisis*.

18 Ibid.

19 Ibid.

20 Credit Report Repair, 2003, www.creditreportrepair.net.

21 National Foundation for Credit Counseling, "Credit 101."

22 Source: Loonin and Plunkett, *Credit Counseling in Crisis*.

23 Ibid.

24 Ibid.

25 Internal Revenue Service, "RS, FTC and State Regulators Urge Care When Seeking Help from Credit Counseling Organizations," IR-2003-120, Oct. 14, 2003, p. 2.

26 Loonin and Plunkett, *Credit Counseling in Crisis*.

27 Karen Alexander, "Minefields Abound in Attempts to Reduce Debts," *The New York Times*, September 22, 2002.

28 The Commonwealth of Massachusetts, *Losing Credibility*, Senate Committee on Post Audit and Oversight, April 2002.

29 Federal Trade Commission, *FTC Files Lawsuit Against AmeriDebt*, Washington, DC, November 19, 2003.

30 Caroline Mayer, "Easing the Credit Crunch?" *The Washington Post*, November 4, 2001; and Jennifer Barrett, "Bad Credit," *Newsweek*, October 23, 2003, http://msnbc.msn.com/id/3339644.

31 Mayer, "Easing the CreditCrunch?"

32 Christopher Schmitt with Heather Timmons and John Cady, "A Debt Trap for the Unwary," *BusinessWeek*, October 29, 2001; and the Commonwealth of Massachusetts, *Losing Credibility*.

33 Ibid.

34 The Office of Massachusetts Attorney General Tom Reilly, "Non-Profit Agawam Credit Counseling Agency Funneled Millions of Dollars to Insiders, and Misled Consumers into Paying High Fees," April 5, 2004, www.ago.state.ma.us/sp.cfm?pageid=986&id=1213.

35 Mayer, "Easing the Credit Crunch?"

36 The Office of Massachusetts Attorney General Tom Reilly, "Non-Profit Agawam Credit Counseling Agency Funneled Millions of Dollars to Insiders."

37 CuraDebt, 2004, www.curadebt.com; and Aegis Debt Consolidation, 2004, www.aegisdebtconsolidation.com.

38 Springboard, 2003, www.credit.org.

39 Debt-Tips.com, "Here's How Debt Negotiation Helped Me Get Out of Debt in Less Than 2 Years... and Saved Me $9,937.40!" www.debt-tips.com.

40 Mory Brenner, "Credit Card Debt Reduction & Settlement FAQ," 2002, www.debtworkout.com.

41 Ibid.

42 Ibid.

43 Pure Credit, 2003, www.purecredit.com.

44 Lexington Law, 2003, www.lexingtonlaw.com.

45 Federal Trade Commission, *"File Segregation": New ID Is a Bad IDea*, Federal Trade Commission, Washington, DC, January 1999.

46 Federal Trade Commission, *Credit Repair: Self-Help May Be Best*, Federal Trade Commission, Washington, DC, February 1998.

47 Barrett, "Bad Credit."

48 Quoted in Consumer Federation of America and the National Consumer Law Center, *Credit Counseling in Crisis: The Impact on Consumers of Funding Cuts, Higher Fees and Aggressive New Market Entrants*, Washington, DC, April 2003.

49 The Office of Massachusetts Attorney General Tom Reilly, "Non-Profit Agawam Credit Counseling Agency Funneled Millions of Dollars to Insiders."

50 The Coalition for Responsible Credit Practices, 2004, www.responsiblecreditpractices.com.

51 Travis Plunkett and Joan Entmacher, "As the Economy Stumbles, Diverse Groups Urge House Leaders to Reject Unbalanced Bankruptcy Legislation," Consumer Federation of America and National Women's Law Center, Washington, DC, March 4, 2003, www.consumerfed.org/bankruptcy_houseleaders.html.

52 Marcy Gordon, "Senate Passes New Bankruptcy Legislation," *The Washington Post*, March 11, 2005.

53 National Consumer Law Center, "What's Wrong with H.R. 975, Let Us Count the Ways...," 2003, www.consumerlaw.org/initiatives/bankruptcy/hr975.shtml.

54 Ibid.

55 Debra Cowen and Debra Kawecki, *Credit Counseling Organizations*, Internal Revenue Service, CPE 2004-1, Washington, DC, January 2004.

Chapter 11: What Can Be Done to Control the Fringe Economy?

1 John P. Caskey, *Lower Income American, Higher Cost Financial Services* (Madison, WI: Filene Research Institute, 1997).

2 Industry Pages, "Check Cashing—Federally Regulated, State Regulated or Unregulated?" April 24, 2003, www.industrypages.com/clmman/publish/article_33.shtml.

3 For a fuller discussion of poverty see William J. Wilson, *When Work Disappears: The World of the New Urban Poor* (New York: Vintage, 1997); Dalton Conley, *Being Black, Living in the Red* (Berkeley, CA: University of California Press, 1999); Katherine Newman, *No Shame in My Game* (New York: Vintage, 2000); Thomas Shapiro and Edward Wolff, *Assets for the Poor: The Benefits of Spreading Asset Ownership* (New York: Russell Sage Foundation Publications, 2001); David Shipler, *The Working Poor* (New York: Vintage, 2005); and Matthew Lee, *City Limits* (Chicago: University of Chicago Press, 1981). Discussions about the fringe economy are in Christopher Peterson, *Taming the Sharks* (Akron, Ohio: University of Akron Press, 2004); Gregory Squires, *Organizing Access to Capital* (Philadelphia: Temple University Press, 2003); Gregory Squires and Sally O'Connor, *The Color of Money* (New York: State University of New York Press, 2001); and Gregory Squires, ed., *Why the Poor Pay More: How to Stop Predatory Lending* (New York: Praeger, 2004). Think tanks and advocacy organizations that are doing excellent work on the fringe economy are referenced in the various chapters.

4 David Cay Johnston, *Perfectly Legal: The Covert Campaign to Rig Our Tax System to Benefit the Super Rich-and Cheat Everybody Else* (New York: Portfolio Hardcover, 2003).

5 Darrell McKigney, *Lawmakers, Regulators and the Consumer Credit Counseling Service Have All Let Payday Loan Victims Down*, Consumers for Responsible Credit Solutions, August 27, 2004, www.responsiblecredit.com/resources/082704 .php.

6 Alan Greenspan, "Challenges in the New Century" (presented at the Annual Conference of the National Community Reinvestment Coalition, Washington, DC, March 22, 2000).

7 Lucy Lazarony, "Credit Card Companies Sidestep Usury Laws," *Bankrate*, March 20, 2002, www.bankrate.com/brm/news/cc/20020320a.asp.

8 Board of Governors of the Federal Reserve System, *Purposes and Functions*, Washington, DC, 1994: 5.

9 Credit Union National Association, "CUNA Testifies on Serving the Underserved," June 26, 2003, www.cuna.org/press/press_releases/cuna_062603.html.

10 For an examination of the Community Reinvestment Act (CRA), see Karger and Stoesz, *American Social Welfare Policy*.

11 Muhammad Yunus, "Grameen Bank at a Glance," November 2004, Grameen, www.grameen-info.org.

12 ShoreBank Corporation, Annual Report, Chicago, IL, 2004.

13 Quoted in Credit Union National Association, *Credit Union Consumer Facts*, 2002.

14 Neil F. Carlson, "Five New Ways to Serve America's Unbanked," *Ford Foundation Report, Fall 2004*, www.fordfound.org/publications/ff_report/view_ff_report_ detail.cfm?report_index=526.

15 "Self-Help: A Model of Excellence in Community Economic Development," *Marketwise* 3 (2003): 34-39.

16 Self-Help, 2003 Annual Report, Durham, NC, 2004.

17 See Michael Sherraden, *Assets and the Poor: A New American Welfare Policy* (Armonk, NY: M. E. Sharpe, 1991); and Carl Rist, "Self-Sufficiency through Individual Development Accounts (IDAs): What's the Role for State Policy?" *Housing Facts and Figures* 4, no. 1 (Fannie Mae Foundation, 2005).

18 Consumer Affairs News, "Judge Upholds Racketeering Complaints Against H&R Block, Household," April 2004, http://consumeraffairs.com/news04/hr_block_suit2.html.

19 China Daily, "Household International to Settle Suit," November 26, 2003, www.chinadaily.com.cn/en/doc/2003-11/26/content_284932.htm.

20 AIB Corporate Banking, Investment Centre, HSBC, 2003, www.aibcorporate.ie/viewarticle.asp?1047.

Index

About the Author

Howard Karger is a professor of social policy at the Graduate School of Social Work, University of Houston. He is a two-time Fulbright Scholar and has written nine books and more than 80 articles or book chapters in various national and international journals. His articles have also appeared in *The Washington Monthly, The Jerusalem Report, Tikkun,* and *Ramparts.* Howard and his wife, Anna, live in Houston, Texas.

About Berrett-Koehler Publishers

Berrett-Koehler is an independent publisher dedicated to an ambitious mission: Creating a World that Works for All.

We believe that to truly create a better world, action is needed at all levels—individual, organizational, and societal. At the individual level, our publications help people align their lives and work with their deepest values. At the organizational level, our publications promote progressive leadership and management practices, socially responsible approaches to business, and humane and effective organizations. At the societal level, our publications advance social and economic justice, shared prosperity, sustainable development, and new solutions to national and global issues.

A major theme of our publications is "Opening Up New Space." They challenge conventional thinking, introduce new points of view, and offer new alternatives for change. Their common quest is changing the underlying beliefs, mindsets, institutions, and structures that keep generating the same cycles of problems, no matter who our leaders are or what improvement programs we adopt.

We strive to practice what we preach—to operate our publishing company in line with the ideas in our books. At the core of our approach is *stewardship*, which we define as a deep sense of responsibility to administer the company for the benefit of all of our "stakeholder" groups: authors, customers, employees, investors, service providers, and the communities and environment around us. We seek to establish a partnering relationship with each stakeholder that is open, equitable, and collaborative.

We are gratified that thousands of readers, authors, and other friends of the company consider themselves to be part of the "BK Community." We hope that you, too, will join our community and connect with us through the ways described on our website at www.bkconnection.com.

A BK Currents Title

This book is part of our BK Currents series. BK Currents titles advance social and economic justice by exploring the critical intersections between business and society. Offering a unique combination of thoughtful analysis and progressive alternatives, BK Currents titles promote positive change at the national and global levels. To find out more, visit www.bkcurrents.com.

Be Connected